THE CULTURAL IMPACT OF KANYE WEST

The Cultural Impact of Kanye West

Edited by

Julius Bailey

First published in hardcover in 2014 by PALGRAVE MACMILLAN® in the United States—a division of St. Martin's Press LLC, 175 Fifth Avenue, New York, NY 10010.

Where this book is distributed in the UK, Europe and the rest of the world, this is by Palgrave Macmillan, a division of Macmillan Publishers Limited, registered in England, company number 785998, of Houndmills, Basingstoke, Hampshire RG21 6XS.

Palgrave Macmillan is the global academic imprint of the above companies and has companies and representatives throughout the world.

Palgrave® and Macmillan® are registered trademarks in the United States, the United Kingdom, Europe and other countries.

ISBN: 978–1–137–57425–1

The Library of Congress has cataloged the hardcover edition as follows:

The cultural impact of Kanye West / edited by Julius Bailey.
     pages cm
Includes bibliographical references and index.
ISBN 978–1–137–39581–8 (alk. paper)
     1. West, Kanye—Criticism and interpretation. 2. Rap (Music)—History and criticism. 3. Rap musicians—United States. I. Bailey, Julius, editor of compilation.

ML420.W452C85 2014
782.421649092—dc23   2013036142

A catalogue record of the book is available from the British Library.

Design by Newgen Knowledge Works (P) Ltd., Chennai, India.

First PALGRAVE MACMILLAN paperback edition: September 2015

10 9 8 7 6 5 4 3 2 1

To all those whose complexities are misunderstood and rendered pathological when all you ever need and want is appreciation.

Also to a few of the loves of my life: Heather, Sandra, Bianca, Antoinette, and Hip-Hop

Contents

Part II   Unpacking Hetero-normativity and Complicating Race and Gender

Part III   Theorizing the Aesthetic, the Political, and the Existential

Foreword

Davey D

As a contributor to Julius Bailey's inaugural book, *Jay Z Essays on Hip Hop's Philosopher King*, I'm proud to return and pen the opening verse on this sophomore project, which focuses on Kanye West. As was the case with the Jay-Z project, Bailey has done an excellent job compiling an array of scholars, teachers, artists, and practitioners who will help the reader navigate and dive deeply (and at times philosophically) into some of the most intriguing questions surrounding the enigma that is Kanye West.

The year 2013, at the end of the first decade of the twenty-first century, marks 40 years since hip-hop's birth. And it's important that we study the music and culture of hip-hop, especially because it's the most popular music form in the country and perhaps the world.

With respect to Kanye West, hate him or love him, it's critical we study this controversial Chicago native, who, with 21 Grammys under his belt, has more than made his mark as a producer, song writer, rap artist, film maker, and clothing designer. In a society that is seemingly all about celebrity worship and reality TV, Kanye West, like his mentor and label boss Jay Z, has come to understand that at the end of the day it's not only his artistic work that's a business but also Kanye West as a personality. Hence he underscores Jay Z's famous businessman mantra.

Kanye with his outspoken, cocky, brazen persona has established himself as the ultimate marketing tool. With each rant and over-the-top antic, like him bum-rushing the stage to interrupt country star Taylor Swift just before she receives an award or him scuffling with meddlesome paparazzi as he walks hand in hand with fiancé and reality TV star Kim Kardashian or him wearing a skirt (kilt) while performing or his latest antic to sell confederate flags to fans, the Kanye West that I met is well aware of the value of kicking up dust. The result of Kanye's dust-raising is that people talk about Kanye. He is hunted down by a ravenous media who chronicle his every move

and attempt to capture tidbits of his "private" life and splash it across
the tabloids. Kanye's dust-raising keeps him relevant at a date and
time when the currency for success is not so much about talent as it is
about the length of time people keep your name on their lips.

I interviewed Kanye's longtime writing partner and childhood
friend, Rhymefest, for this project and he described him best when
he said that Kanye West is "living art." He is "living art" who is
constantly creating and evolving within a society that is constantly
watching, gathering information, and scrutinizing his and other
Black artists' every move. Rhymefest suggested that Kanye is operating within the confines of a music industry that aggressively mirrors a society that is increasingly hell-bent on (de)magnetizing Black
artists from the community and ultimately making them disposable.
"The one thing that is most feared by governments is people coming
together." Rhymefest asserted

It's a stark reality that Kanye is fighting and the industry is resisting. "These artists are fighting the system and the system is bucking
back," Rhymefest noted, "They're fighting back through how they
are presenting their art, and through fighting the corporate system.
So what is the system doing? It's turning to younger artists now, and
trying to manipulate them, with the last bit of money that it has."
Rhymefest added.

The endgame is to separate artists from the community just as
they are wising up to the game and replace them with younger, less
informed individuals who will play to the last vestiges of influence
the industry can exert. Kanye, who is constantly expressing himself
and marketing himself in ways that many would consider outside the
box, has done good to keep himself relevant while simultaneously still
struggling with the sudden loss of his beloved mother Donda two years
ago who grounded him and counseled him. "Kanye may be making a
lot of noise, but he is still trying to find his voice" (Rhymefest).

During our conversation, Rhymefest spoke at length about what
factors influence Kanye's music and how that gets manifested.

> You can't study Kanye without studying the history, politics, gangs,
> social structure and of course the music legacy of Chicago; from the
> Blues to Curtis Mayfield, and the Impressions, all have informed the
> music and sound that Kanye is best known for. Chicago is a down
> south city set in a metropolis resulting in the music having a "bluesy"
> feel. What Rhymefest and Kanye and other Chi-Town artists do is
> create music that pierces the consciousness and makes you think. He
> described Kanye's music as blue-collar-black-American-music that is
> accented by his willingness to be vulnerable and honest (Rhymefest).

Chicago is the birthplace of House music and Rhymefest explained that the culture around House inspired Kanye to be open and experimental with his music. It influenced his style of dress and it also taught him the importance of being accepting of folks who roll a different way. Kanye has been outspoken (and vulnerable) on controversial topics such as homophobia. The House music scene of Chicago has opened him up. The gangs and rough-and-tumble politics that have made Chicago legendary also taught Kanye the importance of affiliation, order, and authorization. Rhymefest explained that in Chicago, folks "roll" in cliques and that affiliation is tremendously important as is loyalty to your clique. The folks that Kanye grew up with are still the same ones in his clique 20 years later.

In studying Kanye and his music, it's important to note that a song is never just a song, and especially when it comes from oppressed communities where music is such an important expression, it is a tool for healing and a tool of communication; one that connects generations. Music has proven over the years to be a tool that can uplift, inspire, and as Fela Kuti reminded us, an instrument to be used as a formidable weapon. From the banning of slave drums at Congo Square, New Orleans, once it was discovered to be a sophisticated form of communication, to record labels like Columbia refusing to release what they described as incendiary racially charged songs such as Billie Holiday's *Strange Fruit* and jazz player Charles Mingus' *Fable of Faubus*, to sitting governors like Alabama's echoing the concerns of the Ku Klux Klan to ban race music (later known as Rock and Roll) for the fear that it would lead to race mixing and Black boys having sex with white girls, to police departments in the late 1980s, forcing concert venues all over the US to contractually forbid NWA from doing their signature song *F—Tha Police* for the fear that it would embolden concertgoers to bring harm to law enforcement, there's a long history of Black music being something that needs to be feared, controlled, and in some outright banned.

We now know that stellar artists such as Bob Marley were under surveillance by the CIA and rap stars such as the Bay Area's Paris have been visited by the Secret Service for the content found to be threatening to then president George H. Bush after he released the song *Bush Killer*. In fact, in the case of Paris when he premiered the song before 22,000 people in August 1992 at KMEL Summer Jam in the Bay Area, he boldly asserted that his song would help derail the reelection attempts of George Bush. After the Secret Service visited him and what he described as "label politics," the release of his album *Sleeping with the Enemy* was pushed back to January, two months after the election.

From Public Enemy to Ice Cube to dead prez to Scarface to Michael Franti, we can go on for days citing examples of Black artists who had their music removed from the airwaves and who were questioned by government agencies or placed under surveillance by police with their lyrics scrutinized.

Many might argue that Kanye West is by no means the most political artist out there, but he has also been censored. Most notably was his song "All Fall Down," where he describes a number of Black pathologies including self-hate, drug abuse, and the worship of white wealth. He philosophically concludes that White men are the financial benefactors of all Black pathologies. Many radio stations around the country, while airing songs with salacious content and even allowing the N-word and the B-word to be played on their airwaves, censored Kanye's reference to White men's financial gain from drugs and Jordans.

Rhymefest noted that Kanye brings to light certain societal realities in his latest release, "New Slaves," to allegedly make the DEA (Drug Enforcement Agency) and the CCA (Correction Corporation of America) team up with a goal of mass incarceration of Black folks. These not-so-subtle attacks at black humanity and agency under the guise of white surveillence places Kanye, and those who are closely associated with him, under the continuous eye of authorities. Rhymefest noted "I told Kanye; 'Listen man when you talk about the CCA and the DEA, They're watching, they're watching us...and they're collecting information and it's not the FBI, it's also the National Security Agency'..." He furthered maintained, "it also gets noticed by folks in power, who is in Kanye's crew," says rapper Rhymefest. The "crew" includes, (among others) an author, an ex-gang member, someone like Rhymefest who ran for political office, and his late mother Donda, who was a top-tier educator and affiliated with the Black Panthers.

The fact that Kanye appeared on an internationally televised telethon to raise money for Hurricane Katrina survivors and accused then president George W. Bush of not "caring about Black people," ensured that he would always be given a second and third look by the government. Bush, years later, wrote in his memoirs that the low point of his entire career was Kanye's public lambasting, and underscored Rhymefest's assertion that people are paying attention to Kanye West.

The question that we should be asking, and that Rhymefest believes Kanye is struggling with, is: What does an artist do with all that attention? What can an artist be allowed to do with all that attention? When looking at an artist as dominant and as popular as Kanye West, one has to explore the ways in which his music is being used as a tool of upliftment and also the ways he and his music are being used to further systems of oppression; especially when we know that with the right type of marketing and exposure, music can be used as a tool to redirect and dumb down. Music can be a tool to turn folks into consummate consumers or be a tool of oppression that sparks fear and hatred.

In 1968, on WBAI radio in New York, former Black Panther and SNCC leader H. Rap Brown noted that entertainers dominate the field of entertainment but rarely control it, and thus they are often used as tools for the white power structure. He went on to add that the community and its movements will have to push entertainers to do right by us as Black people. He then referenced James Brown's "Say it Loud, I'm Black and Proud" song and noted that it was the result of pushback from the people after Brown did a Pro-American song called "America Is My Home."

During the Black Arts Movement and into the 1970s, "the people" pushed their artists, but nowadays the artists are seemingly pushing the people and are backed by a corporate agenda.

> The artist has been demagnetized There seems to be a disconnect and we see that playing out in Kanye West's work and public actions. One minute we see and hear degrees of brilliance and excellence and in the next we see and hear utter wretchedness and contradiction to the values we know Kanye was raised with.
>
> Some Kanye fans cheered when he spoke out against George Bush as negligent toward Black people during Hurricane Katrina. Others cringed when he apologized after Bush complained. We love many of the songs on his new album where he mentions social justice issues on one track but cringe when we hear misogyny and outright wretchedness on the next. Kanye has been fighting to find that grounding which his mother once provided which in turn will allow him the find his voice. (Rhymefest)

The question we are left with is: Are we grounded? Are we trying to be grounded and where is our voice? Maybe through this collection of essays on Kanye will answer some of the questions that are important for the twenty-first century.

Preface: The Cultural Impact of Kanye West

A Preface to the Anthology by Julius Bailey

The Cultural Impact of Kanye West includes critical essays that highlight the importance of the artist in the study of Hip Hop, Culture, English Literature, Philosophy, Gender, and the Africana/African American experience.

This project is divided into three sections that will guide readers through analytical approaches, theoretical frameworks, and pedagogical strategies required for reading and teaching Kanye in the classroom. The only way to study Kanye, according to Rhymefest, is to study history:

> Like we have to study the movement where people come from... Well, for him [Kanye] it starts with Dr. Donda West and then it extends to the Chicago experience, then it expands to his affiliations. Who does he affiliate himself with and why? And I think that's what's important for academia... well; I think it's more important. Maya Angelou said, "It's a shame that the people I write my books for, may never read them." And when she said that, it was profound for me.[1]

On another level, the function of this collection of essays is to give students, especially the college student, a lesson in history and its three-dimensional character: past, present, and future.

Kanye's Cosmo

The cultural theorist Harold Bloom (1973) writes in *The Anxiety of Influence: A Theory of Poetry*, "Poetic influence... always proceeds by a misreading... an act of creative correction that is actually and necessarily a misinterpretation. The history of fruitful poetic influence... is a history of anxiety and self-saving caricature, of distortion, of perverse, willful revisionism (30)." With a noteworthy reputation

as a versatile "beatmaker" and innovative producer for Roc-a-Fella
Records, Kanye West encountered major obstacles when he decided
to shift from music producer to recording artist. West was initially
considered unmarketable as a rap artist due to his clean-cut and
seemingly soft image in a musical genre that celebrates a collective of
street-wise hardcore rappers.

When he finally burst into the music industry as a solo performer
in 2004 with his groundbreaking album, *The College Dropout*, West
filled an as-yet-unnoticed void in rap music and hip-hop culture.
The hip-hop audience, apparently tiring of an endless string of inter-
changeable gangster rappers, found Kanye West's college boy image
and intellectual musical narrative a refreshing change. Rhymefest was
not surprised at this as he cites Kanye's mom as heavily influencing
the breadth of the rapper's voice:

> So what she did was say "Hey, you know, I think it would sound bet-
> ter if you kind of moved into the realm of…talking about…what
> means something to you, and your family life, and not just…money
> and not just this and that." And what's interesting is when she would
> talk like that, Kanye would stop everything and look at her like God
> was speaking.[2]

West's debut album was a critical and commercial success making him
an overnight sensation, in high demand not only as a producer, but
also as a recording artist.

Despite his continuing success as a solo performer, and fashion and
cultural icon, Kanye West has struggled to establish a consistent and
concrete persona or branding image in the American public sphere.
While his music industry contemporaries, Jay-Z, T.I., Lil' Wayne,
and several others have effectively carved-out recognizable hip-hop
brands, West's brand is craftily chameleon as it shifts and changes.
His public and professional image is sometimes at war with his own
highly publicized personal demons or self-perceived defects.

After about a six-year stint as a producer in the industry, Kanye,
within a relatively short period beginning in 2003, has wrestled
through multiple representations of his public self, his perceived
image, and his self-selected branding. He has veered wildly from the
clean-cut good guy to angry militant activist, from fashionable lady's
man to eccentric ego-driven artist, and to bad boy wannabe thug. His
recent incarnation as one-half of an entertainment power couple, with
reality television star Kim Kardashian, reinforces West's place in the
public imagination and marketplace. More often than not, however,

Kanye West's shifts in public brand are not so much driven by changes in the music industry or by market demands, but more by West himself. He seems to be deeply dissatisfied with his well-established position as one of the most talented and critically acclaimed artists in rap music. He appears determined to become not only a larger-than-life personality in comparison to his current contemporaries in rap music, but also a more memorable and marketable public brand than the most well-known icons in hip-hop—Tupac Shakur and The Notorious B.I.G. West's unyielding quest for a particular kind of brand identity suggests that he seeks a kind of public-figure status like music icons, Prince, Madonna, and the King of Pop, Michael Jackson. Such a position has arguably eluded most hip-hop artists.

The Cultural Impact of Kanye West is a study of the artist within a philosophical framework that intersects with his brand. The freedom of the artist is somewhat appropriated by the public in the marketplace. The public who identify with the artist's message feel a sense of ownership that the artist himself cannot escape. The artist who is able to embrace fame while maintaining the power to control his or her public face becomes iconic. However, this position is imaginary. If we consider the late Michael Jackson, then we understand how fragile an iconic position is when brand is at stake. Jackson was unable to control his public image thereby unable to construct and reconstruct his brand. Conversely, West's human elasticity allows for nonracial positioning of virtues and values often associated with the quest for success, a positioning that Jackson failed to master.

Kanye's corpus is of interest to cultural theorists for his challenges to racial stereotypes, and social structures. Further, his worldview can be seen through the lens of a picaresque novel where the reader encounters a rogue character that uses his wit to overcome follies in a world that is always undermining him. The picaresque worldview in America is exemplified by Mark Twain's *Huckleberry Finn*. In Kanye West's hands, the book would have "Nigger Jim"[3] talk as if he were able to claim his agency over the author. West adopts this picaresque attitude in his sophomore album *Late Registration*, in his song "Crack Music," in his next album *Graduation* in the songs "Good Morning" and "I Wonder," and in *My Beautiful Dark Twisted Fantasy* with "Gorgeous" and "Power"; with their references to Malcolm X.[4]

Kanye, much like the philosopher Diogenes,[5] is sprinting in broad daylight with a torch in search of credibility in the form of humanity. Each song is what we encounter as we run with Kanye on his race. What we are asked to understand in our journey with him is that the human race has a recent history of violence from world wars to racial lynching, from uprisings and revolutions in Africa, the Middle East, and South America to youth violence in his hometown of Chicago and other urban areas., We take a walk with the bastards of Marquis de Sade: those males exercising unremitted violence against their mothers and their daughters behind closed domestic doors and open microphones. Kanye contiguously gives voice against both the tacit and blatant attacks upon Black maleness that seek to render an essentialized ontology of it as pathological, and that dismisses the analytical violence that these micro and macro aggressions create within and outside of the Black community. Engaging in a Kanye song is often a free-for-all of violence, porn, horror, gangster proclivities, and revisited memoirs from pimps, prostitutes, and intellectuals alike serving tragicomically as lament that unstables the psyche yet elucidates amusement. A careful look at Kanye's work recapitulates the Du Boisian question of being seen as a problem[6] and in Richard Wright fashion, brashly revolts against Black man's acceptance of an identity that is a menace to society.[7]

For Nobel laureate Toni Morrison, the child wears the mask of the comedian attempting to make sense of the world, yet for the adult the tragedy is realized in our inability to take possession of the world. Kanye asserts from his first album, *College Dropout*, to his most recent, *Yezzus*, a a complex child-like, yet sophisticated nihilistic analysis where there are no social guidelines to help us cope with inequities and racism. As adults, our lives become a full-blown tragedy primarily because the expectation is that we must reconcile ourselves to the fact that follies come with a price and they are burdens we cannot evade. Thus, the family structure is essential in its ability to be a buffer between the child and society so that the child can experience the world in its multifaceted nature and learn to develop a character, personality, and attitude to wear in order to face the world for the rest of his or her life. The ideal cannot be actualized by everyone. So we understand through Morrison's work that what is tragic about youthful comedy is the ignorance toward the experiences of the parents in their search for approval and love. Parents are acutely aware that the ability to create freedom for youth comes with tragic responsibility. It is this same disposition that is Kanye's cosmos in his music. He is a jester in the form of the child attempting to come to grips with the world through the memories he shares with society. It is through the tragedy of the duality of freedom and responsibility and the inability to reconcile them in adult time and space that we share in Kanye's story.

Kanye's life embodies art. Rhymefest puts it this way: "Some people, when they look at Kanye's life, hate him, or they love him, and it affects how they feel about his music. You know, he's a living piece of art. He just is."[8] Kanye West primarily uses music that provides what essayist Albert Murray (1976) called "the blues impulse"[9] in his collection titled *Stomping the Blues*. It is one of the most universal antidotes of the human experience we have that combats misery and sustains hope. The American blues is not limited to Black "folk" but provides to all an existential response to the death shudder of misery, failure, loathing, feeling unloved, and the schism between the American dream and the attempt to reach it. Kanye's blues was birthed in the American South in Georgia and then migrated to Chicago where it was reborn as urban blues. The blues are like Saturday night gospel and like the character Leeve in August Wilson's (1982) play *Ma Rainey Black Bottom*;[10] we must learn to stomp the blues before they muffle our voices. Hip-hop is the most misunderstood arbiter of this blues-like condition and, at its best, is one way we enter into dialogue with the world and people around us. All instruments lead back to the natural instrument of the human body—the voice. Humans come to know the world through two modes; the world as experience belongs to the "I-It" world, whereas the basic "I-You" establishes the world of relation.[11] Yet, since we are surrounded by a world with other human beings, the "I-You" experience takes primacy. Hip-hop is the predominant I-You relationship and the mode of dialogue between artists and fans, fans with other fans, critics and fans, artists with critics, and artist with artists. Hip-hop is a visceral art form that comes from the bellies of global youth in search of Dionysian wisdom.[12] Hip-hop, much like its jazz predecessor, is an improvisation of the eclectic music scene that gave birth to it. Yet, what is distinct about it is the multilayered form of storytelling the emcee wields on tracks. The language can be brash, full of braggadocio, violent, sexist, and tragic partly because the genre is derived from extending the worldliness of language (in context).

Hip-hop solicits extraction of beauty from the ugly, a perquisition of telos in drugs, prostitution, death, poverty, absence of education, and faulty upbringing. But what kind of I-You relation do we expect to hear from kids attempting to find meaning beyond the nihilistic conditions that urban youth, that Kanye likes to refer to, find themselves in and how do we come to deal with the worldview of these youth without dismissing them as arch examples of vulgarity? Thus, we assume that language as a homogeneous mode of expression in any culture carries a homogeneous code of ethics that the subjects speaking that language articulate. Unfortunately, this is why the genre of tragedy is often seen to be universal as the code of ethics we assume to be part and parcel of the world as a divine order has not been experienced the same by everyone. What we see in the tragic figure is one who is cursed and thus justified in cursing the world. Since much of the poetics hip-hop uses include language some refer to as vulgar, in most respects realistically communicates, ranging from the linguistically plebian to the sophisticated, how one relates to the world. In a 2012 interview with *The Fader* magazine,[13] Kanye said it clearly and introspectively, "I'm like a vessel, and God has chosen me to be the voice and the connector." It seems therefore that hip-hop in general, and for Kanye West in particular, has a license to follow in the trajectory of American obscenity in the public sphere that evolved from comedians such as Lenny Bruce, down to Red Foxx, Paul Mooney, Richard Pryor, George Carlin, Chris Rock, and Dave Chapelle, while simultaneously tapping into a speculative realm that dreams for human decency and equality.

The Challenge of the Project

We take for granted the comedian's ability to make us laugh, the poet's ability to inspire, the orator's ability to move us, so that the issue of expressing oneself to others while articulating individuality and the experience of belonging to a particular group is often pushed to extremes. Should a poet be political, entertaining, and inspirational? Hip-hop scholars face a challenge of interpretation—listening to formulation of a text. The challenge is threefold. How do we interpret the voice we hear layered under emotions augmented by instrumentation? How do we describe the use of language and conjecture of words that not only direct the song but also serve as a narrative for the listener? How do we underscore the environment and the silence of language to fully explicate it? The distinction between fiction and testimony is the entry point for the hip-hop scholar, as we maneuver through the world of the voice on the album while being cognizant of the demarcation between being a fan and a critical listener/scholar.

The Cultural Impact of Kanye West examines the content and forms of hip-hop expression as well as the assessment of performance, lyrics, brand, and media images. The critical essays are interdisciplinary. They are studies of the impact of Kanye West by dynamic teachers and proven facilitators who seek to provide a blueprint for curriculum modules for fellow teachers, youth-group directors, and other youth influencers to engage in an organized learning space, utilizing several fields of study.

Section 1 Revisiting the Pharmakon: Artistic Gifts/Human Complexities provides accessibility to this project that broadens hip-hop Studies. This section opens with one of the most respected cultural theorists in America, Mark Anthony Neal, as he engages the reader in a cultural history of soul music and Kanye West's foray into its legacy. Akil Houston takes on the issue of genius in Art and wrestles with the public's many references to Kanye as an artistic genius. David J. Leonard, as he most often and deftly does, challenges those who deny the insurgency in political protests that are not conventionally packaged in the expectations of the dominant white culture. He also raises the question of whose consciousness gets to be deemed as respectable within dominant media discourses. Contributors like visual artist John Jennings and Reynaldo Anderson take us into the Afro-futuristic world by critiquing the digital-mediated cultural production of the visual images and lyrics produced within the artist's videos and demonstrate how the power of software is creating new spaces where cultural forms collide or coexist. Heidi Lewis provides a very accessible reading of the Kanye-trilogy (*College Dropout, Late Registration,* and *Graduation*) and how the poetics impact society and the historical tradition of black musical expression.

Section 2: Unpacking Hetero-normativity and Complicating Race and Gender situates Kanye's image within a tradition of inquiry using race, masculinity, and hetero-normativity as various points of departure. This section demands that the reader delve deeper into some, possibly untapped mental spaces. Philosopher Tommy Curry provides what may be the most polarizing essay of the project. Never deterred by conformity, he argues that Kanye West is adamant that Black men should be the interpreters of the Black male experience, and as such responds not only to Black and but also to white feminist mythologies of Black masculinity. Sha'Dawn Battle presents a critique of Kanye West arguing that he "at times challenges stereotypes of the construction of blackness," while simultaneously conforming to a hip-hop misogynistic status quo in his treatment of women, thereby "questioning the authenticity of the revolutionary discourse he offers." Tim'm West's essay takes a decidedly homo-centric approach as an effort to focus on the precise nature of anxiety produced when hip-hop artists such as Kanye are confronted with questions about their relationship to gay men. While Regina Bradley suggests that West reflects a type of sonic cosmopolitanism that uses sampling and sound to illuminate his views that may conflict with the normal impulses of black masculinity seen and heard in commercial hip-hop. These discussions aim for more carefully developed arguments and a circumspection of popularized views of race, class, gender, and identity theories.

Section 3: Theorizing the Aesthetic, the Political and the Existential aims to focus on arguments that expand the theoretical framework of studies of hip-hop. It is the cornerstone of the work I do in hip-hop, namely, providing tested ways to teach Kanye (and by default, hip-hop) in the classroom. Literature aficionados will be dazzled by teacher and artist A. D. Carson's essay where he creatively, and in a prosaic fashion, fancies himself as Nick Carraway.[14] In his imagination, Jay Gatsby[15] is Kanye West. Monica R. Miller suggests we bypass unnecessary debates about moralism and the "rightful" place of religion as confined within, and tied to, fabricated normative notions of "good," "truth," and "value" and begin to see these notions as products in the competing marketplace of social and cultural interests. I provide a humble reading of Kanye and his quasi-Nietzschean sensibilities. Nicholas Krebs suggests that West continues to master the meritocratic merry-go-round with a pragmatic and relative form of humanism while Dawn Boeck treats three artistic periods of West and proposes that in each the aesthetic products and West's lived reality become a global commodity. She makes the claim that West's dynamic artistic platform is created through various social, historical, and cultural influences, which have empowered him to construct future visions, or models of modernity

Mikhail Bakhtin (1982), in his book *Dialogic Imagination*, describes four criteria to view the use of language in the novel, two being dialogic and heteroglossia. In hip-hop, the dialogic can be heard through the sampling of other music while heteroglossia can be heard through puns, irony, and satire, ad-libs of other artist's work or the real world. The challenge to hip-hop scholars is compounded by the reverence the academy has for writers over musicians so that an attempt to explicate a philosophy for music has to run through literature then to the music as opposed to grappling with the music itself as a literal critic would with a book, digging through its allusions, characters, motifs, contradictions, reverence, and the author's worldview. This study is not like a class on Beethoven where students might expect to engage in the music and its complexities by playing the piano to get a feel for the song. Hip-hop studies the voice of the poet as an instrument and we give credence to sound. To that end, hip-hop, in the academy, is often regarded as material for philosophical and sociological study rather than a subject for the music department. Yet the hip-hop scholarship in *The Cultural Impact of Kanye West*, just like the hip-hop artist, is versed by various academics, music professionals, and cultural connoisseurs using different cultural and theoretical approaches. These chapters will engage you, the reader, with actual studio producers, university professors, poets and rappers, journalists and visual artists in an effort at creating a democratic space for learning and Socratic engagement and provide a substantiated claim for the bourgeoning area of academic inquiry in response to those who resist "academic hip-hop" as a field of study.

Hip-hop scholars, much like producers, avid fans, or backpackers,[16] must roll up their sleeves and dig down into the volumes of the music that inspire us. Hip-hop scholars learn to appreciate the poets and the conditions they attempt to articulate, even when their work doesn't fit nicely into our canons, so that our best work comes from speaking on artists who influence us. The medium is equally important. We have to take the question of technology seriously. From new technology comes a new sense of being. Books transformed our sense of time the way we think of character and their emotions. Movies transformed what we see and don't see in the world, and now the Internet transformed what we know and what is still to be discovered, waiting for us like artifacts in digital clouds.

Here is the crisis for our generation. If books have come under attack by realist critics, movies faulted for feigning reality with talking robots and aliens, and the Internet slammed for its vast and uncensored knowledge, what serves us best as a mirror of our condition? Or precisely, how will we speak about the conditions of our bodies and the moods we embody in the technological world we find ourselves in? With the fight over what constitutes the appropriate knowledge within our institutional walls, books, movies, the Internet, no wonder education has become less relevant for a contemporary-generation feelings cheated by pricey fragments that are qualified by a diploma. Yet one of this generation's most influential figures, Kanye West, a college dropout from American Art Academy and Chicago State University, explicitly expresses his discontent with US educational practices. But before we dismiss Kanye West as being egoistic or pompous, we must excavate his catalogue and uncover the best of what we can learn from him even in his most outrageous escapades. He extends the trajectory of hip-hop beyond the comic style of Biz Markie,[17] and artistically situates himself among the late African American painters Romare Bearden,[18] Jean-Michel Basquiat,[19] and the New York painter and social activist Keith Haring.[20] These experiences provided a springboard to his worldview and continue to propel his career. Sit back and enjoy *The Cultural Impact of Kanye West*.

Notes

1. Interview with Chicago Rapper Che "Rhymefest" Smith. **This was a personal interview specifically for this project. It was taken by phone on July 15 and 23, 2013.
2. Ibid.
3. "Nigger Jim" is a freedom seeker and a friend of Huck's in Mark Twain's *The Adventures of Huckleberry Finn.*
4. The chorus to power is a rearticulation of a famous line in the 1993 Spike Lee movie *Malcolm X*, in which a police officer says to another, while watching hundreds of Nation of Islam gather, that this much power should not be in the hands of one person.
5. Diogenes of Sinope was a philosopher and cynic in ancient Greece. Lore claims he would walk around in the daytime with a torch looking for wise and honest men.
6. Found in W. E. B. Du Bois's *The Souls of Black Folk* (1903), Chapter 1, "Of Our Spiritual Strivings."(New York, NY: Penguin Group, 1995).
7. Menace to society should be taken both literally as well as an equivocation on the 1993 Allen and Alvin Hughes aka "Hughes Brothers" of the same name.
8. Interview with Chicago Rapper Che "Rhymefest" Smith.
9. Term influenced by Albert Murray's, *Stomping the Blues.*
10. Levee is a young trumpeter, in prominent playwright, August Wilson's Ma Rainey's Black Bottom navigating his way in a band of older members attempting to articulate his (blue) condition with new music.
11. Martin Buber, *I and Thou*, Charles Scribners, 1970; 36th ed. (1970), 56. For Buber, the I-You relationship is through language, or as he argues, language creates an inter-subjective. In other words, I cannot know how a cup feels on the inside when I pour hot water in it, but I can know what another human feels on the inside when he drinks hot tea and explains to me how that heat feels. Each experience is meaningful, drinking too hot water forces one to be cautious in future encounters with it.
12. According to Craig Hovey in Nietzsche and Theology Dionysian wisdom "is knowledge without grasping, without mastery...the power necessary to endure reality," 31.
13. Mancia, P (2012) Kanye West: I'm Amazing. http://www.thefader .com/2012/11/29/kanye-west-im-amazing/ (accessed August 11, 2013).
14. Nick Carraway is the narrator in *The Great Gatsby.*
15. Jay Gatsby is in search for a past in the present, a reliving of a historical euphoric moment.
16. The urban dictionary defines a Hip Hop backpacker as "A snob who prides him/herself on being a fan of all the hip-hop you never heard of. Considers any artist not selling CD's out of a Backpack on the

train a 'sellout'. Usually a college-aged suburban kid of any race (dreadlocks optional) who discovered his consciousness at school and dives blindly into underground hip-hop and hates all commercially successful styles of rap music, not realizing that the artists he worships are trying to sell records too."

17. Twentieth-century American rapper, DJ, and beatboxer, who is also credited to have set in motion the legal challenges against rappers for copyright infringement for his (mis)use of Gilbert O'Sullivan's 1972 number one hit "Alone Again...(Naturally)" in his own "Alone Again" (1991).

18. The late Romare Bearden, one of America's most popular African American painters, was also a cartoonist and collagist. One of his famous works that is widely found is "Jammin' at the Savoy."

19. The late Jean Michel Basquiat, painter, social commentator, and graffiti artist, has been repopularized, now within Hip Hop, thanks primarily to Jay Z who has quoted him in "Ain't I" and "We Kings" and many references are found in his newest release *Magna Carta Holy Grail* as well as his 2011 book, *Decoded*.

20. The late Keith Haring was an American graffiti artist and inspired lore from subway stations to later be exhibited in museums.

Acknowledgments

(In my Kanye-voice) The proliferation of the arts in America as agent of the counter-establishment through figures such as Walt Whitman, T. S Eliot, Erza Pound, Phillis Wheatley, Frederick Douglass, Harriet Jacobs, Jean Toomer, Frances Harper, James Weldon Johnson, Lorraine Hansberry, James Baldwin, and others, setup a market for creating a more democratic America challenging and loosening the myopic sense of nationalism defined through the historic albatross of white, hetero-normative maleness. Hip-hop as a culture and Hip-Hop Studies continue to push back at the lingering legacy of pedantic isolationism and provides a space for those lost voices that are tragically yet triumphantly American and deeply human.

The criticism of Hip-Hop Studies as a vital and viable mode of inquiry lands within one or both of the following camps: one camp rattles the cages of the ghosts of history's past where hip-hop, and black culture in general, are undermined and undervalued. Think of a literal "Murder to Excellence" that Jay-Z and Kanye West depict on their 2011 album *Watch the Throne*, and another camp of detractors who are wedded to an intellectual canon in which, they insist, Kanye or anything hip-hop has no place.

Those of us who "profess" to educate the whole person would be remiss if we ignored the lived reality and organic cultural productions, mentalities, and moralities of today's student. So I give myself credit for finding the courage to look the academy in the face and expend the energy and resources to bring you this absolute gem of a read. If this book doesn't win a Pulitzer or sustain itself on the *New York Times* Best Seller List then the readership totally fails to recognize the value of creative pedagogy and sound scholarship!

(Back to reality)This project begins with the vision of two dynamic students, Dalitso Ruwe and Adam Schueler. Both have served as teaching and research assistants for me over the years. The vigor and enthusiasm with which they have prodded and probed me and other audiences propelled us to pursue the unique idea of Kanye West as a subject for academic inquiry. Thank you to the founding members of "Degreed Money Entertainment" as we continue to share and engage the world with ideas.

To omit the very obvious would be misanthropic, thus I thank the 14 contributors who took part in the project and those who began the journey in December 2012 but who could not complete it. You took the vision, accepted it, and made it into a reality.

To Dr. Carmiele Wilkerson, who calmly endures my ranting, my frustrations, my joys, and my pains—my great thanks. Your helpful support and collegiality is never ending.

Shout out to my homeboy in the struggle, Che "Rhymefest" Smith for the interview and the bay area's own, "Davey D" for facilitating such a remarkably honest discussion.

Special thanks go to the following colleagues, students, and friends who also served vital roles in this project (in alphabetical order): Dr. Timothy Bennett, Kate Greene, Dr. Kamasi Hill, Dr. Bettina Love, Jonathon McFarlane, Dr. Nicole Hodges-Persley, Dr. Matthew Smith, Dr. Stephany Spaulding, Dr. David Stovall, Meghan White, Dr. Joycelyn Wilson, and Ytasha Womack.

Also my warmest thanks to my employer, Wittenberg University, and its fine faculty/staff/students who push me to be the best teacher/scholar that I can be. To Chaunta Banks and the Fall 2012, "Kanye West and the Jay-Z" course, the dynamic 2012 and 2013 students in my "Philosophy and Hip-Hop" course, and the Summer 2012 research grant from Faculty Development Board.

Lastly, a heartfelt appreciation is extended to Palgrave Macmillan and the office of Robyn Curtis and Erica Buchman who entrusted this project to its listing.

Part I

Revisiting the Pharmakon: Artistic Gifts / Human Complexities

Chapter 1

Now I Ain't Saying He's a Crate Digger: Kanye West, "Community Theaters" and the Soul Archive

Mark Anthony Neal

Kanye West's first collaboration with Jay Z on *The Dynasty: Roc La Familia* (2000) gave an early inkling on what would be the producer's contribution to the sonic excavation of the Soul music tradition of the late 1960s and 1970s. The track "This Can't be Life" features Beanie Sigel and Scarface (whose *The Fixx*, West would later contribute production), and is based on a sample from Harold Melvin and the Bluenote's "I Miss You." Though the song is not significant within the larger scope of West's career, it placed Jay Z in a distinctly soulful context that would form the basis of the rapper's career-defining *The Blueprint* (2001) as well as frame the early stages of West's own solo career. At the foundation of West's music prior to the release of his 2007 recording *Graduation* is recovery of the aesthetic possibilities of Soul music—a broadly conceived attempt to elevate Soul music as a classical American form, rooted in what Guthrie Ramsey Jr. calls the "community theaters" of Black life.[1] Additionally, West's attention to the Soul archive was also a method to balance his status as one of the most recognizable mainstream rap producers—a legitimate Pop star—with his creative devotion to laboring as a "Crate Digger," as evidenced by famous lyrics that reference long periods of seclusion and a Cosby show reference to living in a different world.

Otis Redding was mining a popular music archive when he recorded "Rock Me, Baby" (1965), loosely based on Lil Son Jackson's "Rockin' and Rollin'" (1950) and "Try A Little Tenderness" (1966), a 1932 tune originally recorded by the Ray Noble Orchestra. But it was also recorded by a young Aretha Franklin and Sam Cooke prior to Redding. That Soul music emerged as the definitive soundtrack of the Black Freedom movement of the 1960s (Free Jazz notwith-standing) explains, in part, Redding's intent: Soul music remains the clearest example of a genre of music that spoke across Black genera-tions—a ripe site to serve the needs of "Movement" politics. Tommy Tucker's "Hi Heel Sneakers"—a 12-bar Blues that would have been on-the-record players at virtually any "quarter party" in 1964 and whose melody you can hear in the original *Sesame Street* theme (1969)—is but one example of Soul music's ability to mediate genera-tional divides on a micro level.

One of the dynamics that marked the emergence of rap music in the mid-1970s was that it was thought to be sonically out of sync with the Civil Rights generation—the Soul Generation, if you will, to cite the name of an actual group from the period—a divide that would play out commercially, and in more than a few households, well into the early 1990s. Indeed, the classic retort that rap music was simply "noise" had as much to do with early rap music's lack of melody as it did with how early rap DJs and nascent producers used previously recorded music in ways that older generations of Black listeners might have thought of as strange or foreign; there wasn't a budding DJ in the period, trying to replicate a "scratch," who was not cautioned by a parent to "not mess up the needle." As any number of early hip-hop icons, such as Kool Herc (Clive Campbell), Grandmaster Flash, Grand Wizard Theodore, and Afrika Baambaataa, can attest, rap art-ists were always invested in Soul music, if only to locate break beats—the "get down" part—that they could reconstitute at the park jam or in the club.

The sonic divides that emerge among Black listening tastes—as much generational as it was regional and class based—spoke more broadly to actual divides, in terms of worldviews, political sensibili-ties, relationships with spiritual and religious institutions, and a range of others issues, that musical genres could never really address. Yet the genius of say Eric B and Rakim's "Paid in Full" (1987) was that it sampled one of the few tracks in the 1980s that both Black youth and their parents might have listened to. That song, "Don't Look Any Further, "recorded by Dennis Edwards (with help from Siedah Garrett) featured production that replicated the electro-R&B of acts such as The S.O.S. Band and Midnight Starr, yet Edwards's unmis-takable vocals recalled the classic Temptations's tracks he sang lead on like "Ball of Confusion" and "Papa was a Rolling Stone." It's important to remember that, during this era, it was a regular practice among so-called Urban Radio stations to eradicate rap music from their daytime programming, often only playing rap songs late at night on Friday and Saturday evenings. "Don't Look Any Further," along with hybrid recordings like Chaka Khan's 1984 track "I Feel for You" (featuring Melle Mel), the R&B friendly production of Whodini (courtesy of Larry Smith), and Jody Whatley's 1988 hit "Friends" (featuring Rakim) were important commercial efforts to bridge the listening gap, though most R&B stations were likely more interested in strengthening their audience base for advertisers.

The best depiction of the generational divide in Black listening practices was a 1996 Coco-Cola commercial (produced by Rush Media) in which an older Black father-figure listens to Marvin Gaye and Tammi Terrell's "You're All I Need to Get By," while his son bobs his head to "I'll Be There for You/You're All I Need to Get By," a track that borrows lyrics and melodies from the Gaye and Terrell original.[2] By the time hip-hop producers, notably figures such as A Tribe Called Quest's Ali Shaeed Muhammad, Gangstarr's DJ Premiere, and Pete Rock of Pete Rock & CL Smooth, began mining the archives of Hard-Bop and Soul Jazz in the early 1990s, the sonic generational gap begin to close some, particularly among Black male listeners.[3]

The radio version of "I'll be There for You/You're All I Need to Get By" was remixed by one of the most critical figures of 1990s urban music, who is largely remembered for helping to craft a sub-genre known as "Hip-Hop Soul"—a riff on a style known as "New Jack Swing," often attributed to producer Teddy Riley, where rap music–styled production was melded with traditional R&B harmonies. Sean Combs was the Svengali behind the Bad Boy Entertainment label, which boasted artists such as Craig Mack ("Flava in Your Ear"), Total ("Can't You See"), 112 ("Only You"), Faith Evans ("You Used to Love Me"), and most famously The Notorious B.I.G. In contrast to so-called serious producers—professional crate diggers—who privileged obscure source material, Combs often chose easily identifiable classic soul recordings. As Joe Schloss writes of "digging" in his influential study *Making Beats: the Art of Sample-Based Hip-hop*, "in addition to its practical value in providing the raw material or sample-based hip-hop, digging serves a number of other purposes," including "manifesting ties to hip-hop deejaying tradition, 'paying dues,' educating producers about various forms of music, and serving as a form of socialization between producers."[4]

Though Combs was often chided for lazy sampling practices (and there has long been dispute about how much Combs's work was actually the product of the producers he employed at Bad Boy), his choices made sense with regard to the expansion of his brand; folk, who a decade earlier might have partied to Mtume's "Juicy Fruit" or The Isley Brother's "Between the Sheets"—both found on The Notorious B.I.G.'s debut *Ready to Die* (1994)—or Kool & the Gang's "Hollywood Swinging," which was featured on Mase's break-out single "Feel So Good" (1997), found the music of Bad Boy Entertainment sonically appealing. Combs also used such strategies for pop audiences, using samples from David Bowie ("Let's Dance") and The Police ("Every Breathe You Take") for his tracks "Been Around the World" and "I'll be Missing You." Given the sampling environment of the mid-1990s, in which licensing fees often made it cost-prohibitive for artists to sample some songs, Combs, with the backing of Arista/BMG and Clive Davis, could literally afford to be less creative. For artists and producers with less financial flexibility, they had to design methods that allowed them to undermine the logic of copyright law, notably the Bridgeport case, which effectively limited them to sampling three-notes from songs. These constraints led to practices such as chopping, which scholar Joe Schloss describes as "dividing a long sample into smaller pieces and then rearranging those pieces into a different order to create a new melody."[5]

Sean Combs's offers one of the most compelling frames to understand the emergence of Kanye West in the early years of the twenty-first century. With six solo releases and a duet recording with Jay Z, West is the most well-known hip-hop producer since Combs—and has arguably surpassed him in terms of public recognition. A decade after Sean Combs was criticized for being "all up" in the music videos of the artists he "produced," West is a legitimate pop star and celebrity. Highlighting Scott Poulson Bryant's observation more than a decade ago that Combs was his "own best logo,"[6] West is indeed his own best brand. Yet unlike many before him, West's attention to the craft of production is as much about the narratives associated with him, as are his now infamous public antics. Though few deny West's status as an Artist—in the purest sense of the word—some of West's most notable rants have been motivated by his perception that he, and Black artists in general, are given short shrift as serious artists.[7]

Whereas West has had the financial backing of a major label like Island Def Jam, his artistic strategy has been to balance his access to the most expensive sampling material with the creative ethics of a class of producers referred to as 'Crate Diggers." For West, who was a relative outsider, whose base was in the Midwest, his embrace of the life of a "crate digger" did important labor in terms of endearing him to hip-hop purists. As Schloss notes, crate digging "constitutes an almost ritualistic connection to hip-hop history," as well as a "rite of passage" in the eyes of already established producers.[8] Yet in light Schloss's observation that a "sign of more advanced digging is the ability to find useful material in unexpected places," West has also leveraged his visibility to celebrate a canon of Soul music from the Midwest, that like his own challenge to the hegemony of "bi-Costal" rap music, challenges the status of Southern Soul as the most aesthetically pleasing and historically important form of Soul music.

When Kanye Became a Pop Star

With the release of "Gold Digger," Kanye West's 2005 collaboration with Oscar winner and sometime R&B singer Jamie Foxx, West became a legitimate pop star. Certified multiplatinum, "Gold Digger" topped the *Billboard* charts in the United States and at the time of its release was the fastest selling digital download of all time. Released a year after the biopic *Ray*, which starred Foxx in his Academy Award–winning performance, the song generously borrowed from Ray Charles's 1954 classic "I Got a Woman," with Foxx reprising his "role" performing the song's backing vocals as "Ray Charles." The perception that "Gold Digger" was just a hot rip-off of a classic Soul recording—as part of a broader indictment of sampling practices—and West's subsequent controversial statements regarding then President George W. Bush's response (or lack of) to the New Orleans–based victims of Hurricane Katrina, helped overshadow the genius of the sample, and West's own sampling practices. As Intellectual Property Law school James Boyle would later explain, "Gold Digger" was a crate digger's dream, as the Charles original was as much a product of sampling, as was West's version and "George Bush Don't Like Black People," the Legendary K. O.'s Hurricane Katrina–inspired appropriation of "Gold Digger."[9]

West made a calculated attempt to use Charles's music—he is rumored to have paid Charles's estate one million dollars and 100 percent of the profits generated from the single for the use of the sample—to establish himself as legitimate pop star. "Gold Digger" was the second single from West's second solo recording *Late Registration*, which was released on August 30, 2005, the day after Hurricane Katrina's landfall in New Orleans. The recording sold more than 800,000 copies during its first week of release, and topped the *Billboard* album charts in the United States. *Late Registration* featured samples from other notable Soul artists, including Bill Withers, whose unreleased demo "Rosie" was featured on "Roses," and Otis Redding, whose "Too Late" from *The Great Otis*

Redding Sings Ballads (1965) appears on "Gone" (with Consequence and Cam'Ron). Perhaps the most famous Soul artist sampled on *Late Registration*, besides Ray Charles, was Curtis Mayfield. "Touch the Sky" (with Chicago-based rapper Lupe Fiasco), which samples Mayfield's "Move on Up," represents the closet distillation of a classic Chicago Soul sound in West's music, though ironically it was produced by fellow Roc-a-Fella producer Just Blaze—the only track on *Late Registration* to not feature production for West.

Despite being produced by Just Blaze, who West shared an affinity with regard to the use of Soul samples and the practice of changing the pitch of the source material, "Touch the Sky" offers important insight to West's own compositional strategies. As Robert Pruter notes in his book *Chicago Soul*, "Chicago during the soul era easily ranked as one of the major centers for the production of soul... Yet the city's self-evident role has not only not received the proper amount of recognition by writers on popular music; too often it has been completely ignored."[10] One example of an artist who exemplified this dynamic is Syl Johnson, who until fairly recently—and in no small part due to his longevity and his copyright infringement case against West and Jay Z for "The Joy," which also samples from Curtis Mayfield—had not received full recognition of his role in Soul music. As an A&R executive at several local Chicago labels and as an artist, Pruter writes that Johnson, "never made an impact with members of this nation's critical fraternity... But if one examines Johnson's career closely, one can find plenty of evidence that he created a body of work that ranked in artistry with most giants of the soul field."[11]

West's approach to Soul music is not unlike the road he traveled with regard to the dominance of so-called East Coast, West Coast and increasingly "Dirty South" biases in hip-hop, privileging communities—Soul-scapes, if you will—that have often been overshadowed by acts aligned with Motown (Detroit), Stax (Memphis), and to a lesser extent TSOP (Philadelphia). Choices such as The Main Ingredient's "Let Me Prove My Love," which is featured on Alicia Keys's "You Don't Know My Name," which West coproduced, or his use of The Persuaders "Trying Girls Out" on his production of the remix to Jay Z's "Girls, Girls, Girls," are examples of West's desire to expand popular knowledge of the Soul archive. Even when West has delved into the archives of the "Big Three," as with the sample of Marvin Gaye's "Distant Love" on "Spaceship" or most famously, with Redding's "Try a Little Tenderness" on "Otis" from *Watch the Throne* (2011)—he has done so in a way that marked his uses as distinct artistic statements from the originals.

Many of the compositions on *Late Registration* were collaborations with instrumentalist Jon Brion, most well known for his work scoring films such as *Magnolia* (1999) and *Punch Drunk Love* (2002). It was with Brion in mind that West would later record *Late Orchestration* (2006), a live recording of his music backed by a string orchestra. With his focus on orchestration and ornamentation in music, West desired to highlight the "majesty" of Soul, not unlike similar efforts a generation earlier by Wynton Marsalis with regard to Blues music. Embedded in this desire was not simply the elevation of the music, but the lived realities of the people for which the music served so much purpose. Here West is illuminating what Ramsey has described as "community theaters" or "sites of cultural memory." For Ramsey, these are sites that relish in "communal rituals in the church and the under-documented house party culture, the intergenerational exchange of musical habits and appreciation, the important of dance and the centrality of the celebratory black body, the always-already oral declamation in each tableau, the irreverent attitude towards the boundaries set by musical marketing categories."[12]

Wake Up, Mr. West

Late Registration begins with "Wake Up, Mr. West," one of many vignettes on West's first two solo recordings, that feature a "faculty" whose voices are similar to that of the late Chicago-bred comedian Bernie Mac. The voice, which sonically represents West's conflicted relationship with formal education—as borne out in the titles of West's three solo albums including *College Dropout* (2004) and *Graduation* (2007)—is also a metaphor for West's layered ambivalence for his hometown—and the "community theaters" animated within the city. "Wake Up Mr. West" features a piano line from Natalie Cole's 1980 recording "Someone That I Used to Love." The song, written by Michael Masser and Barry Goffin, who also penned Diana Ross's "Touch Me in the Morning," "The Greatest Love of All" (recorded by both George Benson and Whitney Houston), and the Roberta Flack/Peobo Bryson duet "Tonight, I Celebrate." The song was recorded as a lament for Cole's divorce from musician Marvin Yancy, who in the 1970s, teamed with Chuck Jackson (half-brother of Reverend Jesse Jackson) to write and produce for the group The Independents. The duo later became the creative force behind Cole, when she became a major pop star in the mid-1970s. Jackson and Yancy were products of a song-writing workshop, founded by Soul singer and Cook County Commissioner Jerry Butler. I would like to argue, that with the brief 41-second segment that opens *Late Registration*, West articulates his complex emotional ties with the city of Chicago, as the place that he "used to love," and the axis of experience that places his middle-class background in conversation with, and at times, at odds with, the Black working-class cultures of Chicago.

On the one hand, Chicago is a source of inspiration for West, as examined in his track "Through the Wire," which documents his recovery from an automobile accident in 2002. As a testament to his resilience, West recorded the song while his jaw was wired after the accident and against the wishes of his label. Notably, West chose to sample a Chicago icon, vocalist Chaka Khan's "Through the Fire." Yet, in the grittier aspects of Chicago—read more broadly as a Black urban experience—West's desire to provide sheen to that experience, is grounded in a particularly classed view of Black life in the city. Again Ramsey is useful here, identifying a particularly interesting aesthetic at play in Theodore Witcher's 1997 film *Love Jones*, which frames the lives of a cadre of 20 and 30-something Black bohemians in the city of Chicago. Released just as rap music becomes a dominant force in pop music, Ramsey notes that Love Jones "expands the hip-hop lexicon of acceptable black subjects."[13] Writing about the film's characters, Ramsey observes, "with fluency they pepper their musings on poetry, sexuality, Charlie Parker, gender relations, religion, and art with spicy, up-to-the-minute 'black-speak' rhetoric. Witcher...wants us to recognize these verbal exchanges and their accompanying body attitudes with a contemporary performance-oriented African-American culture."[14]

As a one-time student at the American Academy of Art in Chicago and the son of a college professor, the late Donda West, Kanye West would have been very familiar with the world that Witcher presents. The contribution of spoken word poet J-Ivy on "Never Let Me Down" (with Jay Z) from *College Dropout* is one example of West's affinity for Chicago's Black bohemia. What West does consistently on his first two full-length recordings—and perhaps better than any of his peers—is cut the difference (musically and lyrically) between modes of expression that would be legible to both traditional hip-hop audiences and the middle-class sensibilities of Black bohemians. One example of this is "All Fall Down" from *College Dropout*. The song features vocals from another Chicago performer Syleena Johnson, the daughter of the aforementioned Syl Johnson. In the original version of the song, West sampled vocals from Lauryn Hill's "Mystery of Iniquity," but when Hill refused to grant permission for the use of the sample, Johnson sang the melody instead. Though the song offers a sharp critique of consumer addiction and materialism, West consistently undercuts his own investments in respectability, by acknowledging his own struggles with consumer addition.

West, perhaps, most perfects this balancing act on the track "Jesus Walks." The song opens with West locating the Midwest—"young and restless"—as a distinct site of trauma, poverty, criminality, and police brutality, an invoking lack spirituality as a response. "Jesus Walks" is an interpolations of "Walks with Me," a 1997 recording from the ARC Choir. The Harlem-based choir is based at the Addicts Rehabilitation Center—ARC—which was founded in 1957 by James Allen. The Choir was formed as an a'capella group in 1975. "Walk with Me" was arranged by jazz bassist Curtis Lundy, brother of the jazz vocalist Carmen Lundy, who joined the choir in the early 1990s to battle his own addictions.

Throughout "Jesus Walks," West is not some pious figure simply tossing stones at the sinful—more than half of those stones West tosses at himself. Instead, West makes public his struggles with living a devout life, and attempts to make that life accessible—through his music—within the very "community theaters" that Ramsey documents. Here West functions as a receptacle for those who think of a "Jesus" that is truly of the people. West makes such a point in the obscure third version of his "Jesus Walks" video. Shot in a grainy, black-and-white guerilla style, that West paid for out of his own pocket—the video mocks the idea of a self-centered spirituality, as a White "Jesus" literally follows West around protecting him from danger. This image of "Jesus" is juxtaposed with that of a Black "Jesus," who is seen playing jump rope with a group of neighborhood children. The video begs the question, which notion of "Jesus" matters? A "Jesus" seen as a "personal" savior or one who resided with and among the people?

For West, his first two recordings, represented a balancing act between the bookish, even nerdish artist, who could navigate between a Black bohemia in Chicago and the harder edges of the city, and the high-profile rapper, who needed to live up to the tenets of a rap music life. West was able to negotiate these dynamics musically on *College Dropout* and *Late Registration,* with an attention to the details of "crate digging" and an expansive view of Black life. With his emergence as a bankable pop star with the release of *Graduation*—which moved more than 900,000 in its first week, famously outselling 50 Cent in the process—West's seemingly distanced himself from the very archive that made him matter in the first place.

Notes

1. Guthrie Ramsey Jr., *Race Music: Black Cultures from Bebop to Hip-Hop* (Berkeley, CA: University of California Press, 2003).

2. It should be noted that Combs often only functioned as a producer for largely branding purposes; many of the songs were produced as part of a collaboration from a range of producers who were under the employ of Combs.

3. See Mark Anthony Neal's "'Memory Lane': On Jazz, Hip-Hop, and Fathers," in *Born to Use Mics: Reading Nas's Illmatic*, ed. Michael Eric Dyson and Sohail Daulatzai (New York: Basic Books, 2010), 117–128.

4. Joe Schloss, *Making Beats: The Art of Sample Based Hip-Hop* (Middletown, CT: Wesleyan University Press, 2004), 79.

5. Schloss, 151.

6. Scott Poulson-Bryant, "This Is Not a Puff Piece," in *Step into a World: A Global Anthology of the New Black Literature*, ed. Kevin Powell (New York: Wiley, 2000), 114.

7. In one account of such rants, West specifically complained about the snubbing of his *My Beautiful Dark Twisted Fantasy* (2010) and *Watch the Throne*, (2011) his collaboration with Jay Z in the "Album of the Year" category. See Kia Makarechi's "Kanye West Grammys Rant" in *The Huffington Post* (December 30, 2012), http://www.huffingtonpost.com/2012/12/30/kanye-west-grammys-rant-atlantic-city_n_2385785.html

8. Schloss, 92–93.

9. See James Boyle, "I Got a Mashup" in *The Public Domain: Enclosing the Commons of the Mind* (New Haven, CT: Yale University Press, 2008), 122–159.

10. Robert Pruter, *Chicago Soul* (Urbana and Chicago, IL: University of Illinois Press, 1992), xiv.

11. Pruter, 254.

12. Ramsey, *Race Music*.

13. Ramsey, *Race Music*.

14. Ramsey, *Race Music*.

Chapter 2

Kanye West: Asterisk Genius?

Akil Houston

Kanye West is arguably one of the most talented figures of his generation. In his relatively short career, he has gone from no-name beat producer to one of popular culture's "it" kids. From his successful music career to his paparazzi/fantasy relationship with reality TV "star" Kim Kardashian, West has parlayed his 15 minutes quite well. In this essay, I examine how Kanye West embodies the zeitgeist of this particular moment. In *reading* West, I turn to America's classic past time—baseball. It is in baseball, through another larger-than-life personality, that I consider how Kanye embodies the cultural climate of this era and represents what can be called an asterisk genius.

In 2007, baseball fans critical of major league baseball (MLB) player Barry Bonds held up signs displaying an asterisk in ballparks as he chased hall-of-famer Hank Aaron's 755-home-run record. For the fans, the asterisk was an indication that something was questionable about the seven-time Most Valuable Player's quest for the distinction. An enigmatic and polarizing figure to sports journalists, Bonds was recognized even by his staunchest critics as one of baseball's all-time talents. After Bonds broke Aaron's record, he became MLB's new home run king. However, despite his talent, to many baseball purists his record will forever be tainted by his alleged link to performance-enhancing drugs (PEDs). As a result, this otherwise milestone achievement remains suspended in suspicion. In addition to allegations against Bonds, the overall climate in baseball was clouded by other high-profile players' admission to using banned substances to enhance their playing abilities. Baseball as a whole at this time has been referred to as the steroid era. The steroid era, which lasted roughly from the late 1980s to the early 2000s, left many fans and journalists questioning the integrity and value of achievements during this period. Prior to widespread public knowledge of PED use in baseball and congressional hearings on the matter, the steroid era produced a peak in baseball popularity during the 1990s and early 2000s. Sports television and magazines ran features about baseball power hitters and home run races, most notably between Sammy Sosa and Mark McGwire. Attendance at ballparks increased significantly, network ratings rose, and there was a proliferation of MLB pitchmen advertising anything from automobiles to men's toiletries. However, as news stories broke about PED abuse, the overall integrity of the game suffered. For Barry Bonds specifically, the asterisk loomed large. The asterisk became both an acknowledgment of his home runs and a constant questioning of the dubious legitimacy of how his title was earned. The asterisk served as shorthand for the litany of questions that will forever be linked to Bonds and this achievement. Did he abuse PEDs? Despite his talent, is Bonds' accomplishment diminished by the overall lack of integrity in the game? Did smaller ballparks and weaker pitchers, as some journalists have argued, make Bonds' record an easier milestone to reach (Pearlman, 2006)?

In this essay, I grapple with the notion that Kanye West represents an asterisk genius. Similar to Bonds, West is a "major league" producer. His talent as a music producer, like Bonds's baseball skill, remains largely unquestioned. West maintains a growing list of production credits that include the likes of Michael Jackson, Janet Jackson, Jay Z, Common, Beyoncé Knowles, Alicia Keys, Nas, Britney Spears, and Justin Bieber. Kanye West's body of consistent work and cross-genre success confirms his standing as a top producer. On more than several occasions it has been his "Midas touch" that has lifted unknown new artists out of obscurity or helped increase radio play for veteran art-ists, as was the case with Common's 2005 *Be* studio album. As a result of his ubiquitous presence in popular culture, West's production tal-ents and body of cultural production have been conflated in appraisals of him as a "genius" (Samuels, 2012). Kanye, with very little room for doubt as to his abilities as a producer, embodies the necessary ingredients of genius and creative mastery of his art that transcends others of his time. However, the lingering question is whether or not his remaining corpus of cultural production (e.g., rapper, celebrity politician (Cole, 2010), fashion designer, and label owner) warrants the mark of genius. Kanye is an appropriate subject as social media (e.g., on Twitter with his May 2, 2013, tweet of "June 18"), the press and media outlets have given him so much attention that it borders on oversaturation.[1] Given Kanye's location (i.e., space and time) in the commercial rap marketplace, the idea of genius warrants unpacking. In Kanye's case, the asterisk serves as shorthand, a marker of the era of his achievements. Much like the steroid era in baseball, commercial rap music during West's emergence and his subsequent reaching of iconic status lacks in discursive complexity. While taking nothing away from West or engaging in regressive and mostly useless criticism, it is necessary to pose the following questions:

1. What constitutes his genius?
2. How does his genius compare with others?
3. What is the state of commercial rap that we can offer the genius designation to this artist?

With few exceptions during the time of West's rise to and subsequent status as an icon, commercial rap suffers from intensified commodification and a saturation of mediocre artists. Although there were a few exceptions with artists such as Talib Kweli or Brother Ali, who released debut solo albums at this point, these exceptions do not disprove the rule. Often overshadowing these kinds of productions were the violently misogynist, homophobic, and sexist albums that featured standard narratives of the drug game. Though some would consider these albums, such as the Clipse's *Lord Willin'* or 50 Cent's, *Get Rich or Die Tryin'*, to be quality work, their constant glorification of black on black crime and disdain for women makes this position dubious. Given this state of affairs, it becomes necessary to explore the fetishization of all things Kanye. Due to no fault of West's own, the intensified commodification of commercial rap and the influx of mediocre artists have created an overall weaker game. In this context, I argue that commercial rap typifies the statement that mediocrity is common and excellence is rare. If the presupposition that commercial rap is mediocre is accurate, then in a sea of mediocrity, how can we know whether what we find to be excellent (Kanye) truly is of superior value? Or does what is considered good become excellent by consequence of the absence of greatness? These are intentionally provocative questions that result in even more questions. My interest is less on the merits of West as a genius per se but the space he occupies in order to achieve such a designation. Echoing Small (1998), I am engaging the question of "What does it mean when this performance (of this work) takes place at this time, in this place, with these participants?"[2]

I acknowledge that by questioning the space that Kanye occupies, his genius cannot help but be questioned by association. To establish a framework for the exploration of these queries, I look to an essay by Ralph Ellison, *Living with Music*. Ellison's writing operates as a vehicle to illuminate the discussion of Kanye's oeuvre. Ellison's work serves as a helpful bridge because of his insightful music criticism, influenced by his reading of the nuances of blackness, popular culture, and his great affinity for jazz.

Living with Music

In Ellison's 1995 essay *Living with Music*, he argues that the relation-ship between black life and music is often so intertwined that the two are inseparable. *Living with Music* is not merely a casual description of an activity; it was and is fundamental to existence. As Ellison (1995) explained, "It was either live with music or die with noise, and we chose rather desperately to live" (227). Jazz and the sociopolitical condition of African Americans served as Ellison's muse. Through Ellison's writing, the meaning of the material conditions of black life is examined in complex yet subtle textures. Ellison is also able to capture the quest for individual autonomy despite obstacles of insti-tutional racism and the limits this places on one's vision, both internal (of the self) and external (how others see you). These dichotomies are found throughout Ellison's work. In this piece, among other insights, Ellison manages to maintain a consistent interrogation of the cultural pedagogy of music and the complexity of the Du Bosian twoness[3] of African American identity in these works. Ellison (1995) writes:

> I had been caught actively between two: that of Negro folk music, both sacred and profane, slave song and jazz, and that of Western clas-sical music. It was most confusing; the folk tradition demanded that I play what I heard and felt around me, while those who were seeking to teach the classical tradition in the schools insisted that I play strictly according to the book and express that which I was supposed to feel. This sometimes led to heated clashes of wills. (230)

Though writing specifically about jazz music, Ellison's observations can be extended to the contemporary moment in rap music produc-tion. Hip-hop artists must negotiate identities within these some-times conflicting spaces and choices. On the one hand, they draw on the repository of the Black musical tradition (a tradition both sacred and profane) in an effort to put pain into music in order to draw out the suffering yet make it pleasurable, as the blues tradition has done. In addition to drawing on this tradition, artists have at the same time attempted to remain viable in a commercial marketplace. At best this is a delicate juggling act, leveraging cultural production that maintains a subjective respectability to the long-established musical tradition and securing a level of market-use value in a pop-friendly radio marketplace of consumers and recording industry gatekeepers. At its worse this space of cultural production is relegated to stooping as low as possible to secure profitable demographics. This is what Jhally (1989) might consider the inherent conflict within the culture industry. Jhally argues that primacy of profit affects media content and structure. Taking these issues into consideration, in addition to musical output, an artist's complete body of production becomes as significant as their music. L. L. Cool J as actor and clothing designer is just as relevant or perhaps more so than L. L. the emcee. Dana Owens is more notable to contemporary audiences for her work in film and television than she is as the Flavor Unit's lyrically gifted Queen Latifah. As an example, according to box office data website the Numbers,[4] films featuring Will Smith as a lead actor have grossed over US $5,581,660,135. With this kind of box office draw, Smith carries more cultural capital as an actor than through his period as the rapper of the duo DJ Jazzy Jeff and The Fresh Prince. The ability to offer a variety of goods and services has long been established as a cornerstone of longevity within the market. Businesses thrive on having the next new thing and twenty-first-century rappers are no different. Since the entrepreneurial success of rappers such as Sir Mix-A-Lot, Master P, and The Wu Tang Clan, more contemporary artists are cognizant of the politics of the marketplace. As the oft iterated Jay-Z saying that he is not simply a businessman that he, indeed *is* a business, essentially implying he understands that in a capitalist economy, his name, brand, public presentation, and business dealings outside of the recording booth are for sale and are areas as viable in the market as any of his albums. In order to navigate within this space, an artist is required to provide a product that has mass appeal and avoids direct confrontation with people and topics that have historically created division along class, race, and political lines. Thus, the imperatives of the market seem to dictate at least two things of an artist. First, the market requires limiting the flow of community engagement, and secondly, the market demands an almost accommodationist ideological positioning from artists.

Community Engagement

Community engagement creates opportunities for contact with other artists, scholars, and consumers. This is what Small (1998) calls musicking, or the encounters between human beings where we work out questions of what and how music impacts our activity. With this contact the artist can receive critical feedback for the music and cultural production to improve. Ellison (1995) shows this relationship at work through a feud with his upstairs neighbor in *Living with Music*. For Ellison and the singing neighbor, community engagement sharpens cultural history and music appreciation, and results in a refining of an artist's craft. Though Ellison begins the relationship in an effort to drown out the noise of the "singing," he and the singer ultimately grow to respect each other and their mutual knowledge of music increases. Ellison (1995) admits his "ethical consideration for the singer up above shriveled like a plant in too much sunlight" (234), particularly when interrupted from writing. In response to the disruption, Ellison decided he would "rush to [his] music system with blood in [his] eyes and burst a few decibels in her direction" (234). However, in his frustration and perhaps with the singer's indulgence, the two began a critical dialectic in cultural production. Ellison (1995) writes:

> If, let us say, she were singing "Depuis le Four" from *Louise*, I'd put on a tape of Bidu Sayao performing the same aria, and let the rafters ring. If it was some song by Mahler, I'd match her spitefully with Marian Anderson or Kathleen Ferrier.... If she brought me up from my desk with art songs by Ravel or Rachmaninoff, I'd defend myself with Maggie Teyte or Jennie Tourel. If she polished a spiritual to a meaningless artiness I'd play Bessie Smith to remind her of the earth out of which we came. (234)

The exchange between Ellison and the singer mirrors a contemporary battle of wits in a freestyle competition between two emcees. For the uninitiated, freestyle battles are fundamental to hip-hop culture. For DJs, b-girls, graffiti writers, and the emcee, battling is a time-honored tradition that demonstrates one's skill and right to participate and have a recognized voice within the culture. When both emcees are technically well prepared and lyrically capable, the battle has the potential to develop creative synergy. In this space, the participants raise their game and challenge their opponent to do as well. This kind of engagement transforms the battle and ultimately the art. "The freestyling technique has little to no bearing on commercial viability, which is largely dependent upon factors that have little to do with lyrical craftsmanship" (Ross, 2008:312). The quality of thought, verbal dexterity, crowd mastery, and command of cultural knowledge are keys to success in battles. Although largely "played out" on commercial albums, these are primary reasons classic battles between Kool Moe Dee and Busy Bee, KRS-1 and MC Shan, MC Lyte and Antoinette, Nas and Jay-Z are memorable. The space of community engagement enabled the artists to grow and improve their craft or, for some, rather embarrassingly have to acknowledge that there is someone much more capable. In the case of Ellison and the singer upstairs, their battle prompted them to increase their understanding of music and each other. Ellison (1995) noted that when he and the singer met face to face, rather than being adversarial, they discussed the music being played and the technology used, which ultimately forced him to confront his own anxieties regarding the whole situation. As Ellison (1995) recalled:

> When I met her after my rebellion...she astonished me by complementing our music system. She even questioned me concerning the artists I used against her...although I was now getting on with my writing, the unfairness of this business bore in upon me. Aware that I could not have withstood a similar comparison with literary artists of like caliber, I grew remorseful. (235)

Here Ellison, through his own encounter with community engagement, showcases the potential for transformative art. An art made accessible through his relationship with his neighbor and their shared intertextual appreciation of music. Though spaces for community engagement are currently possible, operating as Hall (1985) would suggest as counter-tendencies that routinely appear in the seams and cracks of dominant forms, they are often undervalued in dominant discourse.

Corporate Hustle: Intensified Commodification

As the commercial rap market has shifted to what Ball (2012) refers to as the colonized rhythm nation, the focus has been less on skill and more on capitulating to market demands. This trend was a feature of commercial rap as early as the mid-1990s. According to Miller (1997), since the decline in CD sales and traditionally strong earning genres such as rock, transnational music companies are investing in the next big thing rather than develop lasting musical talent. Miller (1997) notes that the major labels today "will often sign young performers not for their musicianship but because they're so derivative" (15). Commercial rap was particularly vulnerable as the mid-to-late 1990s offered the tried and true template of pathologized black masculinity—the gangsta rapper. Though often a staple of unfavorable criticism of hip-hop, and an aspect that rightly deserves critique, when fully contextualized, there is more to the gangsta rapper than the corporate-sponsored caricature suggests. What is often missing in critiques of gangsta rap and gangsta rappers is the foresight to extend the criticism further. Rather than see these representations merely as examples of problematic black youth expressions, analysis should unmask these images as links in the matrix of imperialist-white supremacist-capitalist-patriarchy (hooks, 2004). Rather than arbitrary musings of misguided youth, these images and representations deploy a legitimizing kind of logic regarding who remains powerful and who remains on the margins. Yet, despite these entanglements, what is still evident is a voice mired in institutional and cyclical marginalization that is still attempting to be heard. At face value, this image has an oppositional stance to authority, maybe even a "by any means necessary" desire to challenge the status quo on behalf of those equally oppressed. However, songs such as Wale's *By Any Means*, an appropriation of Malcolm X's standard refrain, hardly comes close to the spiritually motivated defiance of the status quo that became Malcolm X's calling card. The exertions of contemporary "gangsta rappers" appear more like versions of *A Raisin in the Sun*'s Walter Lee. For these rappers and the Walter Lees of the world, it is "the struggle between an older version of patriarchy and a new version that is overly informed by the reality of advanced capitalism" (hooks, 2004:16). Rather than being a challenge to the mechanisms of the corporate music structure, this persona actually fits with the model of ideological accommodation the industry prefers. Though limiting in the depth of musical production, the accommodation model provides promise for artists willing to operate within the hegemonic establishment. In his work, the *Nightmare and the Dream Nas, Jay Z and the History of Conflict in African American Culture*, Ross (2008) argues the success of Jay Z is due in part to his use of the accommodation strategy historically illustrated by Booker T. Washington. Ross (2008) writes:

> Jay Z followed the blueprint laid down by Booker T. Washington. At a moment when America was going through one of its cyclical periods of race weariness...rap, as potent a reflection of black American life as ever there has been, became remarkably accommodating to white America's race fatigue...the music gutted itself of political substance to get ahead in the world. (316)

It was in the aftermath of September 11, 2001, that Jay-Z began to crystallize his message of material prosperity and bootstrap hustle.

Jay-Z's career in this moment is instructive. Jay-Z not only provides a remix of Washington's model, but he also provides a blueprint for eager emcees wanting their piece of the American Dream. Post–September 11, Jay-Z begins to refigure the shadow of fallen icon Notorious B.I.G. He is able to refashion himself not just as a rapper, but as the hood's own version of a Horatio Alger narrative. Like many of his fictitious rhymes, Jay garnered mainstream credibility through several strategic moves. Jay's moves included purchasing a basketball franchise, publically endorsing a political candidate for the US presidency, and, the quintessential hallmark of a patriarchal society, marrying. Although Jay-Z was not alone in this trend and September 11, 2001, was not the first signal of this decline in music, it is significant for two key reasons. Jay-Z is arguably the most successful commercial rapper to date, and is therefore the barometer for others wishing to reproduce his material success. Secondly, post–September 11, 2001, serves as a potential marker for increased political activity on the part of commercial rappers. For a brief moment, due to the ill-fated consequences of that early day in September, artists contractually obligated to major conglomerates had the space to offer critically reflective music. Yet, unlike many rappers before them, post–September 11 rappers retreated to being uncritical flag-waving supporters of the state. Whether aware of potential profit or sponsorship loss, or truly a result of a politically neutered consciousness, commercial rap collectively said nothing. The Coup, Dead Prez, and Immortal Technique remain exceptions to this muteness. Though rappers are a source in this shift, a key force in the silencing and destabilizing of rap's once-critical voice lies in the structural changes involved in the commodification of the music.

While this is debatable, the period between 1988 and 1994 is often considered the golden era of hip-hop. During this period, independent labels were still a factor in rap music production and major labels had not quite figured out how to package, promote, and sell hip-hop culture. With few exceptions other than Rick Rubin, Russell Simmons, and the Def Jam camp, major label executives and artists and repertoire (A&R) personnel were still figuring out how to sell this new innovation in urban black culture. As a result of this ambiguity, artists had more range to create and to showcase a variety of skills, topics, and perspectives. The music often provided complex meditations on love, politics, philosophy, and all manner of musings on life. Besides the aforementioned sale and promotion of the gangsta rapper, a critical shift in rap music production came as a result of changes in copyright laws. The copyright laws shifted to address the rules and regulations regarding sampling, a process of using interpolations of existing music to create new content, a prominent feature in rap music production. Copyright law regulates who can reproduce, distribute, or authorize a copy of a derivative text (Schur, 2009). Though many artists during the "golden age" used sampling techniques, their creations were often innovative rather than appearing as poor duplicates. Public Enemy's production unit, the Bomb Squad, Prince Paul, DJ Premiere, and Pete Rock are among a group of producers whose sampling technique demonstrated the creative use of layering preexisting material into innovative new creations. By the close of the 1990s, after several prominent legal cases featuring rap artists (e.g., Biz Markie, De La Soul, and 2 Live Crew), major labels and the change in copyright law interpretation foreclosed its widespread use in rap music production. According to Jeff Chang, interviewed in the film *Copyright Criminals* (2006), the change in copyright laws drastically changed the way music was produced and shifted greater control of rap production to the hands of corporations. Myer and Kleck's (2007) political economic analysis of rap industry charts between 1990 and 2005 postulates that the influence and control of music corporations altered the content of rap music. After analyzing trends in their sample of rap charts, Myer and Kleck (2007) contend that:

> Several trends [emerge]…Beginning in 1997 we found a rise in the presence of the major labels as these companies began buying independent rap labels…We also discovered a change in the way songs were categorized after 2002. Song titles, genres, and even artists became more homogenized. (144)

With ownership of media moving toward oligopolistic control, a process that happens when "a handful of firms dominate a particular market" (Gomery, 2000: 514), it restricts the likelihood of outliers and increases the potential for easily assimilated parts. For rap music production, this means productions that follow more or less a standard format of content and production. As scholars have argued (Myer & Kleck, 2007; Ball, 2011), rap has been corporatized. Four companies, known as "the big four" (Universal Music Group, Sony/BMG, EMI, and Warner Music) dominate the commercial rap market. These media conglomerates, whose focus is on intensified commodification, largely dictate the terms by which commercial rap will be made, rather than artists and consumers. The influence of the "big four" is so pervasive that artists under the "big four" labels produced

38 of the 52 chart-topping records examined in the Myer and Kleck study. In addition to restricting the creative potential in the music, this commodification of rap helped to homogenize rap with other musical genres. While not necessarily problematic, the homogenizing of rap has meant stripping it of its usefulness as a counter-narrative space. The critiques of white supremacy, capitalism, class inequality, and marginalization are not easily transferred across the market; thus, rap music would have to lose its more critical edge. This is not to suggest that rap music—and hip-hop culture for that matter—cannot operate as a site for these tendencies. What it does mean is that these messages will be filtered through a corporate structure that does not prioritize these concerns. Instead, the market's organization results in a proliferation of mediocre artists. With the bar of success being set at how well an artist can crossover, and with relatively few avenues left to explore within the content of rap music, it provided a ready-made conduit for mediocrity. Rap acts that developed catchy hooks and intoxicating beats did not necessarily need to develop lyrically pensive songs. The 2004 release of *White Tee* by Dem Franchize Boys, *Salt Shaker* by Ying Yang Twins, *Right Thurr* by Chingy, and *Get Low* by Lil Jon & the Eastside Boyz, featuring the Ying Yang Twins, serve as examples of this trend. The popularity of these songs led to rap charts dominated by artists with similar content. Prior to Kanye West's debut, it would not be an overstatement to suggest that rap music was in a downward spiral in terms of creativity and diversity.

Paging Mr. West

Every myth begins with its own creation story. Part will be fact and part fiction, but both are necessary elements in the construction of a popular culture icon. Watching MTV in 2004, one was sure to see what is now hip-hop history. Barely surviving a car crash, Kanye West struggled to speak through a surgically wired jaw about his vision for success. Whatever was not clear in his interview was masterfully articulated in his videos (e.g., *Through the Wire* and *All Falls Down)* and debut album, *College Dropout.* Regardless of whether it was a planned or happenstance attempt to reinvigorate rap music, West's debut injected life into commercial rap. Prior to the release of his first album, West offered his take on the state of rap music:

> I feel like the public is stupid. You try to force feed them what you think it is that they want. Just put a throwback on I'm in a fitted hat and let's get an R&B singer and tell them to rap about guns. And I

think it's a lot of people that's tired of that. It's wonderful for me cause now I have a market for it.[5]

Though Kanye West's remarks might have been justifiably better served targeting the structure (corporations) that enables this lack of content in the music, West's frustration with consumers registered with many at the time. The period in which Kanye enters the commercial scene is critical. Had Kanye's entrance taken place a decade earlier, he might not have received as much critical acclaim. The year 2004 was an opportune moment given the overall quality of commercial rap. I want to be clear that I am not criticizing Kanye West, but am instead considering the tendency among critical commentators to uncritically laud him. Various writers have offered high praise of Kanye West. According to Cole (2010), Kanye West maintains a role as a conscious rapper who represents:

> The minority voice of the marginalized...[he] uses his music, knowledge, public relations skills and finesse, in tandem with mass media, to reach key audiences. His use of mass media as a communications vehicle, either through coverage of his public outbursts, public appearances or published documentation of his music sales, is necessary to creating and maintaining his image. (197)

Though Cole (2010) is primarily writing about West's remarks in reference to Hurricane Katrina, the framing of West as a particular kind of rapper extends beyond the Katrina context. In an examination of West's work as a critique of higher education, Richardson (2011) suggests that West:

> Tirelessly demonstrates ways in which the school system in America marginalizes those outside the dominant culture...he points to a history of hope and struggle in African American culture that is often erased in dominant discourse about hip hop. (p. 109)

In an article titled "American Mozart," writer David Samuels (2011) refers to West as a genius, remarking that:

> Kanye West is at least some kind of musical genius, ranking among the top five producers and the top five rappers of the past decade...He has won 18 Grammys—the most of any artist in the past 10 years—while serving as a backpack-wearing icon of black nerd chic...He is the first true genius of the iPhone era, the Mozart of contemporary American music. (74)

While Kanye West has had an impressive career and a string of successful albums from 2004's *The College Dropout* to *Late Registration* (2005), *Graduation* (2007), *808s Heartbreak* (2008), *My Beautiful Dark Twisted Fantasy* (2010), and his collaborative project with Jay Z *Watch the Throne* (2011), this essay's earlier questions becomes central:

1. What constitutes his genius?
2. How does his genius compare with others?
3. What is the state of commercial rap that we can offer the genius designation to this artist?

As a producer, West clearly provides more than tangible evidence of his talent. The ability to craft obscure sounds and hits from yesteryear and fashion them into contemporary everyday rhythms that resonate across the globe is a skill. West's understanding of musical history and human emotion provide a canvas for some of his most thoughtful compositions. Early in his career, his lyrics and accompanying video for the song "All Falls Down" engages existential questions, boldly exploring questions of individuality and the nature of meaning in a seemingly meaningless universe. Much as Ellison had done in his writings, West, consciously or not, looks at the black experience of oppression and prejudice in the United States through an existentialist lens. In the music video "All Falls Down," West's rap content on self-esteem, insecurity, and internalized oppression are augmented by the shifting point of view of the camera. Through cinematic dialogue provided by the composition of shots, the viewer is treated to a perspective that makes her or him both a voyeur and an active participant, as the viewer sees from Kanye's vantage point rather than looking at him. West would return to extending his use of cinematic language through music videos for the song *My Dark Twisted Fantasy* and the much-debated and critiqued *Runaway*. Kanye West must be commended for extending the creative potential embedded in his chosen art. However, questions of how does his genius compare with others' and whether the state of commercial rap is such that we can offer the designation of "genius" to this or any artist still warrant attention. Considering the dearth of commercial rap that transgresses the standard fare of sexism, misogyny, and homophobia, it is difficult to argue that aspects of West's body of work (rapping) is evidence of genius. Simply being better than what else is on offer is not necessarily a proof of exceptionalism, particularly in a context where rising above the lowest common denominator is discouraged. Wahneema

Lubiano (2008) ponders a similar question with regard to realism, representation, and essentialism in the cinematic offerings of Spike Lee. Lubiano (2008) states:

> Any evaluation of Lee's work as radical or counter-hegemonic has to be run past the question *Compared to What?* Against the underdeveloped, stymied state of discussion about race, racism and racialization in the United States at this moment against the paucity of production about African Americans which we could invoke to situate Lee's work and stylizations, evaluations of his and his films' politics require considerably more analysis than has been available. (36)

Though Lubian (2008) is referencing another aspect of media in analyzing West's body of cultural production beyond producing musical compositions, we are left with a similar conundrum. In comparison to what can we accurately gauge the concept of genius regarding Kanye? Should West's public outburst in the aftermath of Hurricane Katrina, his upstaging of Taylor Swift at the 2009 MTV Video Music Awards program, or his endorsement of invidious consumption be the barometer? The creative and diverse discursive politics, representation, and texture of the music have almost been completely clear-cut from the genre. Thus the few spaces that are left embody all of the hopes aspirations. Although artists such as KRS One, Chuck D, Mc Lyte, Invincible, Wise Intelligent, and Dead Prez offer critiques or critical commentary through their music, their contributions are overlooked because they do not maintain the same level of viability in the commercial marketplace. Resultantly, commentators and critical observers appear to be seeking shifts from a largely nonplussed audience. As Neal (2004) has asserted:

> By asking hip-hop to reform, we are essentially demanding hip-hop's primary consumer base to consume music that is anti-sexist, anti-misogynistic and possibly feminist. And in what context have young white men (or black men for that matter) ever been interested in consuming large amounts of black feminist thought? (4)

Although asking dominant groups to reconsider their orientation to unearned privilege is a daunting task, it does not make it a less desirable option. What may be necessary and perhaps help in doing so is not only asking the artist to rethink their relationship to art, politics, and people, but also for critics to refocus their analysis. Rather than arguing one of the most visible artists as genius, it may prove more engaging to assess the quality of the overall climate. In an essay titled *The Little Man at Chehaw Station*, Ralph Ellison is told by his music teacher, "You must always play your best, even if it's only in the waiting room at Chehaw Station, because in this country there'll always be a little man hidden behind the stove" (Ellison, 1995:490). Throughout the essay, it is clear the instructor is offering more than musical advice. Ellison (1995) writes:

> When I am brooding over some problem of literary criticism...the little stove warmer has come to symbolize nothing less than the enigma of aesthetic communication in American democracy. I especially associate him with the metamorphic character of the general American audience. (492)

Ellison goes on to discuss the role of the artist with regard to their relationship with their craft and ultimately the politics of the space in which the music is composed. In the context of Kanye West, in their evaluation of his cultural production critics may want to consider how Ellison's "little man" registers as a signal that celebrations of artists for doing what artists should ultimately be doing are not useful. Absent are the critiques that an artist needs to flourish. As cultural critics, our consideration of an artist's corpus must consider how they transform the art, not necessarily how good they are in a sea of mediocrity. If we return to our contention that Kanye West would not have made such a splash had he come a generation earlier, then we must contend that his undeniable talent is not proof sufficient of the designation "genius." Arguably, the true mark of genius is the ability to inspire others to follow in one's path. Until West demonstrates that his example will raise the standards of hip-hop across the board, it behooves us to temper our adulation with an asterisk.

Notes

1. Kanye West tweeted a single tweet on May 2 and June 18 of 2013. Over 30,000 of his followers retweeted it without clear knowledge of what it could mean. See *International Business Times* article, "Kanye West Twitter: What the Mysterious June 18th Tweet Could Mean." Friday, May 3, 2013.
2. Small (1998), 10.
3. Du Bois twoness refers to his theory of double consciousness for African Americans. DuBois saw it as a useful way to understand the psychosocial divisions existing in American society. The theory is

useful in examining any individual whose identity is divided between being American and Black.
4. See http://www.the-numbers.com/person/770401-Will-Smith for Will Smith film grosses.
5. http://www.chicagonow.com/blogs

Chapter 3

Afrofuturism: The Digital Turn and the Visual Art of Kanye West

Reynaldo Anderson and John Jennings

Introduction

The emerging contemporary cultural logic of Africa and the African Diaspora is reflected in what some scholars refer to as afrofuturism. In the past, afrofuturism was primarily regarded as a cultural mode of expression and philosophically as a form of aesthetics. However, contemporary afrofuturism is maturing in the area of metaphysical components such as cosmogony, cosmology, speculative philosophy, and philosophy of science (Szwed, 1998). Currently, a dominant expression of afrofuturism lies in its aesthetics. What is less understood is how afrofuturism is related to the cultural production of hip-hop music. That is, how afrofuturism is linked to the hip-hop culture that emerged during the decline of urban inner city cores in the latter half of the twentieth century and its digital transition in the twenty-first century, especially in visual culture. Previously, Galli (2009) illustrated connections between technological advances, artistic creation, and hip-hop culture; however, its Eurocentric construction of black culture and limited understanding of the historical development of black music limit its utility. This chapter asserts that the afrofuturist digital aesthetic perspectives, along with hip-hop culture, are impulses of Africa and the African Diaspora. They are both conscious and unconscious manifestations of "black technocultural syncretism" made possible through the proliferation of digital media as part of what some scholars refer to as postmodernity (Everett, 2009; Harvey, 1990).

Afrofuturism emerged in the spheres of literary and speculative fiction and music of the African diaspora artists in the late twentieth century. More recently, afrofuturism and its aesthetic practices are emerging in hip-hop culture proliferating in a world of new technology and communications through social media. Specifically, the afrofuturist digital aesthetic in hip-hop culture is proliferating as a response to the processes of time, space, and urban cultural practices, techno-genesis or coevolving of humans and technology, and a declining public sphere. This chapter will use an Afrofuturist digital hermeneutic to examine the visual imagery around the media hybridization, evolution, and deep remix within the graphic narrative presented by the covers of Kanye West's albums and videos and show how his art descends gradually into an ever-self-effacing nihilism.

Futurism was an artistic and literary movement developed between 1909 and World War I by Italian artists in response to a perceived crisis in modernity that arose as European urban life suddenly changed in the late nineteenth century (Berghaus, 2005). Principal luminaries of futurism included Gino Severini, Giamcomo Balla, and Umberto Boccioni and the poet-critic Tommaso Marinetti. Futurism's goal was to make a distinct break with old cultural or political institutions and exalt the modern creations of electricity, planes, and science. Both Italian futurism and the contemporary French-inspired literary and artistic movement of surrealism were influenced by the African Diaspora art form of jazz. Italian futurist saw jazz as compatible with their philosophy of technological triumphalism, whereas French anti-imperialist surrealist viewed the art form as an expression of the black working class and they believed that non-Western culture had developed communications and methods "That transcended the conscious" (Kelley, 2002: 160). An intellectual offshoot of futurism, Dadaism was founded by Hugo Ball, Tristan Tzara, and others. It drew on Friedrich Nietzsche's writings such as *Beyond Good and Evil* and *Thus Spake Zarathustra*. Dadaism emerged as an artistic response to the mass deaths inflicted in World War I and the transformation of capital that had the effect of undermining long-held cultural values and became a symbol of nihilism. One of the basic tenets of Dadaism was the use of onomatopoeia and collage to express complex ideas and circumstances. Kanye West utilizes this type of expression in his lyrics and he employs practices that could be seen as Dadaist in videos such as "Good Life" from *Graduation* and "Gold Digger" from *Late Registration*. West's performances in these and other videos highlight the fungibility of art. This was also part of the Dadaists' main objective. They challenged the notion of the systems that served to privatize artistic expression. We operate in a pan-fungible system where everything is for sale and West uses his own celebrity to demonstrate this idea.

According to Bennett (2006), the term *afrofuturism* should be used cautiously. It is distinct from the European futurism based on the work of Friedrich Nietzsche that gave rise to social engineering in the Soviet Union, and Fascism in Italy and Germany (Bell, 2002). Many modern Eurocentric futurists focused on the Nietzschean ideas of Will to power and *Übermenschen* or supermen, and some afrofuturists appropriate and rearticulate Eurocentric theoretical constructs to explore the semiotics of some artifacts. Afrofuturism differs from European and Euro-American futurism in one important aspect. Futurism and Fascism in Europe emerged out of the cultural hegemony that was imposed on non-Western peoples in the late nineteenth and early twentieth centuries.

During the period of the emergence of Fascism, aesthetic inquiry into modern media began to focus on the relationship between analog technology, reproduction, and the arts. Walter Benjamin's 1935 essay *The Work of Art in the Age of Mechanical Reproduction* was a seminal work in the analytical practice of media aesthetics. It was written in a period of important changes in technology, particularly in film, which demanded new analytical approaches in art criticism (Buck-Morss, 1992). Benjamin's essay reviewed the history of the aesthetics of art in relation to practice and identified possibilities for critiquing the possibilities of avant-garde cinema and how Fascism appropriated the new media. Benjamin's prescient analysis of the potential dangers of Fascism and Nazism in Europe in combination with cinema and propaganda foreshadows the apocalyptic future of Europe prior to World War II (Buck-Morss). Benjamin's work, highly praised by scholars, offers an approach to reinterpreting aesthetics from a materialist perspective taking into account the interrelated contexts of the cognitive and sociopolitical functions of aesthetics in relation to modern cinematic technologies and the film industry. Although the approach embraced by Benjamin is valid, the Eurocentric underpinnings of the materialist approach are culturally unsatisfactory and do not take into account the interactions between contemporary cultural formations, hermeneutic ontology, and technological advances.

Among the commentators on Benjamin, Vattimo (1991: 54) asserts that his essay is an attempt to catalogue the "end of art," which is, in the modern world, no longer connected to "the utopia of metaphysical or revolutionary reintegration of existence." The act of reproduction of art collapses the differences between the user and producer relying on the technological use of machines negating the "genius of the artist" (54). Vattimo notes that, "The emergence of a paradigm requires much more than its imposition by force from the outside.

It occurs through a complex system of persuasion, active participation, and interpretations...answers which are never exclusively nor principally the effects of force and violence involve a kind of aesthetic, hermeneutic, or rhetorical assimilation"(92). According to Vattimo, the rise of computer science in the latter half of the twentieth century signified a technological shift from modernity to postmodernity and, in hermeneutic philosophy, required an extension of ideas articulated previously by Walter Benjamin. For example, "The internet has brought up changes in our spatial-temporal social experience that were difficult to imagine some decades ago" (Capurro, 2010: 36). Therefore, the productive logic concerning the relationship between human beings and technology is in need of revision. In intellectual disciplines, such as visual communications, it is impossible to impose the kind of "linear specializations in art, video and film, and due to the impact of Networked mass media giving shape to metamorphic *Becoming* is the challenge" (Stafford, 2004: 214–215). This technological shift has influenced what is referred to as a "Digital Turn" in culture reflected in the influence of database logic, networked software, deep remixability, technological interface, cultural analytics, and neurosciences (Negroponte, 1995; Pisters, 2012). The *Digital Turn* permeates aspects of all societies where modern structures, economic and cultural are influenced by software (Manovich, 2013). The position of the *Digital Turn* and technocratic triumphalism tends to conveniently overlook how race, class, and gender "shape the ways computer technology gets used and by whom (Hines, Nelson, Tu, 2001: 1). The Digital Turn tends to render the idea of a physical body as outdated hardware. Software and associated apps are being readily designed and consumed at amazing rates of speed. As a result, we see the ideas of the analog disappearing and finding the content that was once connected to a particular physical mediated object now being accessed by communal "clouds" of information. The idea of transcending the body and its limitations has always been a central notion in Black speculative fiction and we now live in world where the meta-medium of the computer and its software allows us to do just that. Kanye West's debut of the video for "New Slaves" from the *Yeezus* album involved the projection of West's disembodied visage on city walls around the world. In this video West is simultaneously omnipresent and nowhere. The virtuality of his performance demonstrates not only the power of software but also the subsequent loss of humanity and identity. West exposes the fact that his body, even though virtual, is still a racialized form that carries the history of all prior incarnations of the black image in popular media forms.

A similar problem with the analysis of media, technology, and the African Diaspora was identified in the mid-1960s by Harold Cruse in *The Crisis of the Negro Intellectual*. Cruse wrote that the "Negro" leadership had failed to develop a program for moving the African American community forward following the passage of civil rights legislation. He laid out some of the early cultural contours of neoliberalism with respect to artistic production and modern media with its psychological effects over populations. An example of the latter, as Williams Sites points out in his study, *Radical Culture in Black Necropolis: Sun Ra, Alton Abraham and Postwar Chicago*, is that Sun Ra, his partner Alton Abraham, and other black musicians developed a cultural form of production that was a departure from market-based liberal approaches supported by liberal blacks or white elites and would anticipated more radical forms of black culture creative expression. Responding to the growing nihilism within sectors of the black American population in the 1960s, artists such as former Greenwich Village bohemian poet Leroi Jones penned two influential poems that bracketed the impact of the change that came with social unrest and technological innovation between 1964 and the early 1970s. In the poems "Black Dada Nihilismus" and "Technology and Ethos" Jones, A.K.A. Amiri Baraka, articulated the cultural nexus between art, Western technology, and its impact on the African cultural milieu.

The work of Baraka anticipated the early developmental of stages of hip-hop and rap and their response to urban nihilism, benign neglect, and the postmodern condition. Black and Latino youth in the south Bronx community of New York City used new technologically advanced sound systems, cultural manipulation, and appropriation to create new musical forms (Chang, 2005; Potter, 1995). Pioneers in the emerging hip-hop scene of the 1970s and 1980s such as Afrika Bambaataa's Zulu Nation and others would appropriate, and "rearticulate science in terms of black popular culture, or, 'droppin science' in the hip hop vernacular," and adapt them to the needs of their urban constituencies (Chang, 2005: 27). Baraka's intellectual contribution to black vernacular culture prefigures Kanye West's artistic development. In the second Bush administration, social unrest resulting from the American War on Terror, Hurricane Katrina, and the economic downturn disproportionately impacted minority youth. In tandem with the space/time compression of the postmodern era in the digital age, the analog approach articulated by previous scholarly assessments of aesthetics may be of limited utility. An afrofuturistic digital hermeneutic is needed to critique contemporary artistic production. The question arises as to how to approach an epistemological break with Eurocentric ideas of futurism. A plausible analysis lies in the historical underdevelopment of critiquing racism in institutional frameworks or structures, and the limited understanding of the theory and praxis of African or black activists and intellectuals. Patriarchy and heterosexism are also implicated in these structures, but in the interest of brevity the essay will look at the interplay of race in relation to technology and digital culture.

In regard to racism, most Eurocentric scholarship by orthodox Marxists, neo Marxists, liberals, neoliberals, and some feminists has produced some breakthroughs emphasizing ideological and cultural processes (Bonilla-Silva, 1996). However, this brand of scholarship prioritizes the projects of actors and tends to ignore or obscure the character of social collectives or characters of racialized societies (Bonilla-Silva). For example, the notion of racialized social and knowledge systems and the transition from domination during slavery and colonialism to hegemony during the postcolonial and post–civil rights era clearly identify the hierarchal relationship between whites and nonwhites (Bonilla-Silva, Winant, 2004). Therefore, this historical problem is implicated in the lack of awareness or limited exposure to knowledge systems articulated by people of color.

Previously, it has been assumed that the ideas put forth by Black activists and thinkers are primarily a derivative of European notions of revolution and change and should be understood on the basis of "experiences" (Bogues, 2003). This mistaken assumption is due to the way political ideas and thought are studied. Black activist thought may be considered outside the framework of Western epistemology (Bogues). In relation to the orthodoxy of Western critical theory and practice, the black radical commits heresy by creating a new critical discourse when questioning the doxa of Western intellectual formations utilizing "systems of classifications that reproduce their own logic...imposing their own principles of social reality" (Bogues, 2003: 12–13). As well, "black radical intellectual production engages in a double operation...an engagement with western radical theory and then a critique of this theory...breaking the epistemic limits established by the Western intellectual tradition." Furthermore, "For the black radical intellectual, 'heresy' means becoming human, not white or imitative of the colonial, but overturning white/European normativity" (13).

In relation to technology and racialized utopias, the division of access to technology and science is exemplified by the West's colonization of Africa through its technology and distribution of cell phones, film, economic markets, etc. (Olson, 2011). However, an example of a digital counter-narrative to Western technological domination is offered in the film *Saaraba*, directed by Amadou Saalam Seck, that explores the connection between identity and modernity on African terms (Olson). Also with respect to afrofuturism and visual culture, there are numerous examples of heretical rearticulating that include Sun Ra, George Clinton, X-Clan, and the most recent artistic production of Janelle Monae in her concept albums *TheMetropolis Suite* that reinterpret the 1927 film *Metropolis* by Fritz Lang. Monae', like West, uses the visual medium of the music video to critique the privatization of identity in a media-saturated culture. In her video for "Many Moons," she displays herself as a capitalist meme that is constantly reproduced and sold at a fashion show/slave auction. This use of technology as a mode of critique is an aspect of an Afrofuturist perspective.

Afrofuturism emerged as a means to understand the transformation of African peoples as they dealt with the oppressive forces of discrimination, the complexities of modern urban life and postmodernity. Specifically, contemporary Afrofuturist aesthetic practice emerged out of the nexus of transnational capital, migration, international and domestic social movements and conflict, the influences of technology, religion, black music, black literature, and other forms of aesthetic expression. Secondly, and more importantly, the Afrofuturist aesthetic perspective establishes a counter-narrative and undermines or delegitimizes the power of the *Leviathan*, the Eurocentric social contract that institutionalizes and maintains the power of the elite and limits the ability of the *people* to collectively imagine or prepare for an alternative future (Nurrudin, 2006).

The term Afrofuturism has been described by Mark Dery, based on his interaction with the graffiti artist Rammel-Zee, black writers and speculative fiction, and technoculture as appropriated by African Americans (Dery, 1994). Today, afrofuturism examines aesthetics and intellectual terrain of the so-called post-human/post-racial future invented by largely techno-libertarian white futurists. It does, however, remain connected to an African humanistic past, reinventing a visionary discourse that deals with the diasporic experience impacted by technological transformation and geographic location. It has the ability to maintain a counter-narrative of history, progress, tradition, innovation, memory, the authentic and engineered, analog and digital within spaces of African diasporic culture (Eglash, 2002; David, 2007). In other words, afrofuturism and thinking about the future will take on the local characteristics of an African population as it evolves in relation to technology. As Marlo David (2007) notes:

> Afrofuturist thought posts a reconciliation between an imagined dis-embodied, Identity-free future and the embodied identity-specific past and present, which can provide a critical link though which post soul artists can express a radical black subjectivity. (697)

An Afrofuturist is consciously or unconsciously writing, painting, or artistically expressing the lives of African peoples in relation to other sentient beings in the past, present, or future(s), and is released from a static representation of a *particularistic* or monocultural form of identity that is free and yet remains politically or artistically engaged. Afrofuturism is not a subgenre of science fiction but a larger aesthetic mode connecting artists and scholars with an interest of "project-ing black futures derived from Afrodiasporic experiences" (Yaszek, 2005: 2). For example, Paul Gilroy's *The Black Atlantic* juxtaposes the primary ideological difference between the eschatology 'sor "end time destiny" of Western Eurocentric writers with the Afrodisaporic tradition. He argues that within the framework of European moder-nity, the theme of *Utopia* projects the idea that society progresses through rationalism, technological advance, complexity, and materi-alism, while in contrast the Africana tradition of *The Jubilee* involves a striving for perfection regardless of the destination (Gilroy, 1993:68). An example of this worldview can be demonstrated by the fact that in religion, history, art, politics, and literature, Africans and their diaspora have repeatedly chosen to find a way to resist or transform their circumstances rather than to rationally accept their condition.

Kodwo Eshun (1998) states that afrofuturism is "concerned with the possibilities for intervention within the dimension of the predic-tive, the projected...the virtual...the future"(293). Historically, much of African American literature has been regarded in terms of resistance and redemption, but this, considered in the light of Afrofuturism, lacks a *critical* standpoint in relation to future forces of production and social reality (Bould, 2007).Yet, despite its creative possibilities, the continued threat posed by white supremacy in rela-tion to biological process and technology, and a potential future for African peoples, a critical assessment related to struggle and the col-lective survival of the community cannot be neglected (David, 2007). Therefore, the current study takes an Afrofuturist digital hermeneu-tic perspective that intersects theories of time and space, technology, class, race, gender, and sexuality and delineates a general economy of racialization in relation to forces of production and apocalyptic, dystopian, and utopian futures.

Visual Imagery, Hip-Hop, and Kanye West

Previous studies on the connection between afrofuturism and hip-hop have illustrated the key figures, genres, technologies, and tropes in the culture (Galli, 2004). This section will examine Kanye West's visualization of his seemingly gradual descent from a progressive and forward-looking point of view into a decidedly more nihilistic and morbid visual aesthetic in the execution of his videos. This will involve an afrofuturist hermeneutic analysis of the music videos for the songs "Stronger" from his third album *Graduation*, "Love Lock Down" from his fourth album *808s & Heartbreak*, and "Monster" from his fifth studio album *My Beautiful, Twisted Dark Fantasy*. It will also examine and rearticulate Manovich's notion of media hybridization, evolution, and deep remix with respect to the visual images around the graphic narrative presented by the covers of West's albums and how they reflect his progressive assumption of a self-effacing nihilistic image.

Visual images are one of the most important aspects to hip-hop culture. Even before MTV made images of MCs swagger and "around-the-way-girls" sexy style accessible to a mass audience, visual communications were critical to the construction of identity in hip-hop culture. At present, the visual rhetoric of hip-hop celebrities is controlled by the industry and self-censored because any blemish, bad hair, or fashion faux pas is recorded instantly and broadcast via a web of interconnected media services. One of the most powerful triumphs of the music industry was the recontextualization of what was simply a commercial for a hip-hop album into popular consumer content in the music video. This was the genius of MTV—sandwiching ads between ads. By doing this, MTV has influenced an entire generation of teens through the power of visual images. One of the most visually fascinating hip-hop artists is Kanye West. He possesses visual acumen and cleverly uses this skill set in the construction of his identity in his album covers and his music videos.

West's first three album covers "The Education Trilogy" are dominated by the "Dropout Bear" mascot, which is an anthropomorphic signifier of West himself. It's important to note that the first two of these covers "The College Dropout" and "Late Registration" both involve photographic images. Photography implies visual reporting that is associated with depictions of reality while graphic illustrations are used more for the depiction of symbolic concepts (Sturken and Cartwright, 2009). West's covers become illustrative and more abstract after the first two albums. The artwork for "Graduation" was done by Japanese pop artist Takashi Murakami. The cover shows Dropout Bear being catapulted into the future. Like a great deal of Murakami's work, the style seems "happy" or "friendly," but the work also begins to have foreboding undertones. Where does the bear land and will he be safe after rocketing into the "real world"? The next cover seems to answer that query. The cover of *808s & Heartbreak* (2008) depicts a photo-illustration of a deflated balloon in the shape of a heart. The entire album is dedicated to West's break-up with model/actress Amber Rose and grief over his mother's death. The deflation of his ego and his fall into a darker space is reified with this cover. The heart in the cover art isn't "broken" but simply "empty." This empty heart symbolizes West's music that will become bare and stripped down in content.

My Beautiful Dark Twisted Fantasy, Kanye West's fifth studio album, pushes artistic boundaries in virtually every way and, to some, is his best creative effort. The album art features the work of famed contemporary artist George Condo. Condo's style is Pop Surrealist and Cubist. He portrays various aspects of West's album themes. Various options for the album cover were created. In the final version, the main image depicts a monstrous black man with an armless female Phoenix or angel astride him. The cover also has an image of a ballerina in black with a glass of wine. This image relates directly to West's "Runaway" video. The wine is a reference to Christ. The symbols of religion, power, consumption, and subsequent destruction are apparent in the rest of the graphic as well. There is an image of an almost demonic priest and a sword stuck in the decapitated and crowned head of West. The narrative continues with another sword embedded in a patch of grass. His "Dropout Bear" stares angrily at the viewer and seems to become both feral and lethargic at the same time. Finally, the stark rendition of West with four sets of mouths echoing the imagery of his bear avatar completes the beautifully disturbing artwork with gothic themes.

The meanings of the color red are actively explored in the album covers from the *808s & Heartbreaks* all the way through to his seventh studio album *Yeezus*. The art on the cover of *My Beautiful Dark Twisted Fantasy* was framed boldly in royal red symbolic of passion, love, anger, and, of course, blood. The cover is marked by its starkness. We see only a lone reminder of West's visual passion in a single square placed to the right of the clear casing of the CD itself. The stripped down sound of the album is symbolically portrayed by this almost bare and naked illustration of West's current attitudes about himself, capitalism, and the industry around celebrity.

The images of the covers are part of an overarching visual rhetoric that has been carefully constructed by West to complete his artistic endeavors. Videos from his albums tie together an overall deconstruction of his own image. For example, the music video for "Stronger" adds a futuristic visual style to the electronic fusion sample of the French electronica group Daft Punk. The video depicts West in three roles. The first is that of the visual "chorus." He acts as lead narrator. His coolness is symbolized by his isolation against a gray brick wall while he dances and disengages his gaze via white multi-slit eyewear. This is one of the ways that coolness observes without itself being observed. The second persona is that of a digital image. This image operates from the standpoint of opposition. It not only gazes directly at the audience but also revels in its virtual nature. The image seems to desire to be read as artificial. We can read this semiotically or interpret its signs or meanings through the fact that the actual lines that create the image are clear. This directness denotes intentionality. The third persona is that of the "experimental subject." The guest artists Daft Punk are covered from head to toe in their faceless motorcycle helmets and black bodysuits. They can be read as humans, robots, or androids. This ambiguity of identity is juxtaposed with Kanye West's very human, very male, and very black body. West is shown inside an electronic chamber that performs mechanical exercise on his body. Whatever is happening here, this third persona is understood as "other"—enhanced, or supernatural.

Toward the end of the video, a figure in a hospital bed appears dressed in a gown with its head bandaged. This can be read as the result of a laboratory experiment. The result of the experiment is the development of a type of psycho-kinetic ability that is displayed through the illustration of force exacted upon the space itself and also upon other human bodies. This depiction is obviously appropriated from the classic Japanese anime film *Akira* in which a young man named Tetsuo is given an almost god-like ability. These images explore the theme of transcendence in the face of adversity. Transcendence is one of the main ideas in West's music. He had become successful overcoming financial difficulties, lack of education, and a major car accident. The lyrics of "Stronger" paraphrase Fredrich Nietzche's quote: "That which does not kill you, makes you stronger" and continues to add to West's mytho-poetic of survival. In a sense, West is speaking of the African American experience. It is interesting to note, also, that this is the last album that employs West's bear mascot symbol. To reiterate, the first three Kanye West albums formulate a sort of "education trilogy" from *College Dropout* to *Late Registration* and finally to *Graduation*. Dropout Bear mascot is the major player and is finally getting the spoils of hard work. The bear mascot serves as a chrysalis that is then shed to become the avatar of West's next stage of existence as a public celebrity and artist.

With the death of his mother and the break-up with his former lover Amber Rose, the hip-hop star experiences a "fall from grace." With *808s & Heartbreak*, an album dedicated to pain and loss, West shapes his very public break-up into a narrative intended to be an auditory catharsis. One of the hit singles from the album, "Love Lock Down" utilizes a heavily auto-tuned soundscape held together by the mesmerizing and mechanized beat of an electronic drum simulating the beating of a human heart. The visualization of this song is an intriguing amalgam of past, present, and future. It functions as a connection between the Afrofuturistic and what has become a decidedly darker and Gothic visual sensibility. Gothic narratives deal with:

> the legacies of the past and its burdens on the present the radically provisional or divided nature of the self; the construction of peoples or individuals as monstrous or "other"; the preoccupation with bodies that are modified, grotesque or diseased. Gothic has become so pervasive precisely because it is so apposite to the representation of contemporary concerns (Spooner, 2007:8).

"Love Lock Down's" self-deprecating lyrics speak of West's regret in the aftermath of his failed relationship. The video shows West in a room surrounded by a white timeless void. As the narrative of the song progresses, we see an overlapping of West in the present, simulations of what look to be African tribesmen, and a hovering spacecraft. The appearance of the space is reminiscent of the virtual prison occupied by Morpheus to Neo in the Wachowski brothers' highly praised film *The Matrix*. It also brings to mind the "holo-deck" in the syndicated television show *Star Trek: The Next Generation*. In West's imagination, we see a boldly liminal space that is dominated by giant neon-painted women who appear to be worshipped as goddesses by the tribesmen. The space could be read as a representation of the tensions between two readings of a type of Mothership as a means to escape trauma. The fact that both of these depictions function against the backdrop of whiteness is very telling. All of the narratives are an antithesis of a white space. The Africanist presence in the piece is an amalgam of a certain type of "African" that really has no particularly discernible relationship to an actual tribe. The dances of the Africans morph into b-boying and breaking near the end of the video. At the end of the clip, West's self-representation succumbs to his pain as he languishes on an austere couch fully engulfed by white. This whiteness symbolizes the unknown, the unwritten, and the fear of the future. As a result of this fear, West seems to choose to regress into a darker, more familiar soundscape along with an equally recognizable visual palette.

My Beautiful, Twisted Dark Fantasy opens up a vault of tropes that are easily attributed to the Gothic. "Monster," one of the many hits from this album, sees West truly embrace the nihilistic aspects of his psyche and his public persona. This track features guest stars Jay-Z, Rick Ross, and Nikki Minaj, who join West in celebration of the macabre. The video truly embraces almost every aspect of the traditional Gothic movement. It depicts opulence, vanity, sexuality, the doppelganger, the supernatural, and the grotesque. It relates all of these to the black body and how it reifies the alien and the monstrous other. Rick Ross is surrounded by the corpses of women dangling from the ceiling like ornaments. Jay-Z raps in a chic suit while the camera plays with the image of a nude woman tastefully stuffed under couch pillows. The image focuses on her open mouth and her cold blue, and obviously dead, lips. Nikki Minaj appears as a risqué dominatrix and is torturing another woman who has a bag over her face. The bag is taken off and reveals another aspect of Minaj's own psyche. Her doppelganger's voice is high-pitched, playful but by no means innocent. Minaj eventually growls out her amazing lyrics and fuses her two selves into one darkly beautiful visage. West himself is seen earlier in the video in bed with two gorgeous dead models. He poses one like a mannequin or a life-sized Barbie doll as he spouts his lyrics. In a later scene, he stands nonchalantly against a brick wall with the head of woman dangling from his left hand. It is important to note that the majority of the women depicted are white women. West is making a statement about the stereotypes of hypersexuality and hyperviolence that have historically been heaped upon the black male body. West becomes the stereotypical. He transforms himself into the hated, grotesque, murderous, and subhuman rapist. However, he clothes his image in dark, cool, and cutting-edge fashions. His visual statement lampoons commodity culture and points out that all of these constructs are just fetishized images that are ripe to be devoured by the monsters that tune in and watch.

Reading these videos as a sequence, we see West shift from futuristic post-human antihero to a tortured lovelorn hero and finally to dark and repulsive cannibal. West goes from triumph to a dark acceptance that borders on defeat. He is shaped by the media that gives him power and fame. His sensibility and understanding of image, and how they convey power and meaning, is highly developed. This heightened sensibility is shown in the extreme in the video for his deeply introspective and problematic single the "New Slaves." West, when premiering the video, projected his face on walls so that he appeared as a ghost-like prophet predicting the *darkness* to come. He invoked himself as part of the problem of capitalism and likened us all to slaves in this new, hyper-connected global economy. The video's brilliance is that it utilizes technology to illustrate the frustrations of a society swollen with self-indulgence and shackled by the commodity of self. The video mediates the shallowness and ephemeral nature of our current existence.

These specific instances of the dark symbolism regarding West's apparent disdain for his own success are inextricably linked to the system of consumption associated with late capitalism. He demonstrates via his projection of the stark "New Slaves" video that his very body is unnecessary and that the mediation of his celebrity reclaims public and mental space by its simple ubiquity. The CD isn't important anymore. The content isn't either. It's the personification of celebrity; the godlike qualities that we give media stars is the ultimate consumable product. We see West's climb to stardom going from being behind the scenes as a producer to a living spectacle in the form of his becoming the front man, in some ways eclipsing his former self. West laments the images that represent him and he attacks them constantly in his music, his videos, and his album art. The weight of the multiple doppelgangers of identity in the public sphere has forced West to disassociate himself from his own body. He is now just a ghostly Orwellian "Big Brother" looming on screens like some mediated genie. His message is that of a media god who is tired of his lofty perch and longs to be down among the masses, even though his loss of power would be his undoing.

What happens when you get exactly what you want and find that prize inadequate? West's desire to express himself still gnaws on him and, we, as audience, get to see what happens when a star collapses on itself. The only thing that is left is a black maw that pulls in everything. That includes the outer packaging that is the candy-coated lie of the system. West's genius is that, for good or ill, he sees the connections in society and his own place within that system. He also uses that system to warn us of things to come. This includes the sublimation of the underclass via the constant longing to move up and become the envy of the masses. He has become "Yeezus," the shiny, maniacal media deity and he prays to himself knowing that eventually, we will all follow suit. The barbarians are at the gate and West is waiting there to sample the collapse, remix it, and use it against the very spectacle that he loves and hates at the same time. He explores the various layers of identity in the public and uses himself as "guinea pig."

West's visual portrayals of himself indicate that he truly does understand the nature of the image. He understands that it is only a representation of something else. It is re-presenting the thing that actually isn't there; himself. To borrow and remix from Rene Magritte's classic art piece titled "The Treachery of Images," "Ceci n'est pas un Kanye'" ("This is not Kanye").

West's mastery over various software applications allows him to understand just how mutable the perception of reality truly is. We think of technology as the hardware that enables us to perform certain tasks. However, "technology" also encompasses techniques, systems, and methods of organization. In that regard, race itself can be seen as a technology because it innately produces particular effects that organize and shape our society according to prescribed views. An Afrofuturist perspective and aesthetic embraces this notion and sees the world through a "pantechnological" lens whereby artifacts and constructs can be attributed to technology, hacked and change its representation until it becomes a simulation with no signifier or referent in reality. The software that Kanye West has been slowly reprogramming and hacking into is the representation of himself in the public eye. Identity is just another "software package" that we can shift and upgrade to fit the perceptions of the public. Does West see himself as a god or does the audience? In the vocals of "I Am a God" from the *Yeezus* album, West performs what could be interpreted as a panic attack or an expression of trauma. This dramatic and traumatic expression has become interwoven in West's overall narratives of life, celebrity, wealth, politics, sex, and religion. All of these technologies become more and more mutable when the individual "programs" of various perspectives are introduced. Cyber culture treats all things as equitable. A computer only sees code. However, an Afrofuturist perspective engages that code in a critical and radical fashion and seeks to re-appropriate its power in order to facilitate change and acquire agency.

West has shown that his software package or his identity has been constantly upgraded by being overexposed to the public. He has evolved into "Kanye 5.0," and like the software he so skillfully uses to make his work, he can also hack into expressions and alter presentations.

His methods employ virtually every aspect of deep remix from his various alter egos to his introspective videos. His media forms subvert monolithic notions of identity and expose the falseness of the digital constructs of various modes of surveillance and control. West's work is also highly cross-disciplinary, inter-textual, and hybrid. He exhibits various roles and overlapping performances as producer, consumer, celebrity, singer, visual artist, director, actor, and media critic. The power of software creates a space where simulations of various media forms coexist and become, as Manovich states, new "media species." West uses visual portrayals of himself as an answer to the question: "What happens when those species escape into our world?"

Chapter 4

You Got Kanyed: Seen but Not Heard

David J. Leonard

To begin with an anecdote: I own a t-shirt that reads "KANYE WAS RIGHT." In the aftermath of Hurricane Katrina, and Kanye's appearance at an NBC fundraiser, where he called out George W. Bush for the ineptitude of his administration, I purchased this shirt from the organization Color of Change, which in the aftermath of the broken levees formed to unify and galvanize a black political voice. Selling these shirts was part of a fundraising push for them; it was also a statement of support and outrage for the treatment endured by African Americans in the aftermath of this national disaster.

The shirt spoke to me not only because of the backlash directed at West and the power of his words, but because it became a symbolic intervention at the failed policies before, during, and after Hurricane Katrina. It was bigger than Kanye or George W. Bush. His comments and the shirt reflected my own anger and sadness, frustration, and need to voice dissent about the injustice. While recognizing the limitations of consumptive politics or "purchasing justice," it was an intervention against the silence and political paralysis that defined the post-Katrina moment. Kanye's comments represented an interruption of the silence, an insertion of a voice of anger, and an effort to reimagine Katrina as a national tragedy that disproportionately impacted African Americans; for me, the shirt, which invariably prompted stares and head shakes (along with approving nods), was a rally cry for action.

Several years later, while walking the streets of Los Angeles, several young women of color passed by me, apparently randomly commenting that "Kanye was right." Looking down, I realized I was wearing the shirt. Before parting (with one of them photographing the shirt and posting it to Instagram), we spoke about the shirt's message. I quickly learned that for them, the shirt was about Kanye and Taylor Swift, not Kanye and George Bush:[1]

> "He was right about Beyoncé deserving the award more than Taylor."
> Me: "Indeed, but the shirt is in reference to his comments about President Bush after Katrina"
> "He was right about that too."

Within this context, this paper examines the Swift–West VMA encounter, exploring how race, gender, and the performative bodies associated with rap and country music constrained and contained the media discourse. In fact, the racial and gendered bodies of Swift and West overdetermined the reaction and the fallout that ensued. More importantly, West's past disruptions, the purported apolitical nature of modern popular culture, and the power of whiteness fueled a heated response in the aftermath of Bush and Swift.

Rather than seeing West as a political artist who utilizes the platform afforded to him to disrupt and agitate in a political sense, he was reduced to a selfish thug. Whereas Swift (and Bush) was presented as victim, West was depicted as an irrational, selfish thug. These efforts to individualize the protest, to make it personal, and to demonize West erased the very real political and cultural issues at work. As with West's protest against George Bush and his administration's failures during Hurricane Katrina, the efforts to refigure West diminished the very real and important interventions contained in his words.

His greatest sin was not cutting off Taylor Swift or saying that George Bush doesn't care about black people, but violating the expectations of a black male artist. He neither embodied a politics of respectability nor did he embrace the gangsta lean so popular within the white imagination. Had he dropped his pants, made it rain, or simply rapped about rape, all would be good. Had he worn a suit, talked about his rags-to-rich story, and admonished those who "make excuses"/make the wrong choices, picture perfect. But he didn't do anything of those things, and worse, engaged in political challenge to whiteness. In getting political, in challenging whiteness, he violated the predetermined scripts available to black men.

Examining the reaction, and situating it within a larger history of black popular culture and political interventions, this chapter argues that backlash against West is yet another moment where blackness is desired to be seen but not heard.

You Just Got Kanyed

In 2009, Kanye West stepped on stage as Taylor Swift prepared to accept her award for best female video at the MTV Video Music Awards. Impelled to voice his displeasure that Swift received the VMA rather than Beyoncé, West grabbed the mic, announcing, "Yo Taylor, I'm real happy for you, I'mma let you finish, but Beyoncé had one of the best videos of all time! One of the best videos of all time!" (Syme 2009).

While his actions were the sort of thing you have to expect at the VMAs, West was castigated near and far.[2] Beyond mere denunciation of his actions, much of the media discourse recast West as physically threatening and menacing, playing upon long-standing ideas about black masculinity. Jayson Rodriguez, at MTV, described the incident as one where West "stormed the stage" to "cut the teen singer off, grabbing the mic" (2009). Daniel Kreeps, in *Rolling Stone*, identified the moment as one where "West stormed the stage" (2009). Tom O'Neil saw Kanye's action as part of a larger history: "Kanye West has a long history of throwing the best tantrums over award shows...of all time (2009)." John Mosner narrated the happening as one where "he bullied" and "picked on a teen-aged girl."

Artists also took to the airwaves (France, 2009) to defend Swift, and by extension silence West's criticisms of the music industry:

Pink tweeted, "Kanye West is the biggest piece of shit on earth. Quote me"

Joel Madden tweeted, "All i'm saying is Taylor Swift is a young chic and you just walk up and grab the mic."

Perez Hilton tweeted, "Taylor Swift deserved that award, damnit. It is what THE PEOPLE voted! My heart broke for her, she looked so sad at the end of that moment."

Katy Perry offered, "Fuck u Kanye. It's like you stepped on a kitten."

Kelly Clarkson, in a an open letter to West, asked, "What happened to you as a child? Did you not get hugged enough?"

Ironically, Donald Trump, of all people, lambasted West as a selfish narcissist only concerned with his own spotlight. Calling his actions "disgusting" and encouraging boycotts, Trump asserted that "[West] couldn't care less about Beyoncé. It was grandstanding to get attention." Sean Noble captured much of the rhetoric flying around the Internet that dismissed West and his comments as those of an angry thug or child. His protest was not worthy of consideration. Worse yet, Noble used West's purported bad acts to devalue and demonize rap, hip-hop, and blackness as undesirable and disruptive. He became representative of the pathological values and ego-driven bravado that hip-hop brought into the mainstream:

> Last night during the MTV Awards, he interrupted the young Country star Taylor Swift, who was giving some remarks after accepting an award for best female video. Apparently, West didn't think Swift deserved the award, so he walked on stage and grabbed the microphone from her and said that the best video was Beyonce' (does she have a last name?).
>
> The humiliated Swift—all of about 18 years-old—couldn't even finish after he handed the microphone back.
>
> West has a history of outrageous thuggery—and always with a racial twist.
>
> Who can forget this little beauty when Mike Myers and Kanye West were a part of the effort to raise money for the victims of hurricane Katrina. It would be funny if it weren't so outrageous. Poor Mike Myers, one of the funniest people on earth, was stuck on live TV standing next to this guy as he inarticulately (to put it mildly) said that troops had been sent to New Orleans with permission to shoot Black people and inexplicably blurted out, "George Bush doesn't care about Black people."
>
> I couldn't name a song the guy sings—nor if I heard one of his "songs" would I know it was him—so it'll be hard for me to boycott him (2009).

Denounced as a bully, rude, mean, and disrespectful, the reaction was very much influenced by West's past critiques of George Bush, along with his image as an outspoken and confident artist. The framing of Swift as innocent, pure, and sweet clouded the reactions. According to *Time Magazine*, "Taylor Swift barely had a chance to accept her award for Best Female Video at the 2009 MTV Video Music Awards on Sept. 13 before Kanye West rushed the stage, grabbed the microphone out of the startled teen's hands and aired his objections." Over and over again, Swift was constructed as a helpless teenager, incapable of defending her mic and herself in the face of the aggressive and physically dominating West. The language deployed and the varied signifiers attached to West and Swift played out in profound ways. Simon Vozick-Levinson highlights the historic significance of the reaction to West's entry onto the stage as an assault on or violation against the innocent and helpless Swift:I'm talking, too, about all the characterizations of Taylor Swift as a victim of some awful crime. When a black man speaks rudely in the presence of a younger white woman—and that's all Kanye really did—and it gets described as an "attack" or a "violation" or an "assault," you bet that's playing into centuries of racist tropes. When a black man does something impolite, making no reference whatsoever to race, and he immediately gets crucified for "hating white people" or "reverse racism," that itself is a form of racism (2009).

Not only did the framing amplify the reaction and outrage, playing upon historic tropes and hegemonic stereotypes that imagine white women as under threat from black masculinity, but also focusing on West's personality it depoliticized his comments. Turning his action into an excuse to lambaste West for his antiwhite racism, his sexism, his violence, his lack of impulse control, and his antics, the response successfully stripped away the political nature of his actions. By focusing on Swift as a victim and imagining everything through a West vs. Swift binary, the discourse erased the larger context of the music industry and the persistent impact of race within popular culture. In many regards, the interruption was directed not at Swift, but at the voters who in West's interpretation had privileged a white artist ahead of a black artist despite their actual relative artistic merit—nothing new within America's musical landscape.

It Ain't Personal, It's Political

Despite the endless critiques of "Kanye being Kanye," and his propensity for publicity stunts, Kanye's entry on the stage deserves analysis and reflection. Notwithstanding the narrative that consistently positioned West's speech as the result of his drinking too much Hennessey (Stadtmiller, 2009), his childish antics (Syme, 2009), and his selfishness, it is important to dig beyond frames of minimization and dismissal. Irrespective of the outrage that focused on the disrespect he showed during the Grammys, and a narrative that constantly played upon tropes and stereotypes of aggressive black man and innocent white women, Kanye's protest at the VMAs represented a political intervention. Jon Caramanica spotlights the ways that race governs and overdetermines the opportunities and accolades awarded within contemporary music:

> More traditional artists like Adele, Bruce Springsteen, Taylor Swift and Paul McCartney got to perform unencumbered....
> Forget women. Forget black or Latin stars or those of any other ethnic background. In a year in which the Grammys could have reasonably tried to sell progress as a narrative, it chose to end the night with a phalanx of older white men playing guitars, a battalion guarding the rickety old castle from attack, a defiant last stand of yesteryear (2012).

Writing about the Grammys, Caramanica offers an important context for understanding West's intervention and the dismissal of his protest as that of a raving narcissist driven by ego rather than convictions. First, the music industry, despite claims of post-racialness supported by the ascendance of Bey and Jezzy alongside JT, the Boss, and Adele, is rife with racial meaning. "Yet, when 'post-racial' is understood for what it really is, the racial dynamic of this year's Grammy Awards becomes much more complex. For in reality, this year's awards show represents quite clearly that whiteness still can maneuver itself as the apex of cultural iconicity," writes David Kline. "In the end, this year's Grammys was nothing more than an exercise in white nostalgia for a bygone era when white music (much of which was a mirrored version of black creativity) enjoyed its place at the top of the music industry's most privileged spaces" (2012). Given its history and the ongoing struggles over recognition, visibility, and respect, it is naïve to argue that race and the larger issues of racism and privilege did not manifest themselves in this moment.

Secondly, Kanye had a point. At one level, there is no comparison between the two videos in question. The VMAs are intended to be a show to celebrate music videos. While certainly subject for debate, Beyoncé's video is superior. Its scope and depth, its dancing, the complexity of performance, level of choreography, and its spectacle of representation puts it at another level.

At another level, while Taylor Swift is heralded as a musician, songwriter, and artist, black artists have historically been imagined as performers, lacking the same skills and mastery of craft as their white counterparts. White artists are celebrated for their ability to produce and create music, for their ability to write and generate inspiring melodies and compelling lyrics. On the other hand, black artists are accepted as creating great shows or entertaining, which in some moments is stereotypically imagined as naturally able to dance or entertain. Imagined as having a natural advantage in performance yet less capable as artist, singer, or lyricist, the mechanism of assessment separates black and white artists. The "showmanship" of Nicki Minaj or the choreography of Beyoncé is not the same as the musical talents of other (white) SINGERS.

During this same awards ceremony, Dave Grohl waxed nostalgic for authentic artists, who sang without computers or other alterations. They made their stamp on the music world with their voice:

> For me this award means a lot because it shows that the human element of making rock is the most important. Singing into a microphone

and learning to play an instrument and learning your craft is the most important thing for people to do. It's not about being perfect. It's not about sounding correct. It's not about what goes on in a computer. It's about what goes on in here [points to heart] and what goes on in here [points to head] (Parker 2012).

This sort of framing, and the bifurcation of performers between (white) artists and (black) entertainers not only embodies a level of nostalgia for a different era, one dominated by white artists, but also one that privileges the very talents—singing, songwriting, musicianship—that are imagined as unique to white artists.

Thirdly, West must be understood within a larger history of discrimination directed at black artists, white cooptation of aesthetics and styles originating with black artists, and a culture that rewards whiteness inside and outside of the industry. That is, while Swift isn't capitalizing on the "sonic popularity" of blackness in ways that Eminem, Macklemore, Adele, or Justin Timberlake have all illustrated, her place within the industry should be understood within this history. In many ways, country music has capitalized on the history of American Blues music, a genre pioneered by black artists. The aesthetics and popularity of the Blues speaks to America's love for tourist destinations that allow for the erasure of the politics and conditions of the everyday people of those blues-ridden locations, it is no wonder that country music resonates with much of white America. If the blues tradition spotlights the trauma and violence of African American history, country provides "everything but the burden" (Tate 2003). West's intervention should be read against this history, against the history of white theft of black artistry within R & B, and within the context of American culture. Read against this history, and the privileging of whiteness within virtually every genre of music, West's comment proposes a challenge to the currency of American popular culture.

This isn't simply a question of popularity or visibility, but of financial success. According to Mark Anthony Neal, "Black pop is of course not simply a style of popular music, but a commodity, in which someone benefits financially from the production, distribution, consumption and critical gatekeeping of the music, and too often it is not the black folks whose minds and spirits loom large in the creation of the music" (2005, p. 307). While Swift does not fit into the larger narrative of white artists and the appropriation of black musical styles, the frustration over yet another moment of white celebration at the expense of a black artist cannot be understood outside this larger discourse. Writing about Justin Timberlake, Jamilah King argues:

> With production by Timbaland, The Neptunes and P. Diddy, Timberlake's solo debut, "Justified," thrived on his novelty: He was the white boy with the bleached blonde fade and vague hip-hop swagger who could really sing the black music he unabashedly recorded. Image-wise, he picked, chose and performed suave and often provocative black masculinities embodied by the likes of James Brown, Michael Jackson, and Prince. For that he was richly rewarded; the album sold more than 7 million copies worldwide and he won two Grammys, ironically for Best *Pop* Vocal Album and Best Male *Pop* Vocal Performance....Of course, this isn't all Justin's fault. He's just the latest and most newsworthy example of a phenomenon that's existed as long as black people have been making art in the Americas. It's neither a reason not to enjoy the "20/20 Experience" or rallying cry to keep others from doing the same. But as his first album in six years gets the notoriety befitting a Justin Timberlake Experience, it's worth at least acknowledging *all* of the experiences that have gone into making it possible (2013).

As Imani Perry notes, "that there is a sonic preference for blackness, but there is a visual preference for whiteness" ("Justin Timberlake, 'The 20/20 Experience'" 2013). West was spotlighting this reality; he was shining a spotlight on the power of white privilege.

From Adele to JT, from Eminem to Macklemore, the history of the music industry (and other American institutions) is one of white privilege and the cost and consequences of this for black artists. Bill Yousmann, who sees little transformative possibility in the white adoption of black cultural styles, looks at this music industry as not a space of integration or mediated social distance but one that perpetuates inequality and injustice:

> White youth adoption of black cultural forms in the twenty-first century is also a performance, one that allows Whites to contain their fears and animosities towards blacks through rituals not of ridicule, as in previous eras, but of adoration. Thus, although the motives behind their performance may initially appear to be different, the act is still a manifestation of white supremacy, albeit a white supremacy that is in crisis and disarray, rife with confusion and contradiction (2003, 378).

He further argues that the desirability and acceptability of blackness within mainstream is tied to the consumption and fetishizing of a black aesthetic presumed to be authentic:

[W]hether or not the images represent the life experience of most Blacks is immaterial. What is most important is not authenticity but the appearance of authenticity. For Whites who grow up imaging the Black world as a world of violence and chaos, the more brutal the imagery, the more true-to-life it seems to be (2003, pp. 378–379).

Imani Perry, in *Prophets of the Hood*, identifies popular culture not exclusively as a site of stereotypical representations, but as a space where "the love of black culture with the simultaneous suspicion and punishment of black bodies is not unusual" (Perry 2004, p. 28). She notes further that the "attraction to hip-hop is in part a response to the desire for culture which motivates white suburban consumers who believe they lack culture due to the normativity of whiteness in the United States" (Perry 2004, p. 126). The MTV Video Music Awards and the Grammys are emblematic of this tension whereupon blackness is celebrated yet also devalued, demonized, and dismissed. It is made visible yet rendered invisible at the same time. In interrupting Swift, West, who has long expressed frustration over the lack of respect afforded to his artistry, which neither embodies whiteness nor reflects upon white adoration and fetishizing of blackness, is not simply commenting on the award but on the currency and economy of race and the music industry. West's comments must be thought of not simply as a protest against Swift or a celebration of Beyoncé at Swift's expense, but rather an intervention against white co-optation of hip-hop, from top to bottom, from artist to consumer. He actually fits within a larger history of artists, entertainers, and athletes using the platform and visibility afforded to them within a mediated society. From Carlos and Smith, who used the 1968 Olympics to protest human rights violations, to Michael Moore, who spoke out against the War in Iraq during the 2003 Oscars, artists have long used these widely visible spaces. Marlon Brando in 1973 boycotted the Oscars despite winning for *The Godfather*. He instead sent Sacheen Littlefeather to take his place at the podium and explain his refusal to attend the ceremony: a protest against America's portrayal of Native Americans within. Because of race, because of his place in hip-hop, because of Swift's white femininity (these examples above are challenges to power and white male power), and because of West's lack of specificity and clarity, the reaction to West did not mirror those previous incidences. Yet, in each instance, the protests were dismissed as inappropriate, as unnecessary, and as a violation of the decorum of the event.

Erasing this broader context in reading West's gesture is yet another case of black protests being denounced and demonized, reduced to individual rage rather than accepted as part of a larger scheme of resistance and cultural intervention.

The substantive critique of the music industry, of the elevating of white artists, of the history of racism within American popular culture, and of the unfair burden without equal benefit that underlay West's statements was erased through an effort to personalize and individualize them. His subsequent apology made it clear that while his manners may not have been the best, and though he may not have expressed himself as clearly as he might have done, the basis of his protest remained true:

> I'm sooooo sorry to taylor swift and her fans and her mom. I spoke to her mother right after and she said the same thing my mother would've said. She is very talented! I like the lyrics about being a cheerleader and she's in the bleachers! i'm in the wrong for going on stage and taking away from her moment!. beyonce's video was the best of this decade! I'm sorry to my fans if I let you guys down! I'm sorry to my friends at mtv. I will apologize to taylor 2mrw. welcome to the real world! everybody wanna booooo me but i'm a fan of real pop culture! No disrespect but we watchin' the show at the crib right now cause...well you know! i'm still happy for taylor! Boooyaaawwww! you are very very talented! I gave my awards to outkast when they deserved it over me...that's what it is!! i'm not crazy yall, i'm just real. Sorry for that! I really feel bad for taylor and i'm sincerely sorry! Much respect!! (Crosley 2009)

The backlash directed at West, whose protest was dismissed as a sign of his immaturity and jealousy, has not silenced his own criticism. His spotlight remains on whiteness and white privilege. During the musical interlude of his song "Clique" at a London concert, he called out, "Taylor Swift beat Beyoncé at the Grammys? Beyoncé be dancing in heels and s***." While not explicit, it is easy to make his argument in simple terms: Taylor Swift was cashing in on her privileges, receiving accolades because of the meaning of race within American society. Of course, this wasn't the first moment that West sought to shine a spotlight on whiteness and white privilege, to give voice to discontent and frustration over America's ongoing race problem.

In the aftermath of Hurricane Katrina, West denounced the nation's response, enunciating a widespread belief about the separate and unequal response in the aftermath of this disaster. Yet, despite the fact that his critique was based on substantiated fact regarding the difficulties faced by African Americans in the aftermath of Katrina, and the genuine and understandable anger felt by many unhappy with the government's (non)response to this natural disaster, critics dismissed his voice as that of a narcissist intent on stealing the spotlight.

The Proof Is in the History[3]

On September 2, 2005, following the devastation of Hurricane Katrina that in mass flooding, America's attention turned to relief. The loss of life, the dislocated families that resulted from the broken levees, compelled action, which included a nationally televised fundraiser on NBC. Joined by other celebrities, Kanye West was among its participants. Yet, unlike his peers, Kanye did not want to stick to the program, using the platform, spotlight, and microphone afforded to him to speak out. Whereas the event was imagined as a moment of healing and coming together, West sought the moment as one of empowerment and resistance, calling out both the media and the Bush administration for its failures during and after the storm:

> I hate the way they portray us in the media. You see a black family, it says, "They're looting." You see a white family, it says, "They're looking for food." And, you know, it's been five days [waiting for federal help] because most of the people are black. And even for me to complain about it, I would be a hypocrite because I've tried to turn away from the TV because it's too hard to watch. I've even been shopping before even giving a donation, so now I'm calling my business manager right now to see what is the biggest amount I can give, and just to imagine if I was down there, and those are my people down there. So anybody out there that wants to do anything that we can help—with the way America is set up to help the poor, the black people, the less well-off, as slow as possible. I mean, the Red Cross is doing everything they can. We already realize a lot of people that could help are at war right now, fighting another way—and they've given them permission to go down and shoot us! George Bush doesn't care about black people! (as cited in De Moraes, 2005)

Before NBC could cut to commercial, his words would ring from coast to coast. With social abuzz, media commentators taking to the airwaves, and others, from the political elite to the streets both praising and condemning his remarks as "truth to power," "inappropriate," and just plain wrong, Kanye West had yet again struck chord. While eliciting support from those equally angry about the media coverage, about the failure to evacuate those left behind in wake of Katrina, and the otherwise abysmal response, others denounced West as misguided, his comments as inappropriate, and his behavior as typical of a hip-hop generation's willingness to disrespect authority, "play the race card" in almost every instance, and otherwise shirk personal responsibility. Fox News's loudest pundit, Bill O'Reilly, took to the airwaves to chastise West and his hip-hop brethren. For O'Reilly and others, his comments was indicative of a larger problem within hip-hop, evidence of a set of pathologies and cultural dysfunctions that permeated hip-hop and the culture at large. "And the remarks are simply nutty. I mean, come on, West is saying authorities want to shoot blacks? It doesn't get more irresponsible than that. But what do you expect from an ideologically-driven newspaper industry and the world of rap, where anything goes? What do you expect?" (O'Reilly, 2005, n.p.). Several years later, after investigations that resulted in several convictions because of a shooting on the Danzinger Bridge ("5 NOPD officers guilty in post-Katrina Danziger Bridge shootings, cover-up" 2011), West was proven to be correct on a number of levels. Yet, the impossibility of West's analysis was presumed from moment #1, all of which reflected his statements, the hegemony of colorblindness post-racialness, the culture wars and hip-hop's place, and his own history with the media.

Not surprisingly, O'Reilly had friends who were equally outraged. Many commentators, bloggers, and others loaded up on criticism directed at West. Whether denouncing his unfair attacks on President Bush or his decision to use the apolitical and purportedly race-neutral fundraiser space for his own agenda, West was summarily criticized in the days following. For example, during an interview on the American Urban Radio Network, Laura Bush labeled West's comments about her commander and chief and husband as "disgusting." She further noted, "I mean I am the person who lives with him. I know what he is like, and I know what he thinks, and I know he cares about people" ("First Lady," 2005, n.p.). Former president George H.W. Bush, during an appearance on *Larry King Live*, similarly took up for his son, vocalizing his outrage about a "particularly vicious comment that the president didn't care, was insensitive on ethnicity.... Insensitive about race. Now that one hurt because I know this president and I know he does care...that's what in his heart" ("Interview," 2005, n.p.). Not surprisingly and perhaps most significantly, few who took to the air to both demonize West and defend Bush actually addressed the substantive issues raised by West. Their defense did not reconcile his concern about the systemic failures of the federal government, the perpetuation of racial stereotypes within the media, and the collective failures on display during Katrina. Instead, they followed West's own lead, turning the discussion into one of intent, personalities, and individual motivations, which most certainly didn't advance the discussion. Instead, it turned the social justice issues at hand into a referendum on Bush v. West.

Many years later, West still faced outrage for his "selfishness" and "unfair criticism" of the Bush administration's response. President George Bush, in fact, described this moment as the worst of his presidency. During an exchange with Matt Lauer, Bush furthers the narrative of West engaging in ad hominem attacks that were personally hurtful and without any basis:

> "He called me a racist. And I didn't appreciate it then. I don't appreciate it now. It's one thing to say, 'I don't appreciate the way he's handled his business.' It's another thing to say, 'This man's a racist.' I resent it, it's not true."
>
> Lauer quotes from Bush's new book: "Five years later I can barely write those words without feeling disgust." Lauer adds, "You go on: 'I faced a lot of criticism as president. I didn't like hearing people claim that I lied about Iraq's weapons of mass destruction or cut taxes to benefit the rich. But the suggestion that I was racist because of the response to Katrina represented an all-time low.'
>
> President Bush responds: "Yeah. I still feel that way as you read those words. I felt 'em when I heard 'em, felt 'em when I wrote 'em, and I felt 'em when I'm listening to 'em.
>
> Lauer: "You say you told Laura at the time it was the worst moment of your presidency?"
>
> Bush: "Yes. My record was strong, I felt, when it came to race relations and giving people a chance. And it was a disgusting moment" (Chappell, 2010).

Similarly, John McWhorter dismissed West's protests about Katrina as little more than self-serving rage one that told people more about West than injustice or the Bush administration. He then argued that West's disrespect for Swift illustrates the baseless nature of his critiques at Bush:

> West knew very well what he was doing in pushing that button. He was not nobly speaking up for the powerless or presenting a moral analysis. He was being, quite simply, a bully. This was the same bully who grabbed the microphone from Taylor Swift. This was the same performative indignation behind West's pretending to think white scientists created AIDS to sterilize black people on the opening track of, wouldn't you know it, the very CD he had just released while calling George Bush a bigot.

In the end, if history repeats itself first as tragedy and then as farce, we could call Jim Crow the tragedy and Kanye West squirming and sputtering in that NBC studio the farce. Only when occasions to level the racism charge in earnest have become rare does one feel safe getting off on "calling someone a racist." The litmus test for deciding whether someone is genuinely a bigot is whether you would feel comfortable telling the person so to their face (2010).

The widespread condemnation of West embodied dominant expectations of today's celebrities. In exchange for a sizable platform and compensation, athletes, musicians, and actors are required to be quiet as it relates to politics. In general, those within entertainment or popular culture are not supposed to comment on politics or social matters. There's this idea that because you make your living as an artist, you have no right to comment. In many regards, this transcends race evidence in the reaction to Bono, or to the Dixie Chicks. West's Bush comments (as opposed to his comments about Swift) exist within the general framework that artist exists to escort people away from the REAL WORLD. As they are little more than fantasy tour guides who don't know what they're talking about, they are obligated to just shut up and entertain people without thinking. Yet, race is also omnipresent because the tone and rhetoric directed at West, but also because West became a stand-in for demonizing and criticizing hip-hop and black masculinity. It is no wonder the defense of West was widespread as well.

Amid the demonization and condemnation of West in the aftermath of the NBC fundraiser commentary, many within the hip-hop community came to his aid. In fact, artists, fans, and others worked to drown out the criticism because of the value seen not only in West's comment but also in the anger at his (and by extension their own) presumed silencing. Citing his right to free speech, praising his courage, celebrating his willingness to use his power to give voice to many who were frustrated and outrage, he provided voice to many who felt silence before and after Katrina. Reflecting access and the lack of gatekeepers, the Internet emerged as ground zero. It wasn't simply about coming to his aid but lending credence to his words. In some parts of the nation, supporters donned "Kanye Was Right," "Vote for Kanye," and "George Bush Does Hate Black People" t-shirts to share their thoughts about West and their feeling of outrage about the Bush's administration handling of Katrina. West had provided a level of agency amid a cloud of powerless. For activists, his comments were not disrespectful but one based in love and respect for the black community. He was a rallying cry; where his words would be the

catalyst for people to share their pain and anger, for people to mobi-
lize and demand accountability and justice.

His supporters were not limited to fans and activists; it was not
limited to those who co-signed his comments or rallied around him.
Other artists additionally came to the aid of the beleaguered star,
focusing on his first amendment rights, free speech, and the power
of artistic expression. More than that, several individuals within and
outside the hip-hop community celebrated him for his truthfulness.
Etan Thomas voiced his support for West, using the moment as
yet another opportunity to protest the mistreatment of the African
American community in New Orleans. "Had this been a rich, lily-
white suburban area that got hit, you think they would have had
to wait five days to get food or water? When the hurricane hit in
Florida, Bush made sure people got the help the next day," Thomas
noted. "But now, when you are dealing with a majority poorer class of
black people, it takes five days? Then you still don't send help instead
sending the National Guard to 'maintain order?' Are you kidding
me" (Zirin, 2005, n.p.). Others, like Jay-Z, Diddy, and David Banner,
labeled West a hero, thanking him for giving voice to the frustration
of many within the African American community (Holmgren 2005).
In their eyes, West had provided counter-narrative to the media narrative and political spin. Young City, a New Orleans rapper, defended
West by shining a spotlight on the veracity of his arguments. Whereas
West didn't provide specifics, others stepped into the void, arguing
that because the Bush administration was so concerned with Iraq and
increasing profit margins for America's elite, black communities had
literally been left out in the cold. "I just think that it's real crazy that
our government ain't kicking in to send something to New Orleans.
He's [President Bush] talking about how we need to help people in
Iraq but he isn't even concerned with people in our own country"
(Hamilton, Williams, and Strong, 2005).

The aftermath of Katrina and Kanye West's comments was not only
marked by the hip-hop community demanding justice, accountability, and answers, but also by artists challenging the black community
and hip-hop itself for their own failures. Michael Eric Dyson (2006)
reflects on this important and often overlooked element in West's
comments. His challenge of the president served as a reminder of the
political courage needed within hip-hop, especially in this moment
of crisis. He was a reminder of the history of hip-hop and its role as a
truth-teller. "Not only did West redeem the sometimes sorry state of a
hip-hop world careening on gaudy trinkets of its own success—booze,
broads, and bling—but his gesture signaled a political courage on the

part of the black blessed that is today all too rare" (p. 154). His words served as a denunciation of the Bush administration and American racism; his actions served as source of critique of hip-hop and inspiration for the hip-hop community. It was a rebuke of not only injustices surrounding Katrina but also the demands of silence. As with black athletes, black rappers are instructed to just "shut up and sing." This reflects the stereotypes regarding black intelligence and narratives that depict African American males as focused on parties, women, and hyper-materialism. In other words, had West stayed in his lane—bling, booze, and sex—his visibility and desirability would have been preserved. Warren Sapp may have said it best, "If you a black man in America who makes money, you're supposed to just shut up." Kanye violated this "deal" and therefore faced tremendous opposition.

The criticism was not simply directed at the media and the government but also inward. Hip-hop was now under the microscope. Southern Rapper T.I. blasted hip-hop for aiding and abetting the government, for its own selfishness and disregard for the poor: "I called everybody's bluff who is talking all that ballin' shit," stated T.I. "Popping all them bottles in the club...talking about how much girls and jewelry and cars they got. Let's see how much money they've got for a good cause. Basically, I told everybody to put their money where their mouths are, and if you ain't got no money to give to the cause, I don't want to hear that shit no more" ("T.I, David Banner," 2005, n.p.). Twista, a Chicago-based rapper, concurred, arguing that it was a given that the government and the vast majority of America would show little concern for the despair of America's underclass, particularly those who are black and brown, demonstrating the necessity of hip-hop and the black community as a whole intervening through action and art: "They've been bogus, so what is everybody so shocked about.... I feel the response was real slow, but I look at my own harder than I look at them" ("T.I, David Banner," 2005, n.p.). In this regard, West's comments opened up a space for both outward condemnations of American racism and inward critiques of hip-hop culture. Just as America had failed black America during Katrina, rap had failed not only the people but it also had betrayed the transgressive and political history of this art form. West's stand was not only significant because of his refusal to be silent, but also because of his efforts to create a space of dissent, opposition, and action directed at the media, the Bush administration, and hip-hop itself,

Kanye West's words and those of the figures who supported him suggest that not nearly enough of us are invested in consistently raising our voice for the voiceless. . . . Too many of us are safe until all black people are safe, Kanye West saw his identity tied to the identity of the poor, and realized that the people were drowning were "my people". . . . If Bush and black elites had forgotten the poor, black artists from the Delta have remembered their peers with eloquence (Dyson, 2006, p. 157).

In fact, artists and activists who embodied the hip-hop generation accepted the challenge established by West. In the months following Katrina, they fought to make the injustices facing New Orleans visible, giving voice to the experiences of those who had been erased within the mainstream media. While this was short-lived and often took the form of songs about Katrina, it pointed to the importance of West's courageous stance against George Bush and the silence from many within hip-hop to speak truth to power. West ushered in a moment of change.

Privilege Personified

In disrupting Taylor Swift's speech and George Bush's presidency, Kanye West defied the expectations of a black artist (whereas his remarks on Michelle Obama; his promotion of conspicuous consumption and his hundred-dollar T-shirts; his misogyny; and even his narcissistic claims to the Confederate flag, each has elicited limited national outrage, seemingly fit the expectations of a black artist and therefore receive a pass). He challenges white privilege and societal silence about black suffering. Dismissed as evidence of his ego, narcissism, or troubling personality, framed as yet another reminder of the lack of civility within hip-hop, his protests have not been fully heard. He has never been fully seen. While the reaction and the demonization has hurt his brand, and his career, leading to lost endorsements and, more importantly, to a narrative that haunts and clouds his every move, it also opened up a space for him that was previously unavailable. Kanye made his career on being the "exceptional" one, with his middle-class background, his propensity for wearing sweaters, and even his narratives on college and other universal themes (or themes that white suburbia connected to their own experiences). Being repositioned as a thug, an antiwhite racist, or an angry black man allowed Kanye to redefine himself with fewer questions about his authenticity. Joining forces with Jay-Z or rhyming about blood diamonds cannot be understood outside of the changing expectations surrounding Kanye. It also changed the trajectory of Swift's career, who in the aftermath of being Kanyed found herself framed as the quintessential victim. Depicted as the girl-next-door bullied by the big and bad Kanye, Swift found greater popularity within the American landscape. Kanye helped her crossover in ways that hadn't been fully realized. Her place within hip-hop was a strange but understandable manifestation of her interaction with Kanye West. From her collaborations with TI and Nicki Minaj, to her song with T-Pain, Swift converted her Kanye moment into a lifetime "ghetto pass" that encapsulates the power of whiteness. In "Thug Story," donning sagging pants, a hat tilted to the side, and a chain, Swift ironically raps about how her life, despite its privileges, is that of a "thug."

> I'm like 8 foot 4 Blonde hair to the floor
> You shorties never thought I dreamed about rapping hardcore
> No I ain't got a gun
> No I never really been in a club
> Still live with my parents but I'm still a thug
> I'm so gangster you can find me baking cookies at night
> You out clubbing?
> Well I just made caramel delight T-Swift and T-Pain rapping on the same track
> It's a thug story, tell me can you handle that? (Swift & T-Pain 2009)

The irony and the remaking of her image are telling because at one level she is solidifying the authentic connection between blackness and thug, whiteness and all-American girl. It's ridiculous to think of her as a "thug." Yet, at the other level, the song reimagines "thug" as a state of mind, as simply challenging conventional wisdom. In both cases, her engagement with West seems to provide her "street cred" while at the same time insulating her from criticism about this minstrel-like performance. More than this, the juxtaposition of Kanye as "thug" in the aftermath of Bush and Swift with Taylor Swift "pretending to be a thug" is yet another reminder of how race operates within American culture. Swift can pretend to be a thug, and Bush can ignore the needs of New Orleans because it is "full of thugs," but West cannot step outside of the scripts of black masculinity without becoming not just a thug but also an unwanted presence within white America.

Notes

1. This represents the best recollection of the conversation and is certainly not a word-for-word replication on that day.

2. A 2003 article ("Stage Antics Upstage Winners at Annual Video Music Awards," *The Daily Gazette,* August 27, 2003) describes the VMAs in the following way: "Typically MTV's annual celebration of music videos take a back seat to wacky antics, barely there outfits and eye-popping performances." Retrieved May 21, 2013, from http://news.google.com/newspapers?nid=1957&dat=20030827&id=WXo hAAAAIBAJ&sjid=8okFAAAAIBAJ&pg=2583,6927965

3. This section was inspired, contains material, and builds from a previously published work by the author: "George Bush Does not Care about Black People: Hip Hop and the Struggle for Katrina Justice," in *Through the Eye of Katrina: Social Justice in the United States,* ed. Kristin Bates and Richelle Swan, 261–283. Durham, NC: Carolina Academic Press.

Chapter 5

An Examination of Kanye West's Higher Education Trilogy

Heidi R. Lewis

The NBC sitcom *A Different World*, a spin-off of *The Cosby Show*, aired from 1987 to 1993. Watching that show every week undoubtedly influenced my desire to earn a college degree, but it was not the source of that desire. My dream actually began with *The Cosby Show*. Not knowing Dr. Huxtable was an OB/GYN, I wanted to be a pediatrician, because I thought they delivered and cared for babies. I will always be indebted to Bill Cosby for giving young blacks like myself a glimpse into college dormitories, cafeterias, and classrooms on *A Different World*. Because of him, I saw black professors for the first time. I believed that I could be a doctor. Since Kanye West is only four years older than I am, I can assume he also watched, or at least knew about, *The Cosby Show* and *A Different World*. The difference between the two of us, however, is that he didn't need a television to witness blacks working in higher education. His mother, the late Dr. Donda West, was a professor of English at Clark Atlanta University and Chair of the English Department at Chicago State University before retiring to serve as his manager. Especially because of his background, then, many of individuals with strong academic sensibilities may be inclined to take offense to what appears to be an anti-academic stance infusing his first three albums: *College Dropout* (2004), *Late Registration* (2005), and *Graduation* (2007), hereafter referred to as "the higher education trilogy" or "the trilogy."

For example, West travels down a familiar road by situating college and romantic relationships as mutually exclusive. We saw this assumption before in 2011 when The Champ and Panama Jackson of The Very Smart Brothas published *Your Degrees Won't Keep You Warm at Night: The Very Smart Brothas Guide to Dating, Mating,*

and Fighting Crime and again later that year when comedian Steve
Harvey published *Act Like a Lady, Think Like a Man: What Men
Really Think about Love, Relationships, Intimacy, and Commitment.*
We've also seen this trope in several Tyler Perry stage plays, films,
and television shows. These aren't the only examples, but they are
certainly some of the most popular. "School Spirit Skit #1" operates
within this tradition by denigrating college for ruining one's chances
of developing meaningful and fulfilling romantic relationships. In
the skit, the narrator sarcastically cautions graduates that they may
never have sex but that their degrees will keep them satisfied. This
is another reminder that many of us—in this case, those of us with
college degrees (sometimes several) and healthy and fulfilling romantic relationships—are continuously being erased from conversations
regarding the challenges faced by people of color in higher education.
Seldom do our narratives find a home in mainstream discourse about
all things blackness.

At the same time, however, a closer examination reveals that West
is offering critiques of higher education discourse and practices that
are especially important for those within and outside of the academy
to acknowledge. Specifically, he is critical of a continually perpetuated mis-education about the purposes and benefits of college: the
narrow and unrealistic ways in which we conceptualize and validate
the path to economic success as inextricably linked to college, the
fallacious and dangerous insider/outsider dichotomy that permeates
much of our discourse on the matter, the low expectations for black
males when it comes to education, success, and communal value, and
finally, the sometimes mundane and arbitrary bureaucratic aspects of
college. In this essay, I argue that academics must confront and begin
to mitigate these critiques in order to reconcile some of the tensions,
real or imagined, that exist in the relationship between the academy
and various peoples and communities, especially those existing on the
margins.

In his trilogy, West levels strong challenges to communities that
exist both within and outside of the academy related to a lack of
clarity regarding the purposes and benefits of higher education. It
is especially important for these communities that often overlap, to
acknowledge the ways in which he is advocating for more deliberate
and intentional relationships between the families and communities
that love and support college students, the students themselves, and
the institutions at which these students are being educated. Such an
approach seems likely to alleviate a lot of the ambivalence and frustration being expressed in the trilogy lyrics. In *College Dropout's* "All

Falls Down," for example, West raps about a young woman having no idea why she's in college and being insecure about choosing another path, one outside of higher education, out of fear of her family's reactions. West problematizes the ways in which college is often considered to be a "cure all" in one's quest to find a secure place in the world. St. John, Hu, Simmons, Carter, and Weber (2004) write, "Major choice is an important decision for African Americans because of its immediate impact on persistence. Campus leaders need to consider how academic programs link to employment opportunity if they want to increase persistence by African Americans" (227). While there is validity to this conclusion, which seems to be supported by this examination of the trilogy, I would argue that this strategy for increasing black student persistence in college must be elaborated beyond simply explaining how black students can secure jobs after college. Uncertainty and insecurity is, in fact, an especially valuable component of the college experience. Like the muse of "All Falls Down," I changed my major and ideas about my career path numerous times while I was in college. I started as a Finance and Economics major and graduated an English major. Throughout those changes, I admit my uncertainty and insecurity left me scared, because I had been brought to image that college was a relatively static and unilateral experience. It is important, then, for leaders within the academy to shape narratives about college that will leave those with little to no experience in higher education with a better understanding of the myriad paths we nurture and shape in these spaces.

In much the same way, the trilogy painstakingly reminds academics that we have failed to communicate our own values to our communities. In the "Li'l Jimmy Skit" from *College Dropout*, we learn about a child who resents his father for being more committed to his role as a learner than his role as a provider. Jimmy, the protagonist, sarcastically ruminates about being the smartest dead guy because degrees are all his father left him when he died. This is an especially important problem to consider for those of us who are committed to liberal arts teaching and learning. I grew up in Alliance, Ohio, home of the University of Mount Union (formerly Mount Union College). My high school football team played games under the Friday night lights on the Mount Union field. Even still, as hungry as I was for and as close as I was to higher education, I had no idea that Mount Union was a liberal arts college. I didn't even know what a liberal arts college was. The only differences that I knew existed between colleges were related to location, size, and demographics. Colleges were big or small and white or black. The trilogy takes that ignorance

and communicates it to mainstream America through hip-hop, and
we have to pick up the ball and do the work. Alemán and Salkever
(2003) writes,

> Liberal education has never been a static enterprise in America. Its
> faculties and campus administrators often enacted change to better its
> societal fit [...] These examinations of the educative value of differ-
> ence for the American college will seek to assess the potential for effec-
> tive change, change that will revive its democratic character and equip
> the learner with the knowledge and skills by whose means he can come
> into empathetic realization, sympathetic understanding and coopera-
> tive association with individuals, occupations, and cultures different
> from one's own. (589)

As a liberal arts professor, I can articulate these and other characteristics of the liberal arts experience in detail. While it is no better
or worse than any other form of higher education, it is significantly
different – it values communal intimacy, exploration, adventure,
curiosity, experimentation, creativity, difference, uncertainty, and
insecurity, among other things. We must understand that it is our
responsibility to communicate to our communities what it is we do,
so that our children are able to make well-informed choices based on
a variety of options rather than on default expectations about what
they are or not expected to contribute to the world.

The trilogy appeared almost a decade ahead of the current conversations in mainstream America about the perils of student debt.
Already, Kanye challenges the myth that a college education always
leads to financial security and our failure to carefully communicate
the financial difficulties that many students will face during and after
their education. In "Skit #1" from *Late Registration*, we are introduced to a (fictional)newly founded fraternity, Broke Phi Broke, in
which the members highlight their inability to buy clothes and cars.
On first listen, the skit sounds like yet another example of hip-hop
materialism, which is undoubtedly one of its aspects. Yet on the other
hand it reveals a chasm between student expectations and student
realities regarding finances during the college experience (including post-graduation), a chasm that we, as leaders in the academy, can
easily work to mitigate. St. John, Hu, Simmons, Carter, and Weber
(2004) found:

> African Americans persisted at lower rates than Whites, and they
> placed greater implicit values on major that had immediate economic

returns [...] When we use Bourdieu's theory as an interpretive frame, it is not only apparent that economic forces are of more immediate concern to African Americans but that these economic considerations also influence the way African Americans value cultural capital (and educational attainment). (227)

If we examine the trilogy alongside this type of sociological study, we can begin to have more realistic and ultimately effective conversations with black students about college and finances. These conversations will ultimately add the necessary complexity to the all-too-simplistic existing model that suggests black students should go to college to earn a lot of money. Before I graduated high school, I made the choice to attend a small, private college in Pennsylvania. I won't detail the reasons I made the choice—admittedly, many of them make little to no sense to my adult self—but it's important to remember that I am from Ohio. I had no business attending a private out-of-state school. While I am extremely happy with the way my life is developing, I can't help but think someone—a guidance counselor, a college recruiter, a church member, a family member, someone—should have warned my young and naïve self that I could potentially be in debt for the rest of my life because of one ill-informed choice made as a teenager. Along these lines, the trilogy emphasizes these kinds of narratives in order to emphasize the importance of deliberate and intentional approaches to higher education.

Many academics encourage this approach to higher education within the classroom, but the trilogy begs us to consider doing our job even before students get to our classrooms and even if they never make it to us. To be fair, many academics are committed to educating people who are unwilling or unable to attend college, but some of us also fear the ways in which our respective institutions do not value this work. Most institutions require academics to excel in three areas in order to earn tenure: teaching, scholarship, and service (not necessarily in that order). Rarely ever is service to the community included in tenure requirements. April L. Few (2004) acknowledges this issue in "Balancing the Passion for Activism with the Demands of Tenure: One Professional's Story from Three Perspectives" when she writes, "Other minority professors have told me they could not help anyone else because they were their own diversity project" (50). Further, she writes,

Service is a genuine outlet for activism that defines our selfhood and altruism and supports life-giving connections. It is the glue that

connects the university, community, and world. However, I also suspect that is is valued in most research universities about as much as the
mother work women perform to maintain the household and family
well-being. (56)

Along these lines, the trilogy asks academics to resist such repression by demanding that our work in our communities be valued and
accepted in ways that they often are not. For example, "School Spirit
Skit #1" from *College Dropout* is a cautionary tale about the myth of
meritocracy. An unnamed individual graduates from college and ends
up making a $25K annual salary working as a secretary for another
secretary who has less education but makes more money. This is possible because the latter secretary is the boss's niece. One shouldn't
be, but often is, first introduced to familial affirmative action and
the myth of meritocracy *after* one graduates from college. These are
the kinds of things that should be taught to our children from the
moment they have the ability to understand fully constructed sen-
tences. Along these lines, Hoffman (2003) writes:

> Even though underrepresented students are taking greater advantage
> of postsecondary options while enrolled in high school, these benefits
> remain unevenly distributed. Many underrepresented students are shut
> out of participation in such programs by the lack of rigorous curricula
> at the high schools they attend, lack of information about the many
> options for earning college credit that are currently available, and by
> substantial fees for participation in some states. We need to know far
> more systematically than we now do what the barriers are for these
> students, and how they can be overcome (48).

Granted, community activism is being done, particularly in areas with
strong populations of people of color, such as Chicago, Philadelphia,
and Oakland. For instance, the White Privilege Conference conducts
the Youth Action Project (2013) in order to "provide a safe and challenging space, geared toward youth of ALL ethnic backgrounds, who
are committed to understanding and dismantling white supremacy,
white privilege, and other forms of oppression." Additionally, *The
Feminist Wire* is in the process of further developing the Emerging
Feminisms campaign, which is committed to educating and learning from young people in order to inspire social justice at all levels.
These are the kinds of community activism and social justice projects that have the potential to inspire academics to work with the
people that we too often only imagine ourselves working for and/or
on behalf of in order to affect change. These are the kinds of projects

that can mitigate some of the tensions that exist between those that work within and outside of the academy. Lilla Watson, in collaboration with the aboriginal activist group Queensland, once said, "If you have come here to help me, you are wasting your time. But if you have come because your liberation is bound up with mine, then let us work together." Working with our communities is more valuable than working for and/or on behalf of them, especially because the latter approach assumes that academics exist apart from their communities and are unable to learn from the communities that they claim to serve.

Similarly, the trilogy also provides a salient critique of the insider/ outsider dichotomy—real and imagined—that exists in many discussions about higher education. I especially appreciate the ways in which West is careful not to hold academics or nonacademics primarily accountable for this dichotomy. Rather, the trilogy challenges the dichotomy by requiring its listeners, regardless of academic training, to consider academic and nonacademic communities as inextricably linked. In the "Intro" to *College Dropout*, late comedian Bernie Mac lends his voice as a fictional faculty member asking West to do something (produce and/or rap on a track, most likely) for kids at graduation to sing. Here, West shows the relative ease with which those within and outside of the academy can collaborate, illustrating the existing potential to build bridges that provide effective creative opportunities for youth. On "We Don't Dare," also from *College Dropout*, West further draws attention to the ways that academics and nonacademics already collaborate in an effort to support students who dream of attending college. More specifically, he raps about hustlers "sittin' in the hood like community colleges," because the "dope money here is little Tre's scholarship." Similarly, on "We Major" from *Late Registration*, West relies on the oft-used hip-hop trope of his experiences tipping a college student moonlighting as a stripper to pay tuition in order to make the same point. In these cases, West demands that we come to terms with our connectedness, even when it may be uncomfortable. In their analysis of academic integration, Eimers and Pike (1997) point out the ways in which integration is especially important for minority students. They write, "For both minority and nonminority students, academic integration was at least as important as entering ability in predicting academic achievement, and for minority students, academic integration was more important than entering ability in predicting first-year achievement" (91). If students with little to no access to higher education prior to entering college conceive themselves as outsiders, their academic success is severely compromised. Hence, acknowledging our connectedness is especially important as we continue developing ways to affect change.

The trilogy reminds us of this when Kanye travels down a familiar road by situating college and romantic relationships as mutually exclusive. We saw this assumption before in 2011 when The Champ and Panama Jackson of The Very Smart Brothas published *Your Degrees Won't Keep You Warm at Night: The Very Smart Brothas Guide to Dating, Mating, and Fighting Crime* and again later that year when comedian Steve Harvey published *Act Like a Lady, Think Like a Man: What Men Really Think about Love, Relationships, Intimacy, and Commitment.* We've also seen this trope in several Tyler Perry stage plays, films, and television shows. These aren't the only examples, but they are certainly some of the most popular. "School Spirit Skit #1" operates within this tradition by denigrating college for ruining one's chances of developing meaningful and fulfilling romantic relationships. In the skit, the narrator sarcastically cautions graduates that they may never have sex but that their degrees will keep them satisfied. This is another reminder that many of us—who have college degrees (sometimes several) and healthy and fulfilling romantic relationships—are continuously being erased from conversations regarding the challenges faced by people of color in higher education. Seldom do our narratives find a home in mainstream discourse about all things blackness. I've been unable to find any significant data set that proves that these limiting narratives actually deter black youth from attending college, but I do think it's important for us to challenge these fallacious portrayals by continuing to communicate with our communities about how we all face marginalization, allowing us to all work together to eradicate the oppression we face.

The trilogy also highlights the bureaucratic aspects of higher education that students often experience as frustrating and sometimes debilitating. By the time I was a junior in college, I knew that the beginning of the fall semester was always going to be especially challenging due to the red tape I would have to navigate regarding financial aid. It never failed. I would find myself checking the status of my aid online, realizing that numbers weren't adding up and/or that deposits weren't being made on time and that I was close to being dropped from all of my classes due to issues that were not my fault and that seemed to be beyond my control. Near tears the first couple of times this happened, I would trek over to the Financial Aid Office in order to resolve things with my counselor. What I realize now is that I had, and still have, a knack for doing whatever it takes to get what I want, which sometimes means going to places and talking to people who are unfamiliar and scary. But I am aware that not every student is like me, and that none should have to be in order to get the kind of support they need to be successful in college. Yes, college is about learning to be resourceful as much as it is anything else, but we need to take into account the fact that colleges, especially the administration, are unfamiliar and scary for some students, and we may need to go the extra mile to help these kinds of students succeed in this space. Even though I grew up near Mount Union, I had never set foot on that campus. I visited my older cousin at Ohio State, but it wasn't the same. In addition to that, I started my higher education career at a small school. I can only imagine what it would have been like starting at a larger school like Purdue, where I earned my PhD, where the lines are longer and the classes are bigger, and the situation can be even more unfamiliar and terrifying.

The trilogy challenges academics to prepare students for these difficulties and help them in overcoming them if we are to be successful in helping them to succeed. In "Late" from *Late Registration*, West raps about the sometimes-arbitrary nature of choosing courses, which can ultimately result in students not being able to take classes that help them to fulfill the requirements necessary for their major(s). This indicates that leaders in the academy must better communicate the value of uncertainty, flexibility, and change. While John Bohte (2001) explores the impact of bureaucracy on student education at the K-12 level, it's important to consider the impact of bureaucratic difficulties students experience at the college level. I experienced this personally with one of my advisees who were upset that she may not be able to major in Psychology. Psychology is a popular major at my institution, and it's difficult for students to secure spots in classes that are required for that major. As an advisor, it's important that we skillfully and patiently convince our students that their goals should be flexible and that they should be open to the wonders of change, which can lead to unexpected success. The trilogy, though, is asking us, again, to go beyond doing the job we are required to do on our campuses. As mentioned above, these kinds of conversations should be happening *before* students get to college, especially when those students have not had the kind of access to the higher education environment that most of my students have. Doing so would most certainly alleviate at least some of the unfamiliarity and fear that stifles student growth.

In the trilogy, West additionally offers a critique of the narrow and unrealistic ways in which economic success is often conceptualized as inextricably linked to college. If we take some of the trilogy lyrics at face value, we find that West received these kinds of messages from his mother. For example, on "Graduation Day" from *College Dropout*, West raps about breaking the rules (i.e., dropping out of college) but being afraid that someone would tell and subsequently anger his mother. This isn't necessarily surprising, given her position as a professor. What may be more surprising is "Get 'Em High" from *College Dropout*, where West raps about his teacher calling him a "loser" because of his desire to leave college. On the surface, both of these reactions to a student leaving college may be understandable, especially when one considers the ways in which leaders in higher education understand college to be a relatively secure path to financial stability. However, an alternative reading suggests that we would benefit from meeting students where they are and helping them to develop in healthy and productive ways regardless of their desire to attain a degree or lack thereof. Jenkins (2006) wrote:

> Hip hop, as an alternative male structural system, has welcomed the rage and embraced the strongly negative critiques of the American power structure by Black men. Where black men have been silenced and severely penalized in the classroom for their modes of expression, they have been provided a microphone and immensely rewarded in the hip hop arena. This cultural structure has been one of the few spaces in which Black men can truthfully tell their own story in their own voice. (149)

On "Graduation Day," West raps about being confused about his future. Our education should prepare us to help students navigate similar kinds of confusion regardless of the outcome. Not every aspiring rapper will become a successful artist—in the mainstream or otherwise—but we can help them realize other ways they can be successful in the music industry, as a Field Promotion Coordinator, Music Director, Social Media Administrator, Journalist, Artist Manager, Promoter, Agent, Producer, and/or Art Designer, just to name a few. Admittedly, I personally do not know enough about these careers to determine whether or not any of them require a college degree, but if a student came into any one of our offices frustrated and confused about wanting to pursue music outside of college, we should be prepared to help them do the research so that they can make the most informed decisions possible regarding their futures.

The trilogy also calls our attention to the low expectations placed upon young black men, particularly regarding higher education. What is more interesting for this analysis is that West is especially critical of intracommunal tensions along these lines. For example, on *Late Registration*, West once again calls on late comedian Bernie Mac to lend vocals for the skit "Wake Up, Mr. West." In the skit, Mac, acting as a teacher or administrator, admonishes a young Kanye, a fourth grader, for carrying a book bag, suggesting that the book bag has no value. Mac goes on to tell young Mr. West, "You ain't got nothin' else to do. You ain't doin' nothin' with your life." This fictional interaction illustrates a level of internalized racism that sometimes prevents even intellectual blacks from having the ability to interact with youth who may navigate the culture of education in ways that are often uncomfortable and/or unprecedented. While this is certainly not a new focus for academics, this examination of the trilogy should serve as a reminder that it is important for black leaders in the academy pay careful attention to the ways in which we interact with young blacks, regardless of the paths they are imagining for themselves. Otherwise, we run the risk of alienating ourselves from the communities we claim to serve. Marina Barnett (2004) contends that successful black students receive "plenty of encouragement early in their academic pursuits" and that this encouragement "was expressed in several forms: motivation and praise during childhood, having books and reading materials around the home, discussion of career choices or choosing toys and books which reflect particular career choices, choice of selective or private schools for their child to attend, and organization of college applications and options" (63). While Barnett focuses on familial support, it stands to reason that additional support from black leaders in the academy would serve as positive reinforcement. I do not mean to suggest that we are to be held primarily responsible for nurturing bonds with our communities, and neither is Kanye. I would, however, argue that we must hold ourselves accountable for these relationships and that part of that process entails engaging those members of our communities who have struggled with us in various contexts, such as Kanye West.

Interestingly, West offers a solution to this problem, suggesting collaboration between those within and those outside of the academy. This kind of collaboration, he suggests, leads to children having more access to higher education. For example, on "Champion" (*Graduation*), West raps, "'Cause who the kids gon' listen to? Huh? I guess me, if it isn't you. Last week I paid a visit to the institute. They got the drop out keepin' kids in the school." Whereas some academics may be inclined to exclude an individual such as Kanye West (a college dropout) from the academy, he suggests that doing so might lead to alienating students who are more inclined to be guided by an individual like him than by the academics. At the same time, the "if" in these lines also suggests that he recognizes that some students would be more inclined to be guided by those within the academy. The fact that he claims to have been invited to the institute to encourage students to remain in school suggests that he is not anti-college or anti–higher education. In their analysis of the ways in which college students are mentored, Crisp and Cruz (2009) argue that "mentoring theory should be expanded to include the underpinnings of critical race and feminist theories in an effort to better understand how women or minorities may perceive and experience mentoring differently" (540). An examination of popular culture, especially hiphop, is equally critical to examining and improving the ways in which young people understand and experience college. Similarly, the ultimate concern for West, it seems, is that students be able to explore their ideas without being marginalized for making choices that do not necessarily make sense for academics. This assessment is supported by a theme he visits on "Last Call" from *College Dropout*. On this song, he raps about people in his communities expecting him to fail because of his decision to leave college. It seems, then, that West is arguing for a more nuanced approach to building and maintaining relationships between academics and those outside of the academy, one that entails a more egalitarian type of collaboration in which one path to fulfillment is not privileged over others.

What seems to be an anti-college stance seems to me more of a cry for help. West received a scholarship to attend the American Academy of Art in Chicago in 1997, when he was just 20 years old. He transferred to Chicago State University but left shortly after to pursue his music career. He produced music for Chicago rapper Grav on the latter's1996 album *Down to Earth*, and released his first album (as part of the rap group Go-Getters) in 1999. From the little information available, it seems that West left college altogether when he was 21 or 22 years old; *College Dropout* was released when West was just 26 years old. I consider the trilogy, then, to be the reflections of a young man about the experiences of an even younger man. In order to appreciate these albums fully, we must do some remembering and some imagining. On a personal note, I was not the child of a professor, and hence had even less experience with higher education than did West, but I do remember often feeling like I didn't belong, as if I wasn't good enough to be on a college campus studying anything. I thought I knew what I wanted to do with my degree, but I changed my mind so often that I was more unsure than sure at any given point. It wasn't until I started building a closer relationship with Dr. Connie

Ruzich that my vision became clearer, and it became clearer because she helped to guide and shape my ideas. She paid attention to me during class, listened to me, and helped me decide that being a college professor was my ultimate goal. As aforementioned, I entered college planning to enter the field of Finance & Economics. In the end, I graduated with a degree in English Studies, because an older and wiser woman saw things in me that I was not yet equipped to see myself. She heard and heeded my own cries for help, and that saved my life. As difficult as that must have been for Kanye West's mother, she was eventually able to support and help shape her son's dreams. It is my contention, then, that we all, as leaders in the academy, should strive to be as supportive of our students who may or may not know or understand how college may or may not be the most effective strategy to help them realize their dreams.

Part II

Unpacking Hetero-normativity and Complicating Race and Gender

Part II

Unpacking Heteronormativity and
Complicating Race and Gender

Chapter 6

"By Any Means Necessary": Kanye West and the Hypermasculine Construct

Sha'Dawn Battle

On February 26, 2012, a black male walked home from a convenience store, traversing the sidewalk area of his father's fiancé's gated community in Sanford, Florida. He was carrying seemingly harmless items: an Arizona soft drink, a bag of Skittles, and a cell phone. As reported in a *CNN* article written by Greg Botelho, an armed, non-Black male, Mr. George Zimmerman, was surveying the neighborhood when he discovered the black male, identified as Trayvon Martin. Martin allegedly invoked suspicion, prompting Zimmerman to place a call to the Sanford Police Department exclaiming the following: "This guy looks like he's up to no good, or he's on drugs or something. It's raining, and he's just walking around." Although instructed not to do so, Zimmerman followed and confronted Martin. Minutes later, a scuffle ensued and Martin's lifeless body lay face down on the community's well-maintained lawn, where according to Zimmerman, he should not have been walking.

What really compelled Zimmerman to ignore the directive of the Sanford Police? What societal social codes shaped Zimmerman's consciousness regarding Martin's physical presentation? Was it Martin's hooded, "thug-like" appearance that incited paranoia, causing Zimmerman to regard Martin as an interloper in the conservative community? It has been speculated by the media, by scholars, by the Martin family and others, that the Trayvon Martin slaying was the result of the banal yet relevant phrase, "racial profiling." While those who defend Zimmerman's actions posit that Zimmerman, as head of the neighborhood watch, was merely "doing his job," others, myself included, insist that the Trayvon Martin murder and the trial of Zimmerman are vivid reminders of the existing politics surrounding the black male body.

For many, rap is a raw artistic representation of black American life—namely, the black male body politic. And as these realities tend to morph over time, so too does their reification in rap music. On the other hand, the behavioral characteristics of most rap artists are consistent with historical stereotypes invented by white society. Not surprisingly, rap music is one of the most powerful commercial platforms that thrives on the proliferation of stereotypes that are commercially viable. One of the rap industry's most controversial yet inimitable artists, Kanye West, at times, challenges stereotypes of the construction of blackness. But he simultaneously conforms to the status quo in his treatment of women, thereby questioning the authenticity of the revolutionary discourse he offers. In doing so, he satisfies the industry's capitalist agenda. Therefore, resistance to this art form, by male and female feminists alike, is in part due to the misogynistic lyrics and the disturbing imagery that is so frequently a hallmark of the musical genre, and of black masculinity.

Masculinity portrayed in rap artists like Kanye West seems to be a contingent and a reactionary identification. As such, the goal of this essay is to underscore the politics surrounding the history of the black male body or how black males have used the adoption of a hypermasculine disposition as one particular strategy to resist the feminizing and the dehumanizing characterization of the black male body. I will attempt to provide an explanation of how this paradigm tends to manifest in hip-hop, through the music of Kanye West, and how his music can be problematic because it is made possible through the sexual exploitation of women.

The proliferation of scholarship on rap music has been necessitated by some listeners' need to situate themselves in a comfortable space at the intersection of the misogyny and the artists' outcries against racial injustice. These listeners are put off by the "woman-bashing," but are simultaneously drawn to uncovering the impetus behind the misogyny, how it came to be an arguably central trait of black masculinity portrayed in rap music, and the ways in which it speaks volumes about the neocolonization of the black male mind.[1] The handful of fans, who are a part of the intellectual vanguard community, know all too well the history of oppression that black males have endured within what feminist theorist and cultural critic, bell hooks (2004), in *We Real Cool*, refers to as the "imperialist white-supremacist capitalist patriarchy" (xiii). This "interrelated system of domination that will never fully empower black men" according to hooks, causes them to be feared by whites. And, I would add, it has refused to even recognize the humanity of black males (xii–xiii).

Kanye, in "All Falls Down," recognizes white patriarchy's systematic exclusion of black males from society. He admits that he is "so self-conscious" of the ways in which black males have been rendered invisible in white, patriarchal, capitalist America, that he, himself, refuses to even engage in something so mundane as grocery shopping without adorning himself in lavish attire and gaudy jewelry. He insists that rappers feel inclined to shine and floss to assert their presence, to reverse their erasure, and to metaphorically repurchase the 40 acres of land of which they were dispossessed following the American Civil War.

Oppressed persons are self-deluded in their belief that they can subvert their impositions and disempowerment through the subjugation and oppression of others because, as the Brazilian educational theorist Paulo Freire argues in *Pedagogy of the Oppressed*, they have grown so accustomed to the structure of domination as oppressed subjects, that they co-opt this structure in their attempts to gain liberation. But Freire warns against such a strategy to gain power in that it does not enable the oppressed to become "restorers of the humanity of both [the oppressed and the oppressors]" (44).

Likewise, it appears as if black males have attempted to overcome their victimization through an inversion of the structure of domination. Paulo Freire developed the now widely accepted logic that the oppressed becomes the oppressor.[2] The oppressed is compelled to subject others to the same structure of domination from which he once suffered. And when a popularized art form like rap music appropriates this strategy, oppression becomes normalized in the society in which it is accepted. However, Michel Foucault argues that power cannot exist without the possibility of resistance, meaning it is circulatory, and no single faction monopolizes it (Foucault 1990: 95). When power lands in the hands of many black males, women have paid the price. Black males are well within their rights to resist their oppressed positions, but their strategy for doing so and the misogynistic outcome are problematic. Foucault considers it a misconception to believe that the one who enacts "top-down" power will always emerge the winner (Foucault 1990: 95). Indeed, black males are not victors when they oppress half of their populace. Sexism deployed in rap music certainly reflects this flawed theory that Foucault questions and the inverted power structure that Freire warns against.

There is an undeniable continuity between those who were abused as children and those who were later guilty of violent acts against others. This phenomenon is frequently explained as a subconscious, albeit misplaced, retaliation against the oppressor. Many considered

Kanye's chauvinistic lyrics and behavior following his mother's death as reactions to this tragic occurrence. Others may argue that it is an emotional and psychological response to her frequent but necessary absence during his childhood. In her autobiography, *Raising Kanye*, Donda West (2007) admits to being away from the toddler Kanye, as she worked 15-hour shifts, and interned out of the country for weeks at a time.[3] She recounts how angry this would make Kanye, and how it was part of what disrupted young Kanye's experience of the nuclear family. Therefore, his anger was not directed toward Donda West per se, but toward the representation of the "autonomous wage-earning Black woman," capable of "running her man away" with her earning power. Kanye arguably resorts to misogynistic tendencies in his lyrics as a means of retaliating against this unfortunate circumstance that he endured as a child. Furthermore, and as the central argument of this essay, his sexually oppressive nature is attributable, in part, to a response to the history of black male oppression. In both instances, he may be trying to claim a victory, unaware that "power is exercised from innumerable points, in the interplay of non-egalitarian and mobile relations" (Foucault, 1990:94).

Thus, my concern lies with rap as a discourse or response to non-egalitarian relations and as a space that houses the most visible traces of black masculinity that are themselves created from the long history of racial oppression. Kanye's father was a black panther and his late mother deemed it imperative to instill in him "the courage of Malcolm [X], the wisdom of Martin [Luther King], [and] the tenacity of Marcus [Garvey]" (D. West, 2007: 153). Hence, I firmly believe that Black Nationalism is, consciously or subconsciously, ingrained in his psyche. I am keenly aware of the history associated with the black male body, and that Kanye West's complicated relationship with women may be related to these social realities. Further, I am concerned with Kanye West as an artist who represents an archetype of history defined by traditional forms of masculinity. As a rapper, he mobilizes the history of black masculinity through his preoccupation with the sexual exploitation of women.

Kanye West purposefully situates himself in the margins as one of hip-hop's most potent lyricists, in that he stretches the limits of black male masculinity with his signature pink polo (worn earlier in his career), or with his donning of kilts. Notwithstanding, he occupies temporary lodging within those margins. He repositions himself in the center each time he oppresses women via his lyrics and sometimes in the visuals in his music videos, such as the beheading of women and necrophiliac acts with women, both performed in the

"Monster" video. My religious beliefs made me very apprehensive about purchasing his latest album, titled, *Yeezus*. However, my reluctance briefly subsided as I learned that the title was a misnomer and that very little of the album is sacrilegious. Instead, tracks such as "New Slave" address long-standing racial issues, inciting black male consciousness in the face of race politics, and a need for black male visibility. I may have painted a picture of the ideal socially conscious rap album. Unfortunately, though, I was only able to experience a fleeting moment of optimism in that he uses a sexually exploitative framework as a means of addressing issues of racism.

The Black Male Body Politic: (His)tory

The black body has always been ambiguously and paradoxically regarded. On the one hand, it has been deemed dehumanized and abject, a site of racial difference. On the other hand, its estrangement from "white purity" has caused it to be fetishized, objectified, and subsequently commoditized by white supremacist capitalist culture (hooks "Feminism Inside" 2009: 20). Black male rappers especially constitute a quantifiable presence within popular culture, while white capitalist patriarchs reap the benefits of objectifying the black male body as a site of detestable otherness. For instance, a Mountain Dew commercial aired online transcends what we understand as humor in that its premise involved a frail, battered white woman who has to identify her attacker among a lineup of black men (and one goat, the real perpetrator), dressed in stereotypical clothing: baggy pants, do-rags, and gold teeth. Although the creator of the ad was a black male rapper, PepsiCo, a white-owned corporation, initially released it as a marketing ploy, assumingly endorsing an age-old portrayal of black men as brutes. This twenty-first-century ad was a quintessential example of the objectification of the black male body, as it was on display and subjected to a piercing, scornful white gaze. It called attention to the black male body as a site of racial difference and undesirability. Yet, it was (and is currently) exploited by white patriarchal capitalists, which Kanye comments on in "All Falls Down." Kanye is not only aware of white America's capitalization of black American's—rappers especially—indulgent consumer craves. In addition, he is aware of the ways in which he is more likely to be detained in an airport than is his white male counterpart ("Gorgeous"), because of the history invested in the corporeality of the black male.

The historical feminization of the black race must be acknowledged. As Saidiya Hartman (1997) argues in *Scenes of Subjection*, during

Reconstruction, "the implied citizen of the Constitution . . . was the white male" (154). Thus, black citizenship was contingent upon the mimetic demonstration of "the manhood of the race" (154). Because the legislation and racism prevented the black the man from successfully undergoing this mimetic process, the "manhood of the race" was virtually unachievable. In 1863, in an effort to convince his fellow white countrymen to abandon their fear of blacks, an abolitionist declared, "The negro race is the feminine race of the world" (quoted in hooks "Feminism Inside" 1990:19).

The black male body has also been historically feminized. White supremacist logic has purported and perpetuated claims concerning biological inferiority of the black male body. It signified (and still does) repressed and unrestrained violence and sexuality. Thus, there was a need to literally and figuratively castrate the black male body. Psychoanalytic theory tells us that women are innately inferior to men because they lack and possess "no-thing." White supremacists would appropriate this same essentialist logic to render black males second-class citizens. The black man rejected this feminized characterization, and internalized a hypermasculine image of phallic power.

The advent of intersectionality in the 1970s and 1980s as a lens through which to address the crossing of multiple forms of oppression was certainly instrumental in black feminist theory, and is instrumental in conversations concerning black males, in that the black male body had been "constructed as feminine by white supremacist rhetoric that insisted on depicting the black male as symbolically castrated, a female eunuch" (hooks "Feminism Inside 1990: 20). Hooks recalls her bewilderment at the ways in which feminist theory interrogated the male/mind, female/body dichotomy established by patriarchy, erroneously negating conversations about race, which would have inevitably disrupted the gender binary. She was disturbed because she has been so "acutely conscious of the way in which the black males have always been seen as more body than mind" (hooks "Feminism Inside" 1990: 19). The black male body signified (and still does) unrestrained violence and sexuality that had been repressed during slavery. Opposing his feminized characterization, the black man came to be identified and stereotyped as the brute, the hypermasculine, eroticized symbol of phallic power.

It may seem as if the contemporary expression of black masculinity is the result of black males folding under the pressures of the dominant ideology spewed by white patriarchs. I share Michele Wallace's view found in *Black Macho and the Myth of the Superwoman* (1978) that sometimes black males take the cowardly route when counter-identifying with false epistemic claims about their being, citing Ralph Ellison's narrator in *Invisible Man* and his retreat into the manhole as an example (58). Black male masculinity, to a degree, does not exist autonomously, although it did at one point and still should. This lack of black autonomy is dangerous in that it imprisons men and condemns them to perpetual white patriarchal stereotyping.[4] Even Kanye articulates, in his own rap vernacular, the Hegelian theory of mutual (un)recognition, in his example of a black male purchasing the Mercedes Benz but still being disregarded.

Consequently, white patriarchs fear and internalize the hypermasculine representation of black men and use it as a means to justify their castigation of black males. This archetype has been most notably personified during the Black Power Movement of the 1960s and 1970s, where black males, led by powerful voices such as Eldridge Cleaver, resolved to regain their manhood and access the realm of white male power that had previously been denied them. However, the afro and the raised black fist of the 1960s and 1970s as symbols of robust black manhood to be feared by white patriarchs and their wives, and even black women, have since been supplanted by hooded sweatshirts (like the one Trayvon Martin was wearing), Timberland boots, and sagging jeans. Although rap music has honed this image, Kanye West has attempted to expand this limited representation of black masculinity, and the external presentation of the black male body, with his tight-fitted jeans, and other eccentric styles of clothing. But, despite Kanye's attempts to de-normalize the sedentary image of black masculinity, his participation in the capitalist regime, his lyrics, and even his behavior in some instances, signify his inability to thwart the hypermasculine stoicism meant to oppose the feminization of the black male body. The famous "by any means necessary" epitaph popularized by Malcolm X may have been joined by the "fuck you, pay me" phrase and mentality emphatically proclaimed by Kanye West in "Two Words," but in most albums, Kanye's raps still embrace the Malcolm X-like militancy. He goes so far as to rename himself "Malcolm West" ("Gorgeous"). It is clear in Kanye's lyrics that the BPM and Black Nationalist ideologies have not subsided. They have penetrated deeply into the consciousness of black male rappers.

One of the most notable residual ideologies that manifests itself in rap music and behavior, instantiating Black Power consciousness, is the tendency of male rappers to think through the body. According to hooks, black liberation hinges upon the formulation of "a counter-hegemonic discourse of the body to effectively resist white supremacy" (hooks, "Feminism Inside" 2009: 18). The black male's self-construction has been affected by what phenomenologists refer to as interpolation, which implies a disruption of self-identification. Frantz Fanon, in *Black Skin, White Masks*, explains it as the amputation of the black man. That is, the black man's initial, holistic perception of himself is severed, and he becomes a mere embodied yet soul-less object in the world (Fanon, 1952: 92). The black man's entire being is represented as an amputated limb once it encounters the white male gaze. "A slow conception of [his] self as a body in a spatial world—such seems to be the schema" (Fanon, 1952: 91).

Fanon explains that white men equate black men with their genitals. "One is no longer aware of the Negro," he argues, "but only of a penis; the Negro is eclipsed. He is turned into a penis" (Fanon,1952: 157, 170). Kanye is a metaphorical amputee because he views his soul as cut off from the rest of his corporeal self. He raps about navigating his way through the world by recognizing himself as a black man with an oversized erect phallus. West creates a scenario where he forces a woman to perform oral sex on him as a means of compensating him for her reentry into the Bleau Bar, located inside the Fountainebleau Resort in Miami. She had sipped from the fountain, which, to Kanye's pleasure and amusement, is shaped in the form of a penis, and was consequently ejected ("On Sight"). In 2010, images allegedly of Kanye West's penis taken on his cell phone went virile on the Internet. This incident solidified the hypermasculine persona and brand that Kanye is constructing, and so led him to rap about the penis photograph in the song "That's My Bitch." And if this incident were not enough to prove Kanye's self-identification with his genitals, "Gorgeous explains how Kanye tends to defend himself against the social ostracism that he continually encounters by relying on the existence of his maleness (his testicles), suggesting his inwardness and his artistic capacity to be insufficient and inept, or incomparable. Kanye is creating a genuine "dialectic between [his] body and the rest of the world" (Fanon, 1952: 91). In doing so, he is furnishing his brand with a "masculinist aesthetic" (Perry, 2004: 156), thereby conceding to the exploitative nature of an industry that thrives on an overemphasis on sex-for-shock value.

In the twenty-first century, black males are still acting out hypermasculinity, in their homes, and within the realm of sports and popular culture, as a means to attain equality with their white male counterparts. This reactionary identification has caused black males to be seen as "animals, brutes, natural-born rapists and murderers" (hooks, *We Real Cool*, 2004: xii). So, when Kanye utters lyrics about dismembering female genitalia and burying them in a sarcophagus

("Monster"), or when he associates himself with teen rappers like Chief Keef who encourages Chicago youth to kill and engage in gang banging and decadence, this image of black masculinity is perpetuated and cemented in the minds of white patriarchs. These images of the black male body fuel and justify racist attempts to dispossess black males of their integrity and wills, further colonizing their minds. Unfortunately, Trayvon Martin's body was a site of danger, otherness, and primitivity, to George Zimmerman. As I watched the Trayvon Martin murder trial with images of the victim laying dead, face-down on the grass, I was reminded of Kanye's lines in "Two Words," where he acknowledges the gravity and reality of the black male body politic—the all-too-familiar scene of a black male detained, face-down on the ground, and in cuffs. As it stands, rap music has embraced a discursive framework for black males to continually resist white stereotypes. The problem is that their "game plan" reinforces machismo and hypermasculinity at the expense of female liberation, and as the Trayvon Martin's case proves, at the expense of their own liberty. Hooks corroborates this notion by positing, "As long as black males were deemed savages unable to rise above their animal nature, they could be seen as a threat easily contained" (hooks, *We Real Cool*, 2004: xiii). This containment is furthered in the white-owned-and-partially-consumed rap industry that capitalizes on barbaric representations of black masculinity and the black male body.

Repressed Black Male Liberation: Sexual Exploitation as Social Outlet

The political component of rap music is combined with its aesthetic form, which itself arose from black musical art. Imani Perry argues that given the specificity of its cultural identity, the mere existence of rap music is predicated upon historical and sociopolitical circumstances. It is tethered to a jazz and blues lineage, influenced by francophone Afro-Caribbean cultural traditions and its history is steeped in rich, black American vernacular (Perry, 2004: 10). Rap music, according to Perry, is "100 percent black." It discloses a history of the dual, triple, and, in this case, quadruple identity of black Americans, as many black male rappers are assigned to various categories of identification, all at once. Prior to achieving stardom, a rapper dwells in an amassed bundle of blackness, American-ness, maleness, and, in many cases, poverty. Moreover, as a male-dominated art form, many black male rappers have yet to realize the juncture at which the political existence of the black male body meets aesthetic expression. I think that to some degree, Kanye West has, but he has mishandled this real-ization. Kanye is attentive to how rap, as a political tool, has a didactic function to voice the realities of the black community. He knows that if degree-holding educators fail at mentoring and molding the minds of the inner-city youth, then he is the next best candidate, even as a "college dropout" ("Champions"). But he may be oblivious as to how black masculinity is a subconscious response to the history of black male oppression. Further he probably does not understand the impact of his antifeminist stance on black male youth.

Kanye West appears to be at the forefront of a sexist regime, dis-guised as black liberation in the form of art. In "Gorgeous," he raises black male consciousness regarding stereotypes plaguing the black community. Namely, he identifies the negative portrayal of black males, such as black youngsters "fallin' for the love of ballin'." He critiques the ways in which America polarizes and hierarchizes ethnic names such as "Brandon" and "Jerome," further expanding the gulf that exists between men of different races. Kanye offers a critique of the AIDS epidemic among black males, stating that it is a conspiracy initiated by the government. He also confronts the issues of mass imprisonment of black men and the white stereotype of the black male as an athlete rather than a man with intellectual capacities. But how can Kanye, all in one track, herald such pertinent issues, and simultaneously advocate the consumption of "more drinks" accom-panied by an "American Apparel girl" wearing nothing but tights?

In "Gorgeous," Kanye addresses racial injustices that for the most part affect the black male. Thus, how might black women react to a track like "Gorgeous," considering, as Kimberle Crenshaw (1998) explains in "Demarginalizing the Intersection of Race and Sex: A Black Feminist Critique of Antidiscrimination Doctrine, Feminist Theory, and Antiracist Politics," the "compounding nature of [Black women's] experience is absorbed into the collective experiences" of the race (323). Simply put, the song is created to contest cultural hegemony, but the oppression of black women collapses under the broad umbrella of "racial oppression enacted upon black Americans by white-supremacist patriarchs." Additionally, black women (and white women, since a race is not specified in this particular lyric) are forced to feel the subjugation of their femaleness, in that antiracist rhetoric is laced with sexism. His reference to a half-naked woman used to rem-edy the bruised black male ego counterbalances the serious tone and the revolutionary disambiguation that the song evokes. Kanye makes it appear as if in the face of such discriminatory truths, black males are the natural victims of racialized discriminatory policies, and that black women are unaffected, or have emerged unscathed. The women have only fallen prey to the capitalist system of frivolous spending in order to secure their roles in the performance of what it means to be American.

In "Gorgeous," compulsory heterosexuality becomes an outlet for that which has not been attained; that is black male liberation. "For Freud," Terry Eagleton (2008) posits in *Literary Theory*, "it is by virtue of such sublimation that civilization itself comes about: by switching and harnessing our instincts to these higher goals, cultural history itself is created" (132). This theory therefore involves deferring one's initial desire (black male visibility and equality) for immediate gratification (sexual exploitation of women), as a means of coping with unfulfilled desires. One might uncritically accept such a theory, except in this case, the "social outlet" manifests itself in the form of sexual exploitation in which the woman is reduced to her anatomy and the sexual agency she wields. Also, the black male, who has been perceived as invisible and animalistic, forcibly inserts his being into civilization, through his devaluation of women, which he considers a more "socially valued end" in Terry Eagleton's terms (132). Hence, sexual exploitation becomes an outlet for the frustrated, racially degraded black male subject.

Natasha Lennard (2013), a writer for *Salon Magazine*, explains how "New Slave," a song on Kanye's latest album, anticipates and condemns the burgeoning private prison system, wherein a de facto system of enslaving black male drug kings will occur by mandating these men to perform underpaid labor in order to be of service to private corporations, thus creating "New Slaves." Kanye is rapping about the domination of male labor power by white patriarchy, and by the end of the track, it becomes of necessity to Kanye to invert the power structure by assuming the role of oppressor?

Some may contend that in "New Slave," Kanye is only performing and adhering to the construction of his brand. He has presented himself to the world as one who is impulsive and unashamedly outspoken against what he considers to be racial injustice. He knows that his erratic, combative behavior contributes to his extended stay in the limelight. So, a track like "New Slave" that solidifies his antagonistic nature only boosts his album sales. While this is undoubtedly true, the song is also a form of activism that uses rap as a political platform. Paradoxically though, Kanye appeals to his black male audience by appropriating a rather violent, hypermasculinist tone. In the track, he engages in the process of sublimation vis-à-vis the sexual violation of white women, in order to mitigate his frustrations regarding a system that abets the invisibility and exploitation of black males. Using a queer framework, author Robert Reid-Pharr (2007), in *Once You Go Black*, advocates for a black American intellectual existentialist identity. His premise is hinged upon the dialectic between a sort of obligatory collectivity and the necessity for individuality. In the introduction to this text, Reid-Pharr opposes the widely held claim that black males have attempted to secure their identity through the vehicle of sexuality. He states, "Indeed one might quite easily make the provocative claim that the Black American has utilized sex and sexuality as a means by which to ensure the survival of black individuals and communities to a *much* greater extent than he has utilized violent confrontation" (Reid-Pharr, 2007:4).[5] But Kanye West's body of work and solution offered in "New Slaves" may prove Reid-Pharr wrong. He frequently places his humanity on the chopping block whenever he endeavors to protest against issues of racism and to incite black male consciousness. "New Slaves" and several other songs employ sex and sexuality as a means by which to ensure the survival of black individuals.

"New Slaves" exposes how black males are confronted by a privately owned white corporation that seeks to systematically subject them to exile, much like the goal of the racially exclusive institution of patriarchy. In "Murder to Excellence," Kanye suggests that patriarchy is upholding its purpose of perpetuating the invisibility of black males. Kanye performs an admirable gesture by bringing this to the attention of young black males in both of these songs. However, the sincerity and authenticity of his message can be questioned when he embarks on an oppressive rant at the end of "New Slaves", threatening to sexually violate the wives of these private corporation owners, by forcing them into intercourse, and by ejaculating semen inside of their mouths and on their clothing. I wonder if after listening to this track, as well as entire albums like *808s & Heartbreak* and *My Beautiful Dark Twisted Fantasy*, Reid-Pharr would feel compelled to revisit his claims about the primary means by which black males achieve liberation. Kanye is getting his "by any means on" ("Black Skin Head"), in his resolve to assert his presence and manhood in the most morally dubious fashion, in a white, capitalist, patriarchal society like The Hamptons, where the "one percent" of wealthy capitalists reside—a society in which only his purchasing power may gain him entry.

Black males justifiably attempt to circumvent or subvert unjust power structures. Therefore, I do not wish to silence their voices by requesting that they censor their music and ignore the cogency of postmodern forms of enslavement. I applaud the fact that rappers have created a space where they are relevant, and in which they can elevate the consciousness of young black males. But I caution them against lamenting what society has seized from their black mothers, and reserved for those with "fairer skin," such as the right to clean water supply—by returning the favor vis-à-vis what Jean-Paul Sarte (1963), in *Black Orpheus*, refers to as "anti-racist racism," or even "anti-racist sexism," like Kanye has done in "New Slave." Black American male subjectivity occurs at the moment he resists dehumanization. "The Black American's presence begins...at the moment of his contradiction, the moment at which the slaver must come to negotiate with the enslaved " (Reid-Pharr, 2007: 3). Surely, Kanye is negotiating, as can be demonstrated in his verse on "Mercy" when he demands Def Jam (a white-owned music label), to pay him fifty million dollars to prevent his resignation. However, his other form of resisting exploitation and black male oppression has been at the expense of female liberation. Kanye, and artists like him, must realize that black male ontology and masculinity have to have some kind of a priori existence. Black masculinity does not have to be defined in accordance with its reaction to white patriarchal forces, or in hooks's words, "patriarchal masculinity" (hooks, *We Real Cool*, 2004: 4). It is a reactionary identification, and as hooks argues, it is a co-optation of colonialist, white patriarchal ideology and methodology, which uses domination and exploitation to achieve an economic or political goal. When in rap music, female exploitation and oppression become the answer to racism and black male invisibility, the artists expose the musical form, and the disillusionment of black males to serious criticism.

Conclusion

Despite the charges I have brought against Kanye West in this essay, my iTunes library is filled with every Yeezy album. I find myself reciting his lyrics subconsciously and securing his spot on my "top five alive" list. I embrace feminist thought, but I am also unapologetically a Kanye West fan. Consequently, I have to ask myself: "Have I become desensitized to the promulgation of misogyny in hip-hop?" I tend to use the very platitudinous phrase, "academic inquiry," to justify my interest in his music. This reality implies that as a black woman, even though I continue to support Kanye's music, there is a discomfort that resonates within me. This simultaneous discomfort and endorsement calls into question the black woman's conflicted nature in America. Just as The Combahee River Collective Statement (1997) posits, black women have not been afforded the luxury of adopting a separatist agenda, like white feminists have, for the very reason that "[O]ur situation as black people necessitates that we have solidarity around the fact of race, which white women of course do not need to have with white men " (65). So then, instead of turning a deaf ear to his music, I have decided to take a closer look at Kanye West's performed black masculinism. Such an examination has afforded me the insight into seeing Kanye as what Louis Althusser would call a hailed subject, answering the call to racist sentiments and ideologies—but also as a subject who struggles with disidentifying and counter-identifying with racial and sexual constructions. Black male emotiveness and unadulterated exaltation of womanhood might insanely suggest that the black man is conceding to the feminization of black maleness, thus compelling black masculinity to conform to the reactionary image of manhood espoused by Black Nationalist leaders of the 1960s and 1970s.

According to this logic, Kanye does not represent what Reid-Pharr calls an "anti-traditionalist aesthetic," in that in the art he produces, he demonstrates that he has not been confronted by "the reality of [his] freedom." Kanye cannot dislodge himself from the constraints placed on him by "cultural and ideological apparatuses," which "underwrite so-called racial distinction," as well as a constructed, traditionalist identification of black masculinity. Kanye affirms rather than challenges the racial (and masculinist) status quo (Reid-Pharr, 2007: 7–8). Although Kanye begins "New Slave" with a testament to the black woman's oppression suffered at the hands of legalized segregation, this narrative is uncharacteristic in his music, because it is not the hypermasculinist, sexist portrayal of black masculinity found in his other lyrics.

Yet, sometimes I also see Kanye as struggling to shy away from traditional representations of blackness and black manhood that have been constructed, in part, by exogenous forces and discourses. Kanye occupies both spaces and performs both roles, although the former is more pronounced and pervasive in his work. Hence, one other reason I find myself preoccupied with Kanye's music is because I empathize with him. I realize that he has acknowledged the disadvantages concurrent with what Fanon terms the "fact of [his] blackness," and has chosen an unfavorably vain strategy to resist dehumanization and to cope with an unfulfilled desire to be liberated from white supremacy: sexual oppression and exploitation. Nonetheless, Kanye West sets himself apart from many of his contemporaries because the misogyny he celebrates is followed by a void that must be filled by a woman. In songs like "Blame Game," "Guilt Trip," and "Hold My Liquor,"

Kanye's completeness is contingent upon a woman's presence and embrace. The narrative of "Blame Game" involves a seesaw between Kanye and another woman, in which he calls her "bitch" and she responds with more abrasive language. Once she leaves him, he cannot handle the desolation, so he inscribes her name on the bathroom stall, conjuring passionate sexual acts they once engaged in within his heterosexual imagination. This causes him to admit that she had once given his life a purpose. The misogyny is almost eclipsed by the image of a grieving black male with an ego that has been bruised by white supremacy and his former lover. Similarly, in "Guilt Trip," Kanye laments his abandonment. This time, listeners don't empathize as much with his pierced heart because he slips back into his misogynist role by reducing a new girl to triviality. She becomes a mere "saga" and hot potato to be shared among his clique. In both cases, Kanye displays emotiveness, although in "Blame Game" he implies emotion is commercial suicide for black male "moguls" like himself. Listeners are made aware of his collapsed ego in need of a woman's care, in much of his music. But almost invariably affection is overshadowed by misogynistic rants, arguably because it does not coincide with the connotation of black masculinity that history has promulgated.

I agree with Reid-Pharr in advocating for an existentialist black male ontology, no matter how paradoxical it sounds. If at all possible, the black male must will himself, if he has to, into pure, existentialist subjectivity, untainted and uninformed by white America that views him as "a penis symbol" (Fanon, 1952: 137). That is not to say that he should wear a sporty pair of blinders in the face of the racist white gaze. He must acknowledge and address his objectification by white patriarchs. However, it is vitally important that he does not respond by subjecting women to this same subjugation. Kanye has inserted himself into the lineage of Black Power leaders, but he must follow his own advice and reassess their philosophies ("Power"). In *The Evidence of Things Not Seen*, James Baldwin (1985) declared the need to expunge the habit of seeing oneself as victim: "I refuse to speak from the point of view of the victim. The victim can have no point of view for precisely so long as he thinks of himself as a victim. The testimony of the victim as victim corroborates, simply, the reality of the chains that bind him— confirms and, as it were, consoles the jailer" (78). So then, Kanye West has to realize that inflicting oppression upon another group of human beings doesn't mean he is liberated. In fact, it means he is still thinking as "the victim," and so is still oppressed. It also means that he is corroborating with the exploitative goals of the rap industry, at the expense of female liberation, and black male liberation.

Notes

1. The black male mind embodies genius prior to its encounter with white-supremacist ideology. The black male has an initial perception of his subjectivity, his ontology, his soul, before white America's attempts to monopolize power through racist strategies, repressing his genius, ergo causing him to respond in unfavorable ways, such as the sexual oppression of women.

2. Oppressed persons are self-deluded in their belief that they can subvert their impositions and disempowerment through the subjugation and oppression of others because, as Freire argues, they have grown so accustomed to the structure of domination as oppressed subjects, that they co-opt this structure in their attempts to gain liberation (44).

3. The information in this section is paraphrased from Donda West's book, *Raising Kanye: Life Lessons from the Mother of a Hip-Hop Superstar.*

4. As an example, Michele Wallace recognizes the literary eruditeness of Ralph Ellison's *Invisible Man*, but has voiced her displeasure with the narrator's descent into a substructure to avoid assuming the roles forced upon him by society. Wallace boldly states, "I am often tempted to wonder if that concern with white perception did not help make [the novel] such a huge success. Ellison's hero takes the coward's way out" (58). Comparatively, the black male's masculine disposition where he oppresses women, black and white, can be regarded as "tak[ing] the coward's way out" in order to reject feminized and dehumanized representations of the black male body politic, by conforming to an image that still renders the black male body unwanted and feared in white, patriarchal America.

5. According to Reid-Pharr, those like myself who support this claim put forth a very "basic" and "exhaustive" argument (4). He believes the history of black male combativeness, such as Frederick Douglass's assault on his overseer, is the central force that has formulated black male identity (4). While this is an insightful theory, it is not exhaustive enough. Reid-Pharr may deem this combativeness as operating from an existentialist framework, but he ignores how as a form of resistance, it has the potential to compromise one's role in the advancement of humanitarianism, and as the theme of "New Slave" proves, gender equality.

Chapter 7

Kanye West's Sonic [Hip-hop] Cosmopolitanism

Regina N. Bradley

On September 2, 2005, Kanye West appeared on an NBC benefit telecast for Hurricane Katrina victims. West, emotionally charged and going off script, blurted out, "George Bush doesn't care about black people." Early in his rapping career and fresh off the critically acclaimed sophomore album *Late Registration*, West thrusts himself into the public eye—debatably either on accident or purposefully—as a seemingly budding cultural-political pundit. For the audience, West's growing popularity and visibility as a rapper automatically translated his concerns into a statement on behalf of all African Americans. West, however, quickly shies away from being labeled a leader, disclaiming his outburst as a personal opinion. In retrospect, West states: "When I made my statement about Katrina, it was a social statement, an emotional statement, not a political one" (Scaggs, 2007). Nevertheless, his initial comments about the Bush administration's handling of Katrina positioned him both as a producer of black cultural expression and as a mediator of said blackness. It is from this interstitial space that West continued to operate moving forward, using music—and the occasional outburst—to identify himself as transcending the expectations placed upon his blackness and masculinity.

West utilizes music to tread the line between hip-hop identity politics and his own convictions, blurring discourses through which race and gender are presented to a (inter)national audience. It is important to note that hip-hop serves doubly as an intervention of American capitalism and of black agency. Hip-hop's attraction abroad remains attached to its roots as a voice for oppressed groups. Tropological overlaps of trauma and prejudices about bodies of color—that is, police brutality and poverty—speak to a broader audience than African

Americans. In the same breadth, hip-hop is also a vehicle for understanding (American) blackness as a hyper-commodity. West grounds
his international experiences afforded by his success as a rapper and
producer within localized American hip-hop to negotiate his blackness
and experiences as a cultural commodity. Thus, West's manipulation of
sound allows him to engage hip-hop from a cosmopolitan perspective,
a position of privilege and excess frequently doted in commercial rap.

Jon Caramonica's description of West highlights his complexities
as a cosmopolitan figure:

> No rapper has embodied hip-hop's often contradictory impulses of
> narcissism and social good quite as he has, and no producer has cel-
> ebrated the lush and ornate quite as he has. He has spent most of his
> career in additive mode, figuring out how to make music that's majestic
> and thought-provoking and grand-scaled. And he's also widened the
> genre's gates, whether middle-class values or high-fashion and high-art
> dreams (Caramonica 2013).

As Caramonica points out, West's apt negotiation of oppositional
experiences situates him as a privileged figure within hip-hop. He
utilizes the criticism and fears surrounding his blackness—and his
mouth—as cornerstones of his catalog. However, West departs from
hip-hop's stiff emphasis on a local homesite as a space of negotiating
one's identity politics. His personal conventions and creative complexity allow him to seamlessly move between hip-hop and broader
popular music aesthetics seen and heard in other genres such as progressive rock, electronica, and trip hop. For example, West calls upon
rappers such as Common, Twista, and Chief Keef to sustain his sonic
and creative alliance with Chicago while pulling inspiration from
European musical influences such as Daft Punk and Kraftwerk to
establish himself on an international music stage. It is West's meticulous use of local and international music that positions him as a (sonic)
cosmopolite. Where witty lyrics fall short, West picks up the slack
with his manipulation of sound vis-à-vis sampling or intricate instrumentation. Whether a full-bodied orchestra or the stark and desolate
use of 808 bass kicks and percussion, West uses sound to capture his
emotional vulnerability and relay it to his audience. Because West, as
Caramonica aptly describes him, is "above all, a technician, obsessed
with sound," there is a need to explore his catalog of work through the
perspective of a sound study. A sonic analysis of West's work allows for
the conflicting and oppositional popular cultural discourses through
which West expresses himself to simultaneously coexist.

Building upon Mark Anthony Neal's theorization in *Looking for Leroy* of Jay-Z as a figure of hip-hop cosmopolitanism, I'd like to suggest West signifies what I theorize as *sonic* hip-hop cosmopolitanism. He uses sound to negotiate his stakes (and angsts) as an American, world traveler, and hip-hop citizen. Neal (2013) defines hip-hop cosmopolitanism as "marked in part by a symbolic homelessness from notions of mainstream American morality, political relevancy, and cultural gravitas" (36). Particularly useful about Neal's observations is the literal and figurative detachment of rappers—particularly those in mogul positions like Jay-Z—from mainstream American (popular) culture while still very much influential in situating hip-hop as a site of black agency (or the lack thereof) in the United States. For example, Jay-Z and Kanye West's song "Niggas in Paris" from their collaborative album *Watch the Throne* speaks to their ability to influence American culture while enjoying a materially excessive lifestyle abroad. The track presents a tense juxtaposition between the culturally idealistic representation of Paris as a safe haven for black expatriates such as James Baldwin, Richard Wright, and Josephine Baker to freely indulge their work and hip-hop materialism. Paris provides a site of freer cultural expression that gives rise to the agency and homelessness of early twentieth-century black American artists in ways rarely signified in contemporary commercial hip-hop. Earlier black expatriates utilized their detachment from the United States as both a cultural *and* political expression of their frustration with the treatment of blacks in the United States. This cultural-political agency manifests differently for Jay-Z and West. Their frustrations with America are tethered to their commercial success. Both Jay-Z and West invest in and depict Paris as a nomadic haven of hip-hop wealth (labels, European cars, and champagne) that signifies their Americanness and black masculinity abroad. The opening lines of the track, Jay Z speaks to his ability to literally and figuratively remove himself from their presence. His nomad-ness is a privilege.

Similarly, West speaks of Paris as a dichotomy of opulence and memes of virulent hip-hop masculinity expected by American popular culture. West's rap begs Neal's question of "can a nigga be cosmopolitan?" He writes, "the 'nigga' [serves] as a trope of contemporary transnational blackness" (Neal, 2013: 35). The visibility of "niggas" signifies the (Americanized) blackness in Paris, the epitome of white sophistication. It also translates the use of "nigga" from an American truism for black masculinity to a means to complicate hip-hop cosmopolitanism as a space of (black) respectability. West's verse blurs

the boundaries of the nigga archetype's racial and cultural palpabil-
ity within hip-hop spaces with classed performances of cosmopolitan
privilege. As Neal observes:

> hip-hop identities are intensely wedded to racial truisms that are often
> legitimized by some of the most visible (and highly compensated) hip-
> hop artists, but are often out of sync with those who might otherwise
> reference their hip-hop identities within a broad range of civic, politi-
> cal, cultural, spiritual, economic, and intellectual activities...in this
> regard, a hip-hop cosmopolitanism is undergirded by desires for physi-
> cal, social and economic mobility...a mobility from or even within
> the essential tropes—playa, pimp, hustler, thug, and nigga (37).

In this instance, West literally and sonically teases out the intersections between cosmopolitan and nigga-dom through lyricism and the
performance of his lyrics. A braggadocio-laden yet rhetorical exchange
between himself and the listener, West's verse provides insight into an
experience and lifestyle to which most of his listeners cannot relate.
Indeed, West presents his audience with a "nigga moment," one which
simultaneously subverts the recognizable actions of a "nigga" within
an Americanized construct of black respectability while transcending this construct with access to international travel—and monetary
capital—abroad. Bridging the foreignness of (European) wealth with
the American class disparities that are believed to make commercial
rap authentic, West's cosmopolitanism situates him as a voluntary cultural refugee, a "nigga with options."

West embeds the conflicts and privileges of his hip-hop cosmopolitanism into his sound. His sound work reflects a worldly outlook while remaining attached to the proverbial hip-hop block, lacing
obscure music samples with familiar ones and other aural inclina-
tions of hip-hop aesthetics, such as strong percussion kicks, bass
drops, autotune, deft record scratches, and pauses between verses,
grunts, and moans. Thus, one branch of West's sonic cosmopolitanism exists through his use of sampling. It creates a sonic identity
that mirrors West's growth as an artist and as a man. Joseph Schloss
(2003) argues in *Making Beats* how the sampling used in hip-hop
manipulates sounds to create a specific aesthetic. Schloss writes, "for
hip-hop producers—who *are* highly attuned to the origins of particular samples—the significance tends to lie more in the ingenuity
of the way the elements are fused together than in calling attention to
the diversity of their origins" (66). West's search for the obscure—to
American ears, at least—solidifies him not only as a "dope producer"

but also as a conscious producer grappling for aural control of his listener's negotiation of his position within hip-hop.

In the single "Mercy" from his second collaborative album, *Cruel Summer*, West samples and loops dancehall singer Fuzzy Jones's intro for the song "Dust a Soundboy" by Super Beagle. On West's track, Jones sings about moaning, weeping, and gnashing teeth. His sharp, high-pitched voice cannot be immediately identified on first listening as masculine. This characteristic adds a type of gender ambiguity to the track, graying attempts to categorize "Mercy" as representative of American hip-hop masculinity. Additionally, Jones's braggadocio parallels West's own, emphatically claiming that his sound is the best. Before West's actual verse on the song, the majority of Jones's original intro is played. West's inclusion of Jones's allusions to military precision and agency acknowledges his prominence as a rapper and as a producer and further suggests West's own track record as a successful artist and producer who has been through the trenches of the hip-hop industry with talent left over. Tried and true, the sample blends hip-hop braggadocio and symbolic militancy to relay West's sonic agency and hip-hop influence. His inclusion of the Fuzzy Jones sample provides an example of Schloss's observation about the plight of producers showcasing their knowledge of music and the need for public acceptance to validate that knowledge: "hip-hop production constitutes an ideal value for developing a tactical sense of when to make knowledge public…the constant struggle that producers face between using their work to display their esoteric record knowledge to each other and making beats that appeal to abroad audience that wants to dance" (Schloss, 2003: 81). The obscurity of the sample highlights West's sonic cosmopolitanism as international—his musical influences are not grounded within the United States—and, to an extent, diasporic. The sonic borrowing of Jones's dancehall performance speaks to West's perception of his own blackness as global and uncontainable by American perceptions of black identity politics. Yet West remains attached to the United States through the act of sampling, the use of instrumentation recognized as characteristic of hip-hop—808 bass drops, sparse snare drums—and the (sonic) incorporation of culturally recognizable rappers such as Big Sean, Two Chainz, and Pusha T. West exhibits a consistent awareness of hip-hop aesthetics within his sound work that allows him to stretch the boundaries of those aesthetics. Each album in West's catalog maps his redefinition of and increased sophistication at the process of extending his (sonic) cosmopolitanism outside of the rigidity of hip-hop.

Mapping out Kanye West's Sonic [Hip-hop] Cosmopolitanism

Kanye West's initial sonic branding is rooted in the Soul and Funk genres from the 1960s and 1970s. West credits his parents as influences for his earlier sound: "My dad's generation is a generation of messaging" (Caramonica 2013). A fan of sampling the likes of Curtis Mayfield and Marvin Gaye, West's early soulful blends invoked the cultural memory and angsts associated with the time period. His status as a hip-hop cosmopolitan is one grown from association with influential rappers such as Jay-Z. West's entry point is Jay-Z's album *The Blueprint*, arguably Jay-Z's own initial foray into cosmopolitan status. Sampling from the likes of Bobby Blue Bland, David Ruffin, and the Jackson 5, West lends a soulful credence to Jay-Z's lyricism. His sampling doubly serves the album title: It sonically bridges the audience to past black male artists, who, undoubtedly, influenced West and Jay-Z, but also serves as a template for West's own budding sound production skills. West looks back at his initial sound work as sloppy, though pivotal in establishing himself in a moment of hip-hop where drugs, thugs, and excess materialism ran rampant. About his work on *The Blueprint* West he observes: "It finally gave me a platform to put the message that my parents put inside me and that Dead Prez helped to get out of me and Mos Def and [Talib] Kweli, they helped to get out of me: I was able to put it, sloppily rap it, on top of the platform that Jay-Z had created for me" (Caramonica 2013). West remained closely attached to his black music and black cultural roots. This trend continues through his freshman effort *The College Dropout*, utilizing gospel choirs and samples from keystone black artists, including Curtis Mayfield, Luther Vandross, and Aretha Franklin.

Most notable on this album is the sample of Chaka Khan's "Through the Fire" on the album's lead single, "Through the Wire." Speeding up Khan's chorus, "Through the Wire" resonates as a tragicomic song of triumph about West's resurrection and ability to overcome death, tropes frequently visited in rap. West doubly situates himself within hip-hop's death and capitalist narrative and cracks jokes about the car accident he was then recovering from, laughing about not being able to get through airport security because of the metal in his mouth, skull, and jewelry. Recorded with West's mouth wired shut—the accident left him with a shattered jaw—West delivers lyrics of perseverance and ambition. The sonic intonations of West's accident—slurred delivery, speaking through clenched teeth—literally signify the song title. A sonically traumatic and strained delivery mirrors the trauma of West's accident. "Through the Wire" marks West's initial foray into sonic cosmopolitanism via sound manipulation because he is physically and literally restricted in his ability to voice his fears and frustrations after the accident. West relies on sound to properly communicate the trauma and experiences he cannot put into words. It is his initial foray into tinkering with how sound can be used to translate his experiences into a tangible narrative as a (black) man and artist.

West's sophomore album *Late Registration* begins to stretch his musical influences and sonic hip-hop narrative. Unlike *College Dropout, Late Registration* showcases the production talents of Jon Brion. Notably the producer of singer Fiona Apple, his sonic presence impacts West's own hip-hop agenda and pushes him to be more experimental in the album's sound production. West's use of Brion's access to a variety of pop music instrumentation illustrates a conscious effort to push his sound (American) hip-hop into a larger arena (literally and figuratively) of popular music, including his European influences. For example, West credits English trip hop band Portishead as a primary influence for *Late Registration.* Portishead's hybridization of elements of hip-hop and punk rock impacted West to renegotiate how (American) hip-hop should sound: "Seeing this [Portishead] album cover did so much for me . . . I saw it years back but on my first album I couldn't afford strings. So, after I won those Grammys, the first thing I did was run to Jon Brion, and then I ran and got a string section. Hip-hop never had strings that lush with drums that hard. But Portishead had that. And they sounded hip-hop, and people vibed to that" (Scaggs 2007). West's desire for instrumentation and musical elements that are nonnormative in hip-hop aesthetics carved him a niche where he could demonstrate a mastery of his musical knowledge beyond hip-hop and popular culture knowledge expand his narrative to include influences from outside the hip-hop regime he frequented at the time. On songs like "Celebration," "Crack Music," and the hidden track "Late," a full orchestra is used to give the track more body and push the envelope on what hip-hop should sound like. West's use of the orchestra ups West's lyrical and sonic narrative to refresh delivery of the (black) agency and angst once reserved for bass kicks and piano riffs in hip-hop. Further, West samples Shirley Bassey's singing the song "Diamonds Are Forever" from the James Bond film of the same name in "Diamonds from Sierra Leone." The use of "Diamonds Are Forever" speaks to the hypercommodification and materialism heralded in hip-hop while critiquing the blood diamond trade in Sierra Leone. This track is particularly critical to mapping out West's initial forays into sonic hip-hop cosmopolitanism: It blends hip-hop's cultural disparities with larger international issues. Not only does West critique the use of blood diamonds but he also critiques his own indulgence in jewelry.

West's third commercial release *Graduation,* however, brazenly demonstrates his departure from considering himself as only an American artist and American rapper. *Graduation* signifies West's attempting to connect to a broader, more European audience. It presents West's sonic cosmopolitanism situated in the understanding of his sound being able to reach a broader audience outside of hip-hop while retaining his fan base. *Graduation* demonstrates West's ability to meticulously blend (European) rock and Techno aesthetics from artists including Daft Punk (sampled in "Stronger") and Elton John (sampled in "Good Morning") with his "original sample sound" to create himself a unique niche in American and European popular music as a sonic cosmopolite. West states:

> I went back to songs like "Champion" and "Good Life" and put these type of chords on them that sounded similar to the type of sense that I put on "Stronger." That's why "Flashing Lights," "Champion" all of them have that certain synthesizer, a real 80s synthesizer type of sound. But I mixed it with my original sample sound, so it didn't get too far from what people knew me for, but like created a new form of music in rap...People still bring up "Spaceships" to me. And people compare "Can't Tell Me Nothing" to "Spaceships" saying that's a song that inspires them when they going to work. But the chords itself, is like a Led Zeppelin, rock melody (Laws 2007).

Although sampling and emceeing are still prominent in West's work, he consistently attempts to situate himself in a larger, (European) rock narrative that he indicates sets the foundation for gauging his success as a popular artist. Part of this foundation is in what can be considered as West's arena sound, the ability to attract and move a large crowd. West reconsidered the significance of arena sound and presence after a conversation with lead U2 singer Bono:

> I wanted my drums to bang harder in stadiums. One of my inspirations was I went on tour with U2 and Bono...told me that 'No one from your community has ever figured this out.' And if you think about it, nobody from the black community can really sell out stadiums, like 30,000 seaters, there's not one artist you can think of. I can think of four, you know, white artists (Laws 2007).

After speaking with Bono, West realizes the need to command a crowd through a simpler, although no less brilliant, approach to his music. Situating himself as an arena presence forces him to renegotiate his brand, perspective on hip-hop, and music in general. West "concentrated on speaking volumes without using too many words" (Reid 2007). Simply, West finds himself refiguring the sonic and practical intent of emceeing. During a listening party, West jokingly commented "I'd be saying my super raps, and this 50-year-old white lady would be looking like, 'I can't wait till the Rolling Stones come on'" (Reid 2007). *Graduation* signifies West's simultaneous embarking upon creating and delivering a simplified message and sonic narrative to appeal to the larger European rock audiences. West's sees and hears his European rock as a gateway to the cosmopolitan status he feels his music is headed.

Still, *Late Registration*, like *College Dropout*, is a site of cultural and introspective navigation that West shares with his audience. As stated previously, *Late Registration*'s social-political statements set the stage for West's emotional outburst during the Hurricane Katrina on-air benefit. While West claims that he spoke from a place of emotion rather than logic, West had already established that pathos and ethos do not necessarily remain detached in his work. It is from this perspective that I suggest West's sonic hip-hop cosmopolitanism doubly registers as a tragic space where West's traumatic experiences register sonically. This is especially prevalent on West's *808s and Heartbreak* and *My Beautiful Dark Twisted Fantasy*. The former, released after a series of tragic events in West's life—the unexpected loss of his mother Donda West in 2007 and breakup with his longtime fiancée Alexis Phifer soon after—introduces West's era of minimalism in sound work. Stark, dependent on the Roland TR-808 Bass machine, and the introduction of West's tinkering with autotune, *808s and Heartbreak* sonically reflected its title. West delivers his lyrics by masking his voice with autotune rather than rapping, suggesting an awareness of performing his pain for an audience while working through it. West's autotune performance allows him to sing rather than rap, raising the question of whether or not he isolates his hip-hop audience and roots. There is a demonstrated understanding that West is not only a hip-hop artist and his experiences—sonically and lived—are not restricted by hip-hop aesthetics. As West states in an interview with *Fader* magazine:

> Society has put up so many boundaries, so many limitations on what's right and wrong that it's almost impossible to get a pure thought

out...everyone's born confident, and everything's taken away from you. So many people try to put their personality on someone else. Especially me, they try to suggest what I should do. What I want people to realize at this point is, I don't give a fuck. That's why I made this album. I'm using Auto-Tune because I don't give a fuck. I like the way it sounds. This is the way I'ma put my shit up, this what I like the most. You can't deny me, you cannot deny Wayne, you cannot deny Pain. T-Pain taught me a lot. He just brought a whole vibe and energy when he came down to Hawaii, he was constantly expressing himself (Macia 2012).

More personal and introspective than previous releases, *808s and Heartbreak* is West's sonic experimentation with emotions deemed unavailable to black men, especially black men in hip-hop. On the inaugural single "Love Lockdown," for example, West's autotuned voice is nearly drowned out by the dominant and at times mind-numbing repetition of 808 bass drops. It signifies not only West's emotional unavailability but also the lack of discourse available for West to vent his frustrations. This introspective work takes place sonically.

Yet even with the intense emotional vulnerability, West reveals to his listeners on the album that he remains in the vein of European Rock influence. West samples English progressive rock band The Alan Parsons Project's song "Ammonia Avenue" as the foundation for his track "Heartless." Particularly striking about this sample is the carnival-esque pipe organ that accompanies West's signature use of the 808 machine for this album. The pipe organ aurally signifies West's attachment to the progressive rock aesthetic associated with "Ammonia Avenue" and the circus frenzy surrounding his life. The chorus line "how could you be so heartless?" speaks not only to the undisclosed lover he addresses on the track but also his audience/the public putting him under scrutiny. *808s and Heartbreak* marks West's ascension into his current status as a cocky and arrogant artist. West's solidified position as a hip-hop icon also situates his cosmopolitan outlook, resulting in West pushing his limits and dictating his performances according to the sonic and cultural boundaries he sets for himself.

Although *808s and Heartbreak* demonstrates West's departure from "commonplace" expectations of commercial hip-hop aesthetics, *My Beautiful Dark Twisted Fantasy* marks West's personal and cultural fatigue. In "Critic's Notebook: Kanye West's Growing Pains," music critic Ann Powers (2010) aptly labels the album "the crisis of a jet-lagged cosmopolitan" (n.p.). West himself acknowledges the album as an effort to regain an audience he believed he had lost, referring to the album as "a backhanded apology:" "'Dark Fantasy' was my long, backhanded apology. You know how people give a backhanded compliment? It was a backhanded apology. It was like, all these raps, all these sonic acrobatics" (Caramonica 2013). West's description of the album as "sonic acrobatics" speaks to not only West's creative process but also efforts to simultaneously adhere and dismiss the scrutiny associated with his public and creative self. Notable tracks indicating this tension include "Dark Fantasy," "Monster," and "Power." The lead single best "Power" demonstrates West's meticulous sound production in ways that reflect back to *Graduation*: he utilizes the guitar riffs and ad libs from English rock band King Crimson's "Schizoid Man" and a sample of the introduction to the more obscure track "Afromerica" by French Disco group Continent Number 6. Ryan Dombai (2010) writes: "'POWER' has Kanye internalizing his multiple minds and coming to an ecstatic peace with them. 'POWER' is not a bitchfest. It is an exaltation. All of his various guises—King of the Assholes, drama queen, Red Bull'd 12-year old, Next Chappelle, strangely relatable Megaman—are mashed up in this proudly schizoid roll call. Every sound is ready for the arena" (n.p). Dombai's remarks about "Power" being "ready for the arena" speaks to West's inching closer to the arena sound Bono challenged West to think about earlier in his career. Simple delivery, hard-hitting percussion, synthesizers, and the loop of "AfroAmerica" help West reclaim his initial hip-hop audience while presenting him as a sonic cosmopolite on the brink of the success seen by the white European rockers he admires.

At the moment, Kanye West's meticulous attention to sonic and creative detail situates him in a category of his own. He creates an interstitial existence between the grandeur of European rock and the hyper-capitalism and opulence of hip-hop that has not been emulated in hip-hop. Kanye West's zealous willingness to blend his personal vulnerability and creative process to create an "original hybrid" sound of (European) rock and roll, techno, and hip-hop suggest West as a sonic hip-hop cosmopolitan figure. However, his catalog of music provides an intricate blueprint for future music producers who are daring enough to continue West's trajectory of sonic experimentation as a gateway to musical innovation.

Chapter 8

"Hard to Get Straight": Kanye West, Masculine Anxiety, Dis-identification

Tim'm West

No Homo and Strategic Pauses

In an *MTV News* interview, Kanye West had this to say:

> Man I think as straight men we need to take the rainbow back because it's fresh. It looks fresh. I just think that because stereotypically gay people got such good like style that they were smart enough to take a fresh-ass logo like the rainbow and say that it's gonna be theirs. But I was like "Man I think we need to have the rainbow"—the idea of colors, life and colors and stuff, I mean how is that a gay thing? Colors? Having a lot of colors is gay? (2009)

Straight boys kill me, especially the ones whose heterosexuality is questionable. The word "Gay" too often emerges for them as some kind of litmus test of masculinity. Especially in hip-hop culture, the not-so-smart "smart bomb" in freestyle or battle cyphers is to challenge a combatant's masculinity or sexuality by even the merest suggestion that he's homosexual. One shuts a battle down by calling a straight boy a fag. If the opponent is gay, he'll never admit it; and there is little worse you could call him. It's the most noninventive strategic kill in rap battles. There are other reasons this kills me: beyond the ways it erases the possibility of a nonheterosexual identity as even being plausible among "Real Men" in hip-hop contexts, it conflates gender identification with sexual attraction in a way that denies any viability of queer masculinities. In 2013, understanding the differences between gender and sexual identity, it would seem obvious enough that not all straight men are masculine, and that many queer men are. I am a queer scholar, attuned to my masculine privilege, and passionately connected to the ways heteronormativity similarly and differently affects other demographics in the vast and diverse LGBTQ community. Still, this essay takes a decidedly homo-centric approach as an effort to focus on the precise nature of anxiety produced when hip-hop artists are confronted with questions about their relationship to gay men specifically.

The essentialization of "straight boys" here is necessary to illustrate my point about the excesses of their masculine anxiety. Straight guys who understand the overstatement are seldom offended by a queer "reading" [of][1] straight boys; a distinction that perhaps expresses the difference between straight guys who are masculine and heterosexual and those *invested* in being masculine and heterosexual. The invest-ment offers a failed promise that masculinity or heterosexuality won't be called into question, when it so often already is. A guy who is self-admittedly gay is just gay. With the expected gay-bashing and degradation, why would any guy in the hip-hop context admit he is gay? The emergence of "down-low," secretive, closeted homosexuality in some of the more masculine contexts (e.g., professional sports cul-ture, military, and hip-hop) suggests frustration on the part of many straight men with having to provide proof of their heterosexuality.

The logic of owning an abject identity suggests that one must truly be serious about it; otherwise, it is self-defeating in hip-hop to tell anyone you're queer. Overstating one's straightness almost always incites suspicion that one isn't. Since straightness is the societal default, going to the trouble of openly identifying as straight is gener-ally read as overstatement . . . with one exception: one who, by measure of not following the masculine or heterosexual code, must constantly reinforce his heterosexuality for fear of being mistaken for a queer. Heterosexuality is often a categorical performance that is inextrica-bly, if uncomfortably, bound to its antithesis. Questionable straight boys' relentless reclamation of masculinity, the constant anxiety about "keepin' it real," and the abjectifying distancing from all things gay are testimonies to how necessary it is for straight boys to have gay boys as counterpoint: no homo.[2]

Psychoanalysis and queer theory have both suggested that the instability of the heterosexual identity is verified by its constant (re)iteration. Straightness requires a burden of proof that can lead to the valuation of one as suspect due to the bend of the wrist, wearing pants either too loose or too tight, or paying one of your homies an aesthetic compliment (e.g., "that shirt fits nice, yo") without immedi-ate rebuttal. The viability and durability of masculinity and its reifi-cation of straightness often comes at the expense of a figurative and sometimes literal death[3] of the queer through statements like "no homo." In 2013, NBA all-star Roy Hibbert can be fined $75,000 and forced to apologize for saying "no homo" because of his need to clarify that being "stretched out" by LaBron James was not a sexual reference. The irony lies in the reality that the postmodern black heterosexual has to know a great deal about the particulars of gay sex as precondition for disassociation.

Heterosexual competency of gay sex is among the most frequent ways masculine anxiety emerges in conversation between straight men. Says Kanye West in a 2009 interview on *MTV News*: "Back in the day, people used to have songs like 'Get in That A—' or something like that. Someone would never make a song like that [today] because they'd be like 'Whoa! I can't make no song like that! People gonna call me gay!'"

But there is another fascinating aspect of the Pause[4] or "No Homo" that I believe offers ambivalent promise. Rather than the utter invisibility and absence of the homo in public discourse, "no homo" serves as affirmation, if rendered as derogatory, that homos actually exist. Ironically, one who uses "no homo" as clarification that he isn't gay is actually acknowledging the possibility that he might be. The term "pause"—a term one uses to point to the subconscious gayness of a heterosexual peer—affirms the kind of heteroflexibility that Def Jam poet ButtaFlySoul references in his infamous "Queer Eye." ButtaFlySoul employs a comedic candor, rather than metaphor, to wise his sistas up to the queer eye that enables him to "see gay people"... especially those trying to hide, even from themselves:

> So I leave you with this
> Ms. or whatever you want to call yourself...
> Maybe he's not gay
> maybe he's just heteroflexible
> You know, H-flex, not all the way there
> just suspect

For ButtaFlySoul, the preference for a fruity cocktail instead of a beer or wearing Timberlands as performative cloaking of one's same-sex desire both become other ways that suspect homosexual desire is pronounced. "No homo" is an acknowledgment, though language, of a possibility of being suspected as gay that, for many straight men, must be defended and clarified. If, as many postmodern theorists suggest, we exist through language, if "I speak therefore I am," then a statement like "no homo" offers referential affirmation of what I am by affirming what I am not. The negation and affirmation are inextricably, if uncomfortably, partnered: bro homo.[5]

On Kanye: Bro Homo

So why Kanye? Quite frankly, I've always been intrigued about his ability, by his own admission, to be a more fashionable and flossy man than even most homos. In his rather infamous interview about style on *MTV News* in 2009, Kanye says:

> People wanna label me and throw that on me all the time, but I'm so secure with my manhood. And that's the reason why I can go to Paris, why I can have conversations with people who are blatantly gay.'Cause I used to be scared to talk to a gay person. It's designers that's scared of people in hip-hop. And in hip hop, there's people—and let's not even say scared like homophobic—but they're scared of the way people gonna look at them. If you see a person be like, "I don't wanna stand next to Marc Jacobs 'cause I don't want that to bear on me because I'm just so cool." One of the reasons why, the perspective I come from with my raps and my songs, the reason why can't nobody dis me —no gangsta rapper, nobody can really dis me is 'cause it's so authentic (n.p.)

Not a gangsta rapper, Kanye believes he is exempt from criticisms rebuking his high-fashion flair and colorful style. Continuing, he both admits the influence gay men have had on style while, in typical Kanye fashion, one-upping the gays by validating that he dresses better than many gays.

"That's when I was ignorant to gays. 'Cause there's a lot of gay people who don't dress good at all. There's a lot of gay people that I dress way better than."(*MTV News*, 2009: n.p.)

And I'm guilty as charged, "cousin" Kanye: I'm a masculine, aesthetically dull, jock-rapper. Kanye's straightness enables his ability to appropriate and fetishize the access, via his economic privilege, Fendi, Prada, Jacobs, and a bunch of other labels I wouldn't know if they slapped me on the ass. It's important to own the way my own experiences as both a hip-hop artist and scholar inform my reading of Kanye West. My published scholarship has largely been about the ways patriarchy and heterosexism hurt all men, not just queer men. I sympathize with straight and gay men who feel constrained by the male-box that restricts men's freedom to be fully self-actualized— whether that manifests as critiques that I'm not a "gay enough" hip-hop artist, or emerges as Kanye's sensibilities in fashion and sensitivity about being lazily conflated with gays. Kayne made the GQ top 10 best-dressed men. I need queer eye for the queer guy. I think we both probably understand what it means to be misunderstood, not necessarily by any failure to be "normal" men, but by society's unyielding circumscription of what it means to be a "real man."

I'm challenged and deeply upset by the continued assaults on Kanye's sexuality based on his stylization and queer appropriations. I must also challenge the ways that marking one's flavor for Fendi or penchant for Prada is even a "gay" appropriation to begin with. Doing so feeds into the very stereotyping and essentialization I believe we should be working to deconstruct. Pink sweaters aren't gay, they're pink sweaters. Toting a Glock isn't manly, it's dangerous. Still, there's the undeniable tension between Kanye's own admission of fashionable flair and gays providing some kind of standard for high-fashion, and the attacks of his brave appropriations by the likes of Brand Nubian's Lord Jamar, whose new track, "Lift Up Your Skirt" takes aim at Kanye by lashing insults about his ego and labeling him a fan of queers.

The blatant emasculation that Lord Jamar suggests in his lyrics is layered, for the call for Kanye to "Lift up [his] skirt" might be read as expressing the kind of desire followed by repulsion that is most commonly described as "gay panic."[6] Is the request to see Kanye's piece a move to police his gender or sex—ensure he's anatomically correct(ed)? The call to "lift up your skirt" is generally connotative of heterosexual and patriarchal ownership, a command for the subjugated and submissive partner to enable the man to "see *his* stuff." To that end, the demand that Kanye "lift up [his] skirt" does as much to call Lord Jamar's sexuality into question as it does the subject of his "diss(ed)-identification."[7] Perhaps the criticism of Kanye's leather kilt (which isn't a skirt actually) is a way Lord Jamar can one-up the rap icon, whose skirt hardly seems to be deterring his female groupies or Kim Kardashian from lifting their skirts for "half-f-gs."

This softened gay panic enacted by many or most masculinist and homophobic critics of Kanye seems to be the kneejerk reaction, upon gazing, to rebuke one's voyeurism as iterative affirmation of utter and complete heterosexual allegiance. The Black Nationalist bullying by the not terribly relevant Lord Jamar is a spectacle attack that suggests Kanye is the pioneer of the "queer shit," one who has perhaps ushered in the movement to feminize men in hip-hop. Though media has long regarded another West as a pioneer more appropriately credited for ushering in "Homo-Hop," I have often been considered too masculine to support Lord's claim about an emasculated hip-hop.

Bigger than a personal punch at Kanye's skirt—a Scottish rather than gay appropriation—Lord Jamar aims to warn the hip-hop nation, via tweet, of queer infiltration: "Y'all Cee where the Kanye s–t is takin us right? #halfaf-g." This kind of alarmist policing isn't uncommon or atypical, especially when coming from artists who stand to gain more by saying something blatantly homophobic and making a headline than by their efforts to be lyrically compelling.

Mo Money, Mo Problems: Wake up Mr. West

The defense I will offer Kanye in the subsequent pages neither comes from a Kanye fan, nor one with expert familiarity with his work. I've come to know Kanye through "snapshots" of some of his billboard hits, as well as the regularly eccentric statements and appearances he makes in the media. In 2004, a student I was teaching at Oakland School for the Arts kept making reference to the "Wake Up Mr. West" that woke the world to Kanye. For this particular student, a fan also of my own work with now-defunct Deep Dickollective, "Mr. West" served as an identificatory link between two black hip-hop pioneers he looked up to. Ironically, my first introduction to Kanye West led me to question, not so much his sexuality, but certainly his masculinity. On the Southside of Chicago or in many other American hoods, his eccentric antics and the risks he's taken, both musically and through stylized performance, have led some to the valuation that: "That's so gay!" I found the colorful preppy sweaters and khakis a welcome diversion to the hip-hop uniform requiring all "real rappers" to look as if they just left prison: sensationalistic stylizations that ironically glorify a prison–industrial complex that crudely restricts creative free-dom for many black men.

To be sure, the "gayness" I reference here is as classed as the "homo" money Kanye references in "We Don't Care." Often, there is no examination of the ways masculinity and power is shaped by class position. As noted by antisexist advocate Jackson Katz in Byron Hurt's documentary "Hip-Hop: Beyond Beats and Rhymes," eco-nomic power, especially when wielded by white men, doesn't demand the embodiment of struggle and physicality that seems to define black masculinity. Katz suggests that men generally seek power by "being dominant, being in control, having the respect of your peers," but men with a lower economic status don't have "real power."

The wake-up call is a challenge not to lazily conflate judgments about masculinity with suspicions of homosexuality, but rather under-stand a more complicated matrix where vectors of class, race, sexual orientation, and gender expression all formulate an existential being-in-maleness against which all men are judged. Perhaps Kanye is simply a victim of economic privileges and cultural sensibilities not of his choosing. Unfortunately, perhaps, he operates in a hip-hop culture where street cred eschews the "soft" pleasantries that come with black middle-class aspiration. Any bearing of Kanye's class on his sexuality is, therefore, incidental. That the upper classes are pompous and a little prissy has no bearing on their sexual preferences. Similarly, poverty or a hard life on the street has never prevented anyone from being gay. The reality of the disproportionate numbers of queer youth of color on Chicago streets is evidence enough of that.[8] If Kanye's lyrics provide any parallel between money and queer existence in cities like Chicago, it's that, for queer youth, both are "hard to get straight."[9]

In Kanye's case, the middle-class boy with an English professor mom embraces a class ambivalence that both owns access to the broad music archive that grounds his exemplary sampling, and yet disidentifies with this privilege through appropriations of street culture both lyrically and by associations with the likes of Chief Keef. This teetering between doing "just enough but not too much" to lose favor with the hip-hop masses is something that Kanye has managed to balance with aplomb. In the tension and insecurity that defines much of hip-hop culture, Kanye is the "tell-all" confessional animal who exposes his dirt so that no one else can dig him into a hole. Says music critic and journalist Ernest Hardy (2005) about Kanye in his essay "Up from Middle Class".

At the core of all the innovation is a carefully mapped one-man truce (with all its spiked footnotes on authenticity and viability) on the class angst that plagues Black America. West if from a solidly middle-class background was inculcated with nice, middle-class aspirations. His introduction of himself to the world as a college dropout fanned all sorts of webbed, crippling anxieties around Negro respectability and upward mobility.

Hardy continues:

> By positioning himself as the middle pole swaying between hood rat poses and caviar dreams, he simultaneously reconciles and underlies tensions that simmer in the lives of his fellow Negren. (Hardy, 2005)

Later, Hardy makes reference to the "balancing act [Kayne] pulls off by erasing the sham but powerful borderlines that still exist between 'conscious rap' and 'street shit' between fans of Fiddy or the Ying Yang Twins, and fans of Talib Kweli, Common, and Little Brother."

Kanye's ear for sampling and musical craftsmanship undeniably
led to his expeditious rise to fame between "College Dropout" and
"Graduation Day." To be sure, Kanye goes hard, lyrically, if not physically, when addressing his boys in the hip-hop nation. It is his clever
negotiation of his black male(d) performance that speaks to both a
rejection of heteronormative norms and, simultaneously, a reliance on
them. Kanye reflects both a middle finger to heteronormative constructs and yet submits to these constructs for legitimacy as a hip-hop
artist.

Next Shit: I'm down with you, but Not *THAT* down

In 2013, even with a black president and NAACP National
Headquarters affirming Marriage Equality as a new Civil Right, what
is sometimes misdiagnosed as black homophobia is perhaps better
looked at as an anxiety around black masculinity or black emasculation, as was evidenced by my participation on a recent annoying
radio panel on Chicago's Cliff Kelley Show (WVON) preoccupied
with the "crisis in traditional black masculinity." Largely prompted
by the "coming out" of NBA player Jason Collins, I believed it more
important to divert the conversation to a discussion about healthy
masculinity. As a masculine-identified queer man of color in hip-hop,
a shameless ESPN junkie and coach, I noted seeing no clear and necessary connection between a man's attraction to men, and any assault
or crisis in his masculinity. There is a great investment that many
straight boys have in "ringing the alarm" about a crisis in traditional
masculinity due to black men "coming out" as gay. It is connected
to the heteronormative sexism that allows blackness to be defined
in ways that sustain straight male privilege. It is an alarmist black
patriarchal reaction related to antifeminist interrogations when black
women step out of "their place" to challenge the black order of things.
The patronizing emasculation of gays operates as extension to this
dismissal and disregard for any power that might dethrone black men
as "Kings" of the hip-hop Nation. When in Byron Hurt's "Hip-Hop
beyond Beats and Rhymes" Fat Joe declares that "we the Kings of
this," the connotation might be that both the queens and *the queens*
are second-class citizens at best, invisible or at worse, ignored.

There is perhaps no contemporary figure in hip-hop who better
symbolizes this anxiety than Kanye West. His teetering between gay
sympathizer or "ally" alongside adamant disassociations with homosexuals through his own self-proclaimed "homophobia" offer a met-
onymic exemplar for an angst that especially many black progressive

straight men have around alliances with gays: Progressive straight black men must work to demonstrate a compassion for their gay brothers while evading the "gay by association" burden that happens when one fails to say "pause" or "no homo" and is too fashion-forward, too soft, too flamboyant. The necessity of proclaiming one's heterosexuality becomes all the more necessary for one whose sexuality might be called into question. There is no shock and awe when a gangsta rapper or a self-proclaimed thug hates the gays. It becomes a way that "realness"—a shifting construct I have suggested doesn't actually exist beyond approximations and aspirations—demarcates those who are hard from those who are soft (no pun intended). On a "realness" continuum, terms like "street cred" and "swag" mark an invulnerability that is evidenced by everything from jail time or gunshot wounds, to progeny or number of "hoes."

Whatever alliances he has built as a hip-hop mogul, super-producer, and iconic rapper, Kanye West is not "hard." Still, rappers who don't perhaps meet street codes of masculinity are sometimes able to gain "cred" through their wit, lyrical agility, and proven success of their hustle. Southside Chicago reference aside, Kanye is quite attuned to his relegation as someone who was vulnerable to bullying by those who interrogated not just self-proclaimed "gays" but anyone perceived as a faggot. The vulnerabilities of being a bourgie school boy at Kenwood Academy and a mama's boy against the backdrop of more braggadocio-laden masculinities no doubt led to the defenses Kanye developed around those who, as recent at 2013, question his sexuality and spread gay rumors. In the 2009 interview on *MTV News*, Kanye relays the suspicion that allies to the LGBTQ community are "gay by association":

> [I was] speaking out against hip-hop homophobia, some people were, like, 'Oh, Kanye must be gay! Look at the way he's dressing! And why would he speak about it? He's a gay rapper...and my whole point is, I wouldn't have spoke on that [*sic*] if I was gay or if I was in the closet. I would have stayed so far away from it.

The kneejerk reaction, the disassociation with gays expressed via more politically correct verbiage, still underscores the kind of masculine anxiety that especially straight allies and sympathizers to the LGBTQ community must offer as reaffirmation of and allegiance to their straightness. Denial of gay rumors is the necessary defense (mechanism) that reiterates a necessarily volatile sexual identity, since it's being questioned as suspect to begin with. In Down-Low

(DL)–obsessed social media, there are rappers whose names seldom, if ever, emerge on as "suspect." Straight rappers who embody stylistic eccentricity, or lack hypermasculinity and are open-minded, are especially vulnerable to interrogations about being gay. They must regularly and firmly "set the record straight" for fans who can accept that their favorite rappers don't hate on gays, as long as their favorite rappers aren't themselves gay.

"I'm still homophobic myself to certain extent…you know, I wouldn't go to a gay parade and feel comfortable. I wouldn't ever to a gay club or something and just be chillin' and grab a drink."[10]

Black heteronormative masculinity demands this kind of backpedalling in a culture where there are negative ramifications for homophobic statements or lyrics. It is worth questioning the degree to which public rebukes of homophobia and gay sensitivity are, more accurately, adjustments that rappers make in a market where blatant homophobia could result in a loss of profits or opportunities. Still, the danger is that allying with gays becomes the commonplace polite and politically convenient response, leading many to forego any genuine self-interrogation of homophobia or heterosexual privilege.

In 2012, just before the release of his critically acclaimed debut Channel Orange, Frank Ocean's "coming out" as a man whose first love was a man was met with surprising affirmation and praise from many in the hip-hop community who had previously been ambivalent, at best, about gay acceptance. One such 180 came from Busta Rhymes, a masculine, if eccentric, rapper himself who, when asked about the prospect of a gay rapper in Byron Hurt's "Hip-Hop: Beyond Beats and Rhymes," responded by saying: "I can't partake in that conversation…With all due respect, I ain't trying to offend nobody. What I represent culturally doesn't condone [homosexuality] whatsoever."

Asked by Hurt if hip-hop culture would ever be accepting of a gay rapper, Busta Rhymes anxiously exits. Today he's the subject of an *MTV News* headline that reads: "Frank Ocean Is 'Impeccable,' Busta Rhymes Praises:' I think the whole world is ready to accept whatever people choose to be in life,' Busta Rhymes tells MTV News about Odd Future singer."

One can't help but question the degree to which the support for Frank Ocean, at least by some, is a strategic move to gain favor with fans and a market generally that is a great deal more sympathetic to gays and lesbians than they were just a few years ago. For the love of the almighty dollar, many will be gay-friendly; especially when the barometer for Civil Rights, as legendary Civil Rights activist, Bayard

Rustin, foreshadowed before his death in 1987, seems to be LGBTQ rights.[11] Countless other once-homophobic rappers had nice things to say about Frank Ocean's "coming out," though Chuck D's dismissive "he's not a rapper" suggests that the Hip Hop Nation is still "queer-free"—a concern that blindly denies the hundreds of LGBTQ rappers who've emerged since Alex Hinton's groundbreaking documentary "Pick Up the Mic: the (r)evolution of Homo-Hop" (2006).

"Erry'body's Got a Gay Cousin, Right?"

Kanye West is not the first to reference a gay cousin who opened his mind and heart to a more gay-friendly shift in perspective. For rapper Common, whose cousin is referenced in "Between Me, You, and Liberation" as having been impetus for challenging his own homophobic views, the issues has to literally "hit home" in order for change to occur. For both men, perhaps cousin marks the biological recognition of "gays in the family" despite the distancing and shame that may have otherwise or previously existed. The "cousin" operates as genealogical disidentification; one who is close but not too close. The cousin is almost but not quite immediate family— he approximates relatedness, though could also mark the colloquial designation of any black man with whom one is close as "brotha," "cousin." It is the most committed noncommittal measure of having your boys' back. No homo.[12]

When a black president, largely supported by young people in the hip-hop community, repeals the ban on gays in the military and shows public support for the LGBTQ community, the question of where the more influential members of the hip-hop community stand, or better, *how* they stand, becomes critical. They must be kind yet stand straight and carry a big stick, for fear of bending too much. Kanye represents the almost but not quite "down with the gays" that parallels the rhetorical ambivalence of what it could mean to be "down." It marks the masculine anxiety for emcees who see themselves as political allies, but who don't wish for alliance to be mistaken for allegiance. And this is what kills me about straight boys, especially the questionable ones: They capitalize off their strategic appropriations of queerness in ways that can even sometimes get them cool points with women who'll verify that these men are straight because they've transcended anxiety about or around gays. Yet, few of these gay-friendly rappers have ever put any money where their mouth is to create safer spaces for queer youth, open doors for talented queer emcees trying to break through hip-hop's homophobic glass ceiling, or provide more than lip service about the insensitivity and hurt caused by homophobic lyrics. With the prominence of Marriage Equality being seen as a principal Civil Rights issue, it is fair to question the degree to which support for it by rappers as diverse as Jay-Z or Murs is prompted by what each man stands to lose in preserving a homophobic guard that seems to be waning in influence with each year. When homophobic comments can get one fined or result in the loss of promotional contracts, many homophobes will experience a "change of heart" in order to be gay-friendly enough to keep their paycheck in check.

Flashing Lights: Gay-Friendly Is Fashionable

College Dropout (2004) tackles this tension between flossy straight boys and the gay *fashionegras* they appropriate might be described as "magnetic" for those believing that repulsion to gays, for many straight men, is rooted in their attraction to gay men. There's surely an allure and affinity for the more fashion-forward gays that, in many ways, authenticates Kanye's transcendence beyond his Southside hood and struggle and into both literal and figurative spaces where braggadocio is defined by being "niggas in Paris." Mobility to move across the world in this way marks a shift in the way economic power supplants and overrides the kind of hard-edged, gritty masculinity necessary for hood boys whose influence must be proven via hyper-masculine lyrical flow for lack of cash flow.

In her captivating book *Troubling Vision: Performance, Visuality, and Blackness*, Nicole Fleetwood (2011) devotes a chapter to deconstructing hip-hop fashion. The Chapter "'I Am King': Hip-Hop Culture, Fashion Advertising, and The Black Male Body" mainly deconstructs the history and trajectory of hip-hop fashion (from L.L's Kangol and Run DMC's Adidas to black-owned clothing labels, like Phat Farm or Roca Wear). For Fleetwood, the investment of hip-hop moguls in fashion enables an alternate aesthetic, indicating the access by black businessmen (some of them rappers) to shape and influences aesthetic codes marked by both tailored suits than fitted caps. Referencing Paul Smith's analysis of the relationship between mass consumerism and the co-opting of designer fashion by hip-hop mongrels, Fleetwood writes:

> In Smith's analysis of the Hip-Hop mongrel as cultural icon and business powerhouse, fashion is just one of those areas of capitalist and cultural expansion for [the] entrepreneur. He emerges as one of the successes of the continuous expansion of popular entertainment

cultures and the rise of the New Economy, marked by deindustrialization, technological advances, and the rise of the service industries. The most celebrated are Russell Simmons, Sean Combs, and Jay-Z, all having established very successful fashion lines that topped the market in profits during the past decade (Fleetwood 2011).

Economic ascendance is critical to Kanye's swag and enables him to follow the footsteps like Simmons, Combs, and his comrade in *Throne*, Jay-Z. Kanye foreshadows this obsession with money, power, and respect on "College Dropout," where his sexualization of money as "homo"—a substitute for a more archaic "funny"—still relegates the "gay" as utilitarian marker of social transcendence and power. Kanye's fashion literacy is undeniable; and he frequently has a lot of gay designers' names in his mouth. It's a kind of appropriation that tensely runs alongside the distancing he does to ensure his fans and comrades don't doubt his allegiance to heterosexuality.

The gender-bending mascara antics and stylizations of black artists from Prince and DeBarge to the playfully flamboyant hip-hop acts like the Village people-esque Grandmaster Flash and the Furious Five or early 1990s Kwamé, seem to tell a different story about the acceptability of gender-variant subjects. Michael Jackson or Fresh Prince were not known for their hypermasculinity, but were more often called "different" or "nerdy" without necessarily assaults on their sexuality—with the exception of the endless Michael Jackson pedophilia accusations, which marked him as a sexual freak, though not necessarily gay. My sense is that the increased public discourse about gay rights introduces a social anxiety that produces the kind of witch hunting associated with uncovering which black men are on the DL. Confessions of a gay rapper and the onslaught of media attention attributing increased rates of HIV among black women to suspect gay men, have continued to shape the black social landscape. This broadening awareness is especially complicated by a seeming increase in tolerance for the LGBTQ community that isn't as clearly mirrored in the Black community. Being stylish and fashionable is a marker of success in many black communities where being gay still isn't.

Still, while the skinny jeans and colorful patterns of many rappers in 2013 don't particularly strike many as terribly masculine, they are a far stretch from the transgressive gender play that we saw in the 1980s. If Trey Songs crawled on the floor after a bath with flower petals and bubbles as Prince did in "When Doves Cry," he would be considered "straight gay." The stakes are high for men who wish to push gender boundaries in a gay-affirming culture but who are not gay. This creates an especially strong tension for hip-hop mongrels striving to be fashion-forward without seeming gay-forward.

In the anthology "For Colored Boys Who Have Considered Suicide When the Rainbow is Still Not Enough: Coming of Age, Coming Out, and Coming Home,[13]" retired NFL athlete and LGBTQ youth advocate Wade Davis speaks about a different kind of masculine anxiety. For gay, bi, and queer men, the performative aspects of masculinity become one of the ways they access straight privilege through "passing." Still, passing carries its own angst: the possibility of failure in passing for straight. In sports or hip-hop contexts, not being straight can lead to a kind of social death where homosexuality renders one a "waste" of a man. Being "straight acting" both functions to enable access to straight privilege and problematically suggests masculinity and heterosexuality are necessarily aligned. Wade Davis in his anthology contribution "Coming Out in the Locker Room" comments on the compulsory outfitting that enabled him to secure his standing as a strong black man:

> I'm at the point in my life where I hate that people refer to me as "straight acting." It took me a while to get to this point. Years ago I would act ultra-masculine to overcompensate and act as if I wasn't gay." I thought people wanted this from me as a black man. The black community reinforces this as well...I used to wear thirty-eight size pants when I was thirty-two, or triple X tees, all of this uber-masculine gear because that's what I thought people expected (81).

Hip-Hop in Fashion

In her chapter about the Black Masculine Body, Nicole Fleetwood (2011) accounts for the movement from traditional hip-hop fashion that exploded in the 1990s and marked a movement to stylize street fashion to a new divergence from that movement marked by designers like Pharell Williams.

> Hip-Hop fashion companies that developed after an established market had been secured have moved away from the conservative fashion apparel on which companies like Phat Farm and Roca Wear built their fortune: hypermasculine apparel, namely baggy jeans, oversized outerwear, caps, and t-shirts. Williams' Billionaire Boys Club and Ice Cream combine hip-hop fashion with Japanese animation, skateboarding style, and science fiction and target consumers who are interested in the purchase of hip-hop as hybrid culture (Fleetwood, 2001:172).

This movement away from some of the hypermasculine outfitting of black men is sometimes met with the response of hip-hop police who've come to believe things have become too suspect. The fashion-forward and open-minded straight boys, for them, threaten a space that has, for many, been among the fiercest self-congratulatory bastions of homophobia and gay bashing. I, for one, am thankful for the ways that Kanye has, conscientiously or not, disrupted traditional notions around, not just sound, but fashion and culture. In this way, his creative flair for fashion parallels his musical risk-taking, via sampling, which I believe to be his strongest asset as a hip-hop artist. It's the blending of old and new, couture and street, black power and post-black, street and bourgie, in order to imagine something I believe is more transgressive than any of our categorical imperatives: FREEDOM. In the final analysis, is not this what black men should value: a memory not so distant from shackles and chains—all made to obey orders of masters who did not honor our mastery of music and art?

I came to this essay unsure of whether or not my survey of limited snapshots into his world and experiences would lead me to be more or less ambivalent about the impact or influence of the iconoclast, Kanye West. I had every expectation that he would fortify my doubts about any conscientious positive impact on a hip-hop redefining itself more and more in terms of gender and sexuality. I am left to believe that Kayne, too, is subjected to an insidious and relentless demand that "real men" prove that they are real men—a burden I share with him and a task that seems impossible, since realness seems to necessitate a burden of proof that few escape. Perhaps we have as much in common as the young man who handed me *College Dropout* assumed? And perhaps, someday, Kanye will one day claim me as his gay "cousin," give me a few fashion tips, and in return I'll give him a few lessons in humility—with LPs having gone, a few times, aluminum, I'm in a good position to do so. We can both exchange strategies for how to continue "fighting the power." Only this time, the powers we fight are the old and new ones—allied in the intraracial allegiance to norms ultimately connected to global white supremacy and its dedication to keeping the male-box intact. Perhaps this is just wishful thinking, since there is ample evidence of Kanye's sexism, as recent as the rampant feminist criticism of his "Yeezus" project. As Ernest Hardy once wrote about the superproducer and iconoclast:

> He's not perfect, and he's not the savior of hip-hop. But like the most
> resonant of music icons, he's a charismatic fusion of offstage self,

onstage persona and the music he makes. He's whole, multi-dimen-
sional, contradictory, full of himself, a tad unsteady, within reach of
brilliance, and just plain black at the core (*LA Weekly*, September 5,
2005)

Notes

1. "reading straight boys" is an fairly commonplace execution of wit
   where queer boys undermine, poke fun at, and question inflexible
   heteronormativity.
2. "No Homo" is a phrase made popular by men in hip-hop culture in
   East Harlem in the early 1990s. The term was a way that straight men
   could distance themselves from statements that might be suggestive
   of homosexual desire, closeted or apparent. For example, a statement
   like "he's hot" when a basketball player isn't missing a shot, might
   be qualified by "no homo" following the statement, so that no one
   questions the sexuality of one making such a statement.
3. A 2013 Report from the National Coalition of Anti-Violence
   Programs (NCAVP) corroborates the evidence in local and regional
   settings spanning everywhere from Orange County, CA, to New
   York City. There's evidence that while hate crimes generally have
   decreased, hate violence against LGBTQ persons has skyrocketed.
   The report also suggests that LGBTQ people of color are especially
   vulnerable.
4. The term "Pause" generally references when an error has been made
   in speaking, but in hip-hop culture has come to specifically represent a potential misrepresentation of sexual identity. The Urban
   Dictionary defines it as a statement "used to signify that someone has
   said something homosexual in nature, usually to make [the speaker]
   aware of the sub-conscience gayness." To that end, a Blaxploitation
   affirmation like "Shaft was hot, man" from one guy to another,
   might be followed by "Pause," as a way of suggesting the speaker's
   homo-potentiality. Interestingly and ironically, "pause" draws attention to the homo-potentiality where it may have not otherwise been
   interpreted. In this way, it implicates, not just the speaker being made
   suspect of homosexuality, but the "pauser" who notices it.
5. "Bro Homo" is a song on my 2011 release "Fly Brotha," which was
   an effort to relay the irony and insidious nature of saying "no homo"
   after complements between, especially, black men. Where black on
   black violence still occurs in epidemic proportions, the unnecessary
   distancing between black men created through virulent defense of
   sexual preference seems a far stretch from "fighting the power."
6. Gay panic describes a legal defense in which the defendant suggests
   that they have victimized by romantic or sexual advances, ironically,
   by the victim. The victimizing victim or defendant finds the advances
   so traumatic and frightening that it elicits a violently uncharacteristic

psychotic state. (Summation of "The Gay Panic Defense" in *UC Davis Law Review* [Vol. 42:471] by Cynthia Lee)

7. This magnetism between straight subjects in hip-hop and gays is also central to the concept Jose Munoz talks about in "Disidentifications," and which I have referenced in other scholarship. For Munoz, the double bind of disidentification is that, with regard to any rejection or distancing, a very strong identification must first be present.

8. According to a June 2013 *Huffington Post* article, homeless LGBT youth represent up to 40% of those on the streets. A disproportionate number of these youth, at least in Chicago, come from Black neighborhoods on the South and West sides.

9. This equivocation also lends itself to Kanye's line in "We Don't Care" from "The College Drop-Out" (2004)

10. Kayne West in the *Evening News* story for *Edge New York*. Retrieved from: http://www.edgenewyork.com

11. Ironically, disparities between white gays and gays of color suggest that racial equality is still very much a pending Civil Right.

12. Rapper Kanye West is still wrestling with his "own homophobia"— despite promoting a campaign to stop the use of antigay language in rap records. The GOLD DIGGER singer urged his fellow rappers to put a stop to homophobic lyrics in August (05) after discovering that one of his cousins was gay. But West admits he's still grappling with his own fear of homosexuality.

13. *For Colored Boys Who Have Committed Suicide When the Rainbow Still Is Not Enough: Coming of Age, Coming Out, and Coming Home.* New York: Mangus Books, 2012.

Chapter 9

You Can't Stand the Nigger I See!: Kanye West's Analysis of Anti-Black Death

Tommy Curry

Despite debuting at the number 1 spot on the Billboard charts, the reaction to Kanye West's *Yeezus* (2013) has been diverse (Makarechi, 2013). While some critics have embraced Kanye's brash political commentary on race (Nigatu, 2013), many academics have mobilized an intersectional moralization, pitting his very real material account of the racism that Blacks, especially Black men, suffer against his sexual engagement with women. From being called a violent misogynist (Shird, 2013) to sex crazed (Johnston, 2013), Black progressives and feminists echoing the haloed/hollowed values of their respective disciplinary/political ideologies—ideologies that offer little to nothing to Black Americans, especially the worsening plight of Black men—have condemned Kanye West's message as little more than the patriarchal ramblings of a power-hungry deviant. Such a condemnation, which exceeds the utility of a corrective criticism, does not aim to transform or interpret Kanye's sentiments to more ameliorative ends, but rather seeks to eliminate such sentiments because they allegedly come from a pathological/immoral/Black/masculine mind.[1] Unlike much of the academic criticism that claims to be in the business of antiracism and critical of white supremacy, but is nonetheless approved of by white journals, white readers, and white colleagues, West completely disregards the morality that sustains the academic's loyalty to the preapproved disciplinary rhetoric used to convey disdain, and the bourgeois lexicon of academic pretense created to criticize oppression and social inequity. West's aesthetics shows these disciplinary tropes of discontent, which limit, censor, and overdetermine the content of Black criticism toward less radical ends, to be useless and empty distractions.

Kanye West is disrespectful. He shows little respect for the opinions of others, much less the copyright the academic plantation claims to have over theoretical knowledge. For West, knowledge/theory/experience is a misnomer. They point to idle caricatures of life and an etiquette that only impedes, rather than motivates engagements with the world. Over two decades ago, Sylvia Wynter (1992) exposed the complacency of the academic enterprise to reify rather than refute the onto-anthropological nomenclature of the biological human in her essay "No Humans Involved," or the acronym [N.H.I.] The force of Wynter's analysis surrounding the violence against Rodney King is not simply the infusion of social (nonideal) context, or horror into the vacuous and sterile albatross of knowledge, or an attempt to remind us to think more critically about what we claim to "know" or define what we claim to possess in "knowing" as "knowledge"; rather, Wynter demands that we reject the biologized humanity we claim has the faculty of knowing, and the concomitant apotheosis of disciplinary/conceptual/theoretical knowledge that valorizes Western man as the revelatory vessel of colonial history to the exclusion of Black people—the Non-Humans. Rejecting such ontology is not simply the work of discussions over and writings about the degraded anthropos of modernity. For Black men specifically, the rejection of the human being/Black Nigger is the catalyst for *Black Death*. Wynter urges the reader to consider the relationship between the paradigms of dehumanization that resulted in the genocide of Armenians by Turkish pan-nationalists, the holocaust inflicted upon Jews by the Germans, and the language used to describe, through taxonomy, Black men as a species deserving death. To classify the deaths of Black men as "No Humans Involved," is to reify the sociogenic principle behind anti-Blackness; or as Wynter says "for the social effects of this acronym (N.H.I.), while not overtly genocidal, are clearly serving to achieve parallel results: the incarceration and elimination of young Black males by ostensibly normal and everyday means" (Wynter, 1992: 14). Wynter's analysis of anti-Black death makes the Black male the conceptual paradigm of inquiry; the lens through which this kind of death is best viewed, and the body that should be grasped by the imagination to fully comprehend the ontology and consequence of the violence that perpetuates this anti-Black horror. Destroying the Black male body, murdering the Black life that demanded to be more than the petrified phantasm of the white imagination, extinguishes the idea of the Black human the white supremacist world demands cannot exist. Killing Black men who dare to speak against and live beyond their place erases them from the world, making an example, and leaving only their dead melaninated corpse as a deterrent against future revolts against white knowledge.

Rather than being a calculated articulation framed by the most recent intersectional/apologetic jargon in vogue, Kanye West's race consciousness is reflexive. It is an intuitive/emotive reaction to the racist assaults and imagery in and of the world. West does not apologize for being Black, nor does he care about the moralism of feminists, be they Black or white. West embraces a narcissism that validates his existence, to the dismay of both his critics and judgmental onlookers; a practice not unfamiliar to the academy where scholars who label themselves feminists, radicals, or democratic progressives are isolated from criticism given the supposed virtue and moral correctness of their theories. Since his 2005 outburst that "George Bush doesn't care about Black people," his response to the dereliction of the relief agencies under the Bush administration, Kanye West has built a career that mixes the mythology of (Black) power and racial consciousness with disturbingly accurate, but pessimistic descriptions of America as a police state. West's recent performance of "Black Skinhead" and "New Slave" on Saturday Night Live (SNL) are powerful demonstrations of this modus operandi, a raw aesthetic technique that revealed itself only in glimpses throughout his previous album *My Beautiful Twisted Dark Fantasy* (2010). *Yeezus!* (2013) is an accumulation of this pessimistic rendering of the world. *Yeezus* not only holds the government, the police, the prison–industrial complex, and the racist–capitalist–corporatism responsible for the commodification of commercial rappers (James, 2005) accountable, but dares to hold responsible the lives sustained by this matrix of anti-Black oppression, including the quality of life that racism affords white women. No one is safe! He does not pretend that conversations about racism are constrained by the bourgeois morality that marries it only to white men, or excuses the complacency of Black women in its operation. Skin color (race) and genitalia (sex) are not intersectional shields from criticism or condemnation for West. It's a refreshing aesthetic that holds anyone and everyone accountable: a criticism far more visceral and authentic than the quotidian bourgeois (pseudological) criticisms waged by scholars in the academy, aimed at garnering acceptance from, rather than the destruction of, the oppressor class. West seems to believe that his awareness of the theory behind the necropolitics of the American state, and the racist confinement of ghettos within it, extricates him from this conceptual and psychological enslavement to the mere want of possessions. In a recent *New York Times* interview, Kanye West was asked if he sees things in a more "race-aware way," now, later in his career, than several years ago when he attacked then president Bush for his derelict in Hurricane Katrina. West replied "No, it's just being able to articulate yourself better. 'All Falls Down' is the same [stuff]. I mean, I am my father's son. I'm my mother's child. That's how I was raised. I am in the lineage of Gil Scott-Heron, great activist-type artists. But I'm also in the lineage of a Miles Davis—you know, that liked nice things also" (Caramanica, 2013).

This article is not an apologetic for Kanye West. It does not aim to achieve empathy from the reader, nor recognition from the bourgeois academics who seek acknowledgment for their discursive moralism that pervades contemporary explorations of racism, sexual oppression, and capital exploitation. This article will most likely offend the Black progressive and the Black feminist alike, not because it specifically targets these groups, but rather because it ignores the alleged validity of their intuitions/revelations/faith (merely puritanical beliefs posing as theory) as testaments to a moral superiority regarding the oppressive realities of Black men specifically, and Black people more generally (Thomas, 2007; Thomas 2009). Kanye West is dangerously narcissistic, materialistic, and a heretic, but none of this means his analysis or approach to the world are incorrect. Like the bourgeois academic, he responds to his environment and the demands of the world he is in, but unlike the academic, his life, his disdain is not morality, but blasphemy. He does not honor knowledge, or truth as the ad populum consensus of learned people, but rather takes knowledge to be the "obviousness," no one else dare speak. What this article will do is situate Kanye West's lyrical testaments of American racism within the paradigm of West's pessimism, birthed within Black manhood. The first section will describe and defend his use of Black manhood as the basis of social analysis, while section two will speak specifically to his disregard for (Black) feminist criticisms of his narrations. The final section suggests that Kanye West's pessimism, rather than being a disregard of racial and sexual vulnerabilities, is a testament to an actual conceptual and theoretical disruption, rather than a reification of idle disciplinary dogmas, identity politics, or ideological consensus masquerading as critical social interventions.

Yeezus, the Nigger, and the Trauma of Black Manhood

Unlike many of his academic counterparts who feign an interest in race, class, and gender under the guise of the Black female subject (Kwan, 1997), Kanye West shows no remorse for being a Black man or describing the world from this vantage point. Why should Black men be remorseful for describing and/or indicting the world as it presents itself to them? Their lives are endangered by violence from birth. They see themselves killed and slaughtered like animals by police and criminals alike, only to see their demise made into silent caricatures debated by elite Black women, white society, and state institutions as irrelevant, necessary, or accidental. It is no secret that Black men have been at the bottom of the social structure of American society since its inception (Alexander, 2013; Pettit, 2012). The "terrible spectacles" birthed within Black enslavement that often "immure us to pain by virtue of their familiarity" (Hartman, 1997: 3), the activities of the dire symbiosis between death, Black masculinity, and criminalization, are the background of current conceptualizations/discussions/imaginings of anti-Black death and the consequences of racism. Anti-Blackness is a negating activity; not for its denial of the humanity of the Black, but because anti-Blackness is found in the death of the Black male, his lynching, his castration, his incarceration, his rape, an existence that all other identities are debased and devalued—negated—toward. It is when the Black woman or child is murdered, treated with the violence ensconced within this ontology predicated on the death of Black men, that the oppression violating the virtue of femininity or innocence of childhood is found to be immoral. In other words, it is when Black women are treated as Black men that they are not seen to be women at all; but masculine, or when the Black child is killed because that Black child was seen to be the conclusion of its racial ontogeny, a threat, a criminal—the Black man.

The origin of this system is a direct product of American slavery. Rather than simply being "an event," a historical moment that was abolished/absolved in its entirety with emancipation, slavery substantiated American racism; it gave substance to anti-Blackness—making the presumption that Black people were dangerous racial inferiors natural. In this world of emergent anti-Blackness, slavery divested Black people (the enslaved African) of resistance to the legislative, legal, and societal consensus. As W. E. B. Du Bois stated in *The Negro* (1915):

the Negro slave trade was the first step in modern world commerce, followed by the modern theory of colonial expansion. Slaves as an article of commerce were shipped as long as the traffic paid...The new colonial theory transferred the reign of commercial privilege and extraordinary profit from the exploitation of the European working class to the exploitation of backward races under the political domination of Europe. For the purpose of carrying out this idea the

European and white American working class was practically invited to share in this new exploitation, and particularly were flattered by popular appeals to their inherent superiority to Dagoes, Chinks, Japs, and Niggers (141).

The effect of this colonial theory, the economic/racial/imperial project undertaken was not simply the commodification of Black bodies into an economy; but it is also a process of erasure and substitution. As Saidiya Hartman (1997) has persuasively argued in *Scenes of Subjection*,

> the fungibility of the commodity makes the captive body an abstract and empty vessel vulnerable to the projection of others' feelings, ideas, desires, and values; and, as property, the dispossessed body of the enslaved is the surrogate for the master's body since it guarantees his disembodied universality and acts as the sign of his power and dominion. Thus while the beaten mutilated body presumably establishes the brute materiality of existence, the materiality of suffering regularly eludes (re) cognition by virtue of the body's being replaced by other signs of value, as well as other bodies (21).

The enslaved African/Black body was not simply a commodity to be bought and sold, but commodified into what whites desired, feared, and sought to vacate from (white) virtue into (Black) degradation—creating the darkened/racialized Nigger.

The Nigger is not a representation, a mere phantasm; rather, the/that Nigger (he) is the object; the thing, intended to be subjected to white violence, and dealt with through death, and incarceration. This political/tyrannical practice is a constant theme throughout Kanye West's *My Beautiful Twisted Dark Fantasy*. In "Gorgeous," the penitentiary chances forshadowed by the devil dancing conveys the looming state sanctioned police violence against Blacks who love ballin by selling rocks. They get trapped within the ghetto, and in trying to make it out, they fall; no doubt an allusion to West's lyrical exploration of this phenomenon in his 2004 hit "All Falls Down." With little to no economic prospects, the economy available in the dark spaces that confine Blacks is illegal; and drugs, violence, and incarceration seem like predetermined ends. In other words, West recognizes that the system is set-up and constructed to fulfill the purpose of racial degradation. The disparate treatment of Blacks is about the already present and different realities of Blacks and whites, where individual choices are illusory, and structures/institutions determine the essence/substance/(B)eing of Blackness. West shows the audience that racism is not only about the difference between kinds (Black versus white), but in fact the difference made manifest through engineering society into a world institutionally against Jeromes and historically in favor of Brandons. A world where Black men are killed, incarcerated, and dismissed to protect, and absolve, white men. The Black man is condemned to live the nature whites believe are the biological catalyst behind the violence they see in the inner city, the untamed sexual savagery that pollutes the ghetto with the dark bodies that infest them, and their endemic propensity for poverty and death. West's description may seem cruel, but it points out that the dominant strategy in the academy, the appeal to white moral conscience, is useless. West's aesthetic compilations reveal that it is impossible for discursive appeals to whites to address, much less remedy, Black death. West reminds us of the reality of life. West's pessimism is not simply negativity, but an aesthetic response to America's necropolitics (Mdembe, 2003)—its racist fixation on the death of the Nigger.

The dire conditions that cultivate the pathologies of Black existence have always occupied West's thinking. In "All Falls Down," West highlights the "ghettoized/militarized/corporatized" perils of Black poverty by drawing attention to how hustling might allow us to buy ourselves out of jail, but we can never buy ourselves our freedom. The persistence of surveillance and the naturalized presence of the police, corruption, and Black people's interaction with the police fundamentally negate the liberty of the individual, and the freedom of Blacks in America. West then offers us a surprising analysis of relative deprivation that undergirds his aesthetic presentation of Black materialism and exploitation. In "All of the Lights" (2010), West highlights the symbiosis between the ghettoized existence of Blackness, its policed reality, and the desire for unneeded possessions. The "cop lights, flashlights, spotlights" that define the watching/monitoring/criminalizing confinement of Black people is dealt with at the psychical level. The deprivation of life and wealth "educates" Blacks into a pathology of false expectation, or what West calls the "ghetto university." His lyrics point to an interchangeability in the narratives substituted for the inability of the impoverished to gain material comforts and the recognition of whites. The desire for wealth amidst poverty drives the activities that seek to acquire profit as a means of elevating oneself above the pain of confinement in dark ghettos. West's lyrical provocations mirror the analysis of Kenneth Clark's *Dark Ghetto* (1989), specifically his chapter "The Invisible Wall," which explains how the racist framing of Blackness has redrawn the parameters of the American ghetto.

America has contributed to the concept of the ghetto the restriction of persons to a special area and the limiting of their freedom of choice on the basis of skin color. The dark ghetto's invisible walls have been erected by the white society, by those who have power, both to confine those who have no power and to perpetuate their powerlessness. The dark ghettos are social, political, educational, and above all economic colonies. Their inhabitants are subject peoples, victims of the greed, cruelty, insensitivity, guilt, and fear of their masters" (11)

In "Power" (2010), West explains that the broken system offers Blacks no real chances of social mobility. School closings deny education opportunities Black youth, and prisons are open to exploit these uneducated youth. His awareness of the interdependency of injustice, the failure of the education system, and the path to prison for uneducated, unemployed Blacks, exposes the white supremacist orientation of America hidden beneath the veneer of democratic promise. Like W. E. B. Du Bois's "The Souls of [w]hite Folk" (1920), which argues that "whiteness is the ownership of the earth forever and ever" (30),[2] Kanye West recognizes that Du Bois's theme can only reveal the actuality of the white man's world as irreconcilably cruel and the dehumanizing toward Blacks. West's position obviously parallels the language and ideas of the ghetto introduced through Clark's analysis, but his lyrics demand that the reader and/or audience go further to an understanding of Robert Allen's thesis in the final chapter of his now-famous work *Black Awakening in Capitalist America* (1969), which maintains "to white America, black people were a resource to be exploited ruthlessly—and racism facilitated this exploitation by degrading blacks in the eyes of whites, thereby placing the former outside the pale of normal moral or humanistic compunction" (275). West shows that the potentiality ensconced within humanity and buttressed through education is vacated with Blackness, and replaced with criminality and needing to be confined to the prison.

I'd rather be a Dick: West's Refutation of (Black) Feminism's Bourgeois Morality and the Prison Industrial Complex

Kanye West addresses the sexual and gendered violence largely ignored and overlooked when considering the exploitation and vitiation of Black men. Despite the early work done on Black men's sexual vulnerabilities under American racism, such as Lawrence E. Gary's anthology *Black Men* (1981), or Richard Majors and Janet Billson's

Cool Pose: The Dilemmas of Black Manhood in America (1992), current approaches to Black masculinity, in no small part dictated by the premises of (Black) feminist ideology, pathologize Black manhood.[3] Influenced by the early ethical dicta of bell hooks presented as a project for "Reconstructing Black Masculinity" (1992), Black manhood has come to be understood as a phallocentric endeavor. Drawing from her experience of men in her "southern Black patriarchal home" (hooks, 1992: 87), hooks concludes that "in traditional black communities when one tells a grown male to 'be a man' one is urging him to aspire to a masculine identity rooted in the patriarchal ideal (hooks, 1992, 88). bell hooks's "phallocentric" analysis is an extension of Michelle Wallace's *Black Macho and the Myth of the Super-Woman* (1978), which understands the Black Power movement of the 1960s as little more than Black radicalism for the opportunity to have sex with white women. In Wallace's view, Black Power was a "coming out of black male/white female couples" (Wallace, 1978: 9) driven by the realization that "black was sexy and had unlimited potential" (Wallace, 1978: 10), and white women's desire for "black cock because it was the best cock" (Wallace, 1978: 10). The consequence of this interracial coupling was the ability of Black men who sought education, political recognition, and access to capitalist resources to define Black womanhood through mate selection, since in gaining "recognition," these Black men could be recognized as suitable and/or desirable lovers by white women. bell hooks summarizes Wallace's thesis as Black men's "refusal to acknowledge that the phallocentric power black men wield over black women is 'real' power" (hooks, 1992: 108), which makes this a sempiternal aspiration for patriarchy by Black men since slavery and establishes the basis of Black women's "female" solidarity with white women.[4] Today, the consequence of these historical debates is the popular blogosphere-generated existence of "Black male privilege" (L'Heureux Lewis, 2010; Marsh, 2011). The historical evidence presented by Gail Bederman's *Manliness and Civilization* (1995) suggests that Black masculinity was never a monolithic and mimetic identity taken up by Black men blindly reproducing white masculinity and patriarchy, and Michele Mitchell's chapter on "The Black Man's Burden: Imperialism and Racial Manhood" in *Righteous Propagation* (2004) details the stake *Black women* had in Black men being known to the world as "fighting men," imperialists and patriarchs capable of both war and the defense of their women. Today's theorists conveniently ignore these perspectives, and continue to engage Black manhood as a predetermined, oppressive, outdated, racial caricature.

West rejects such ideological silliness. The phallocentric advantage Black feminism claims exists is an artifice of the actual sexual status of Black men in society. While it very well may be true that Black dick is desired by white women, there is no power afforded to Black men in such carnal debasement to, or a Black man being reduced to, his Black penis. On "Hell of a Life" (2010), West adamantly refutes the phallocentric analysis behind the myth of Black male privilege and Black men's power over Black women by contending that Black dick—fucking Black men—divests white women of worth in society. West argues that sex between Black men and white women is a sodomitic opprobrium, like doing anal, or a gangbang; being penetrated by Black dick is same thing. Michelle Wallace's and bell hooks's analyses incorrectly assert a unilateral perspective on Black men's patriarchal lineage, because they assume that sex establishes power and advantage by men over women. So when the Black dick is desired by white women it becomes valuable, and sex with Black women depreciates. While there may be psychical benefits for Black men in having sex with white women and being recognized as carnally acceptable for, desirable to, white, the sexual activity in no way changes the debasement of the Black male body in a society that is so powerful that it divests white women of their racial capital to white men. West suggests that (the Black dick) stains the white woman, marks her as immoral and her sexuality with deviance (*a freak*) or makes "her price goes down." The sexual lasciviousness of the white woman, her hunger for Black dick, is a relationship long recognized by Frantz Fanon (1967) in *Black Skins, White Masks,* but unlike the Black feminist analysis that sees sex between Black men and white women as an exercise of power over both Black and white women, Fanon's psychological evaluations of racialized subjects reveal this sexual activity to be pathological, the result of colonization, and the imposition of racial inferiority upon the racial/native male.

Kanye West's intervention into the sexual exploitation of Black men has not been considered, much less appreciated by Black academics, or Black feminists, who claim they are interested in the nexus of identity comprised across the categories of race, class, and gender, because they are ideologically blinded to the categorical copyright feminism has on gender. Multiple feminists blogs have claimed that Kanye West's latest album *Yeezus* is misogynistic because it "treats women solely as sexual objects and money-hungry groupies/wannabes" (Menyes, 2013), and "bro rage" because "Yeezus is a relentless spleen-vent against the women in his life—the women he's fucked or wanted to fuck or who fucked him over or lied to him or whatever, that's occasionally provocative thanks to political asides that West has done more with more nuance and humor in the past" (The Spin, 2013). West does not operate from the feminist a priori of these authors and many of the other critics who believe that he perpetuates sexism. *Yeezus* is an album that contrasts the sexuality of Black men as a reference for thinking about sex with white women. The commentators, critics, and academics who consider his lyrics constantly overlook the attention he draws (as in his lyric from "Hell of a Life") to the woman's lust/desire for Black men. In the controversial verse from "On Sight," what provocation is gained by simply stating that Black women like Black dick, and like to have sex with Black men? West has a pattern of attending to the racial/racist contrasts of interracial sex and the *desire for Black dick*. West subtlety reveals Black men as being gendered, vulnerable, and exploitable from the very desire many feminists, both Black and white, claim give him power. West's lyrics make the same point Greg Thomas advances in *The Sexual Demon of Colonial Power* (2007).

> Histories of gender and slavery focus overwhelming on women, as if gender and women are coextensive and men have no gender. This observation points to a problem with the conceptualization of sex and gender across academic disciplines. For if there is a structural neglect of manhood in studies of gender, and if womanhood is misunderstood to be synonymous with gender itself, these this approach signifies an extension rather than an analysis of gender ideology, which traditionally inscribes women as being gendered and men as being generic and beyond gender (45–6).

The current paradigms of gender and sexuality studies in the university, and taken as the pop culture iteration of feminism, simply reproduces this blindness theory has when *thinking about* Black manhood.[5] Here I return to the theoretical intervention made by Saidiya Hartmann (1997) concerning the commodification of Blacks during slavery. While Hartmann gives a rich analysis of suffering, pain, and dehumanization being necessary to and thriving as the condition of enslavement, she too reifies the idea that rape and sexual assault is the province of enslaved womanhood. She says, "Gender, if at all appropriate in this scenario, must be understood as indissociable from violence, the vicious refiguration of rape as mutual and shared desire, the wanton exploitation of the captive body tacitly sanctioned as a legitimate use of property, the disavowal of injury, and the absolute possession of the body and its 'issue.' In short, black and female difference is registered by virtue of the extremity of power operating on captive bodies and licensed within the scope of the humane and the tolerable" (86). Hartman's point is insightful in that it links pain and violence to the definition of enslaved Black bodies, but her analysis is categorically misleading, since there is no reason to make her conceptualization of rape as desire and exploitation a privation isolated to the enslaved female body. Thomas's (2007) analysis of essentializing femininity's vulnerabilities as the concept of gender itself is both instructive in exposing the undisclosed meaning of gender as a category and a corrective, since Thomas dismisses the idea that only women are victimized by rape, key insights needed when evaluating Hartmann's contention.

> It is almost impossible to locate a text of slavery which does not construe rape as the bottom line factor that differentiates the experience of slavery along lines of sex, or gender. Allegedly, the female can be violated, and the male cannot. This assumption is unacceptable, if not absurd, because it perversely requires heterosexuality to recognize exploitation and abuse. Not only is sexual violence reduced to whatever qualifies as rape, narrowly construed, but rape is also to penile penetrations of female bodies, perhaps not even those unless they result in pregnancy and offspring (46).

West's invisibility as a Black man, clearly seen in songs like "Power," demonstrates an aggression toward the silence imposed upon his manhood by academes and journalists alike, whose beliefs stem from this slavery-born assumption that continues to the present day. Simply as a matter of historical accuracy, Hartman overlooks the documented rape and sexual abuse of Black men as being a theoretical center and conceptual core of how one situates anti-Black violence generally and sexual exploitation (against Black men) specifically. Thomas Foster's "The Sexual Abuse of Black Men Under American Slavery" (2011) argues that "The sexual assault of enslaved black men was a component of slavery and took place in a wide variety of contexts and in a wide range of forms...In addition to the direct physical abuse of men that happened under slavery, this sexual exploitation constituted a type of psychological abuse that was ubiquitous" (464).

The accusations of misogyny by critics suggest to readers, the audience, an unjustifiable and seemingly axiomatic proposition; namely, in a world of anti-Black violence and the death of Black men, women should be spared; that there are no valid/moral/ethical reasons for enacting violence against, or displaying anger toward women, even white women. Notwithstanding the obvious ignorance of such a position that holds that despite women's, especially white women's, history of anti-Black violence, they should be spared from all violence, this morality nonetheless seems to be the accepted consensus of gender theory. How, then, should Black men, who have historically been the victims of rape, sexual assault, and lynching by white women's Ku Klux Klan organizations,[6] react to white women? Denying Black men's actual victimization in the history of sexual assault and violence perpetuated against Black men at the hands of white women in an effort to advance a fabricated feminist morality is both intellectually dishonest and racist at its very core, since it construes Black male anger/resistance/voice as synonymous with the fear and criminalization of Black men under the trope of the Black male rapist. In reality, it is the denial of the function of white womanhood and the alliance of Black feminist scholarship with this denial that should give us pause concerning both camps' historiography and normative proclamations. "The traditional denial of white women's sexual agency has contributed to our obscured view of those white women who sexually assaulted and exploited enslaved men. Indeed, the abuse of black men at the hands of white women stands on its head the traditional gendered views of racialized sexual assault. Yet as historians have demonstrated, despite the legal and cultural prohibitions against sex between black men and white women in early America, occurrences were far from rare" (Foster, 2011: 458). Racism was carried out through sexual exploitation, the rape of Black men and boys. It was the central aspect of how white women's virtue, their racial superiority and character, was elevated above barbarous myth of Black sex.

> Wives and daughters of planters who formed these sexual relationships were simply taking advantage of their position within the slave system. Having sex with their white counterparts in the insular world of the white planter class, if exposed, would certainly have risked opprobrium, and even gossip about their public actions might have marred their reputations. Daughters of planters could use enslaved men in domestic settings, however, and retain their virtue and maintain the appearance of passionlessness and virginity while seeking sexual experimentation. In other words, one of the ways that some southern women may have protected their public virtue was by clandestine relations with black men. (462).

West explicitly articulates his awareness of such illicit relations in "Black Skinhead" and offers the listener concerning white society's wish for the death of the Nigger as the political impetus for order. Here he argues that part of the fear of the Nigger, the need to kill the Nigger, is rooted in the disgust of, as well as, the lust for fucking Black men. Psychically, the fear of the Nigger is both: the recognition of the inhuman in the Black man, his animal-like sexuality—the threat a Black dick poses to the white myth of superiority—and the erotic fascinations produced by the white (male and female) imagination enamored by the idea of fucking such a Black creature. Is this psychical fascination with possessing or owning the bodies of Blacks, having Black dick indebted for want of white things, not how he describes this new racism that, while connected to segregation, does not need segregation to dehumanize Black people?

On "New Slaves" (2013), West describes old, or broke, nigga racism of the Jim Crow/segregation era. This racism thrived on the poverty and inability of Blacks to attain what whites had. Notice the parallels this has to his analysis of the ghetto. It is a Black space, segregated from the world, where the Black people in it (broke niggas) desire/crave the material possessions of the white world. But now there is another type of racism. A racism that commodifies Blackness based on its servitude to white economies of production, be they libidinal (Wilderson, 2010) or political. West continues the evident contrast. Rich nigga racism functions at the plateau of social elevation and economic mobility for Blacks. The opportunities given to the "rich nigga" enslave/exploit him/her more, and his access to white women ultimately endanger his life, since it is a symbol of the failure of racism to keep that a Nigger in his place.

For those who suggest that racism is solved by both economic and physical integration, West offers a compelling view of those dangers. There is no change in the mindset of the oppressed; or what Blacks desire/want, be they segregated in the ghetto, or rich, driving Bentleys. Freedom is, as Gil Scott Heron says in "Who Will Survive in America," free doom. How then does West claim he is able to resist this societal matrix, and indoctrination? He says simply: "He knows." He "knows that we the new slaves."

West beautifully summarizes the overarching themes and conceptualizations of anti-Black racism and the violence indigenous to it. Like his reflections on anti-Black death—the death of the Nigger—West suggests that concern over grand schemes of global conquest like the New World Order distracts us from the central issue of racist domination: Black male incarceration. Like Becky Pettit's *Invisible Men: Mass Incarceration and the Myth of Black Progress* (2012), which argues that "the promise of the civil rights era has been undercut by a new form of invisibility manufactured by mass incarceration and the prison industrial complex" (p. 3), Kanye West's analysis strikes at the core of any and all beliefs about Black progress and the emergent postracial transcendence of America under Obama. Since the economic prosperity of white America—yes, even white America under Obama—relies on the profit extracted from Black male bodies when they are caged, and the markets/economies/policing/surveillance spawned by the corporatization/privatizing of American prisons, Kanye is correct in reiterating the connection between, or better yet seeing the extension of, Black enslavement and the prison–industrial complex. The Drug Enforcement Agency (DEA) is in an industrial partnership with the Corrections Corporation of America (CCA). The governmental agency convicts and captures, while the private corporation incarcerates and benefits from free labor. This relationship, articulated over a century ago by W. E. B. Du Bois (1901) in "The Spawn of Slavery: The Convict Lease System in the South," gives credence to the extremism conveyed in West's lyrical, jingoistic tones, because it displays an actual understanding of the economic motivations facilitating anti-Blackness, and the deliberate production of new slaves: Black people, overwhelmingly Black men, isolated away from society, and divested of any political and economic power to resist the social organization of society. In other words, the new slave is the basis of America's social and political order.

How then does Kanye West cause disruption/rupture to the codified economies of racial exploitation and imprisonment? He says he will hold the business owners and their white wives accountable. The profits from that privately owned prison allows the white capitalist to afford their house in the Hamptons, and it is this immorality, which profits from the death and suffering of Black men, that West attends to. It is this injustice that he sees as necessitating his revolt and attempt to "tear shit down." His lyrics signal his disgust and disregard for the possessions of whiteness, both materially and symbolically. West reproduces the symbolic relationship the Black man has to the ogre—the white woman found in Eldridge Cleaver's *Soul on Ice* (1968). In destroying the possessions that symbolize white power and social status above Blackness, West must address what the white woman represents, but unlike Cleaver, West is not trapped within a psychological neurosis that both hates and craves the white woman. For West, the sexual assault of the white woman, in both its literal and fictive rendering, addresses her culpability for the rape, murder, and dehumanization of the Black man, and the impotence of the Black community.[7]

We're Human Enough: West's Rejection of the Disciplinary Castration of Black Manhood's Theoretical Utility

The aesthetic provocations of Kanye West fill a lacuna in the academic scholarship, which shuns obvious social awareness about American racism and the violence enforced upon Black men for rhetorical pleonasms that utilize idle theoretical complexities to express a predetermined morality of integrationism and postracial hope. The condition of Black men in this country is dire (Edelman et al., 2006; Mincy, 2006). Despite the death, imprisonment, and political isolation of this group, the academy creates disciplinary incentives to ignore and actually rebuke scholars and scholarship seeking to highlight these physical and academic erasures of Black men. West has a blunt honesty about the racist (necro) political organization of America, and rather than being interpreted as making a radical public commentary on Black oppression, he is criticized for not internalizing the bourgeois morality enforced through the identity politics of the academy. Are white women not culpable for their rape, exploitation, and role in the death of Black people? Why are Black feminists the self-appointed mediators between white women and the Black community, as if the particular ills and violence white women have inflicted upon Black men are without consequence? Kanye West regards the white woman, like her white male counterpart, as being beyond moral suasion and without vindication. In short, they are irredeemable, given that the alleged morality of the white man's world is actually sustained by its immorality—its racist dehumanization of Black people—the consequence of which is the death of the Nigger. The color of West's skin, just as much as the shade of his dick, is of material and conceptual consequence for his articulation of death, dying, and the world that constrains what he actually is or potentially can be.

West's theory originates at the corporeal juncture between himself and the world. Rather than being an abstraction from the world, West's theory is an immediately empirical, concrete, and submerged aesthetic, which situates the lives of Black Americans, at the center of reflections upon Black existence. This aesthetic submergence (Curry, 2010) makes the listener engage the materiality of anti-Black racism instead of retreating into abstractions far removed from the ugly realities of racial oppression. The incongruence between his Black skin and the white world breeds his pessimism. As a Black man, West is simultaneously constituted by knowing/(B)eing Blackness and the processes in the white world that demand his life be extinguished to

preserve order and profit. Racism is not a series of mistaken charac-terizations and stereotypes irrationally embraced by white individu-als; rather, racism is the lens that intentionally fixates the world on the supposed biological deficiencies of Blackness. Black manhood, its beauty and its degradation, is conceptually orienting for West, and it is because of this unapologetic stance, which takes Black manhood as a foundation from which the world can be viewed, that Kanye West is both hero and heretic. The university will continue to ignore his lyrical interventions because Kanye West simply does not believe the academy is the exclusive purveyor of theoretical, much less moral, knowledge. His disregard for gender politics and his focus on the vis-ceral sexuality of America's racist logics will continue to elude disci-plinary identification. To understand West is to embrace amorality—it is a brutal realization that your white oppressor has no actual worth, since their existence necessitates your death. It is not to pretend that revolution, or simply "talking about" oppression is meaningful activ-ity. It is to realize that any attempt at moral engagement with whites that requires their recognition of Black humanity is ultimately an impossibility, necessitating Black death to preserve social order. West's message, at its root, is an indictment of all knowledge production that seeks to inquire into Black reality with love, compassion, and equality as predetermined ends, since these values are vacated by whiteness to sustain anti-Blackness. Recognition is not what is at stake for West, the realization of dying and the propensity for death is.

Notes

1. For a worthwhile treatment of Kanye West's view of gender, see Ebony Utley's (2013) "Kanye West's Yeezus May Be Sexist, But Is Not Blasphemous," which an extension of the analysis presented in her book *Rap and Religion* (2012).

2. It is my belief that the capitalization of the word "white" incorrectly conveys to readers that term is neutral and descriptive. [w]hiteness does not refer to a historical group of people that can be or should be thought of as separate from its dehumanizing colonial relationship with African-descended peoples and other peoples of non-European descent. To capitalize [w]hite suggests that the object and concept marked by [w]hiteness is absolved from its tyrannical racism against non-[w]hites and can be thought to have equal standing with the specific cultural and liberatory identity captured by the word "Black" and the concept of Blackness. The de-capitalization of the word "white" next to the word "Black" by the author is the grammati-cal problematization of this relationship that exists in our linguistic structure and cultural discourse and aims to convey to the reader that

the relationship [w]hiteness shares with other racial terms is marred by its history of racist domination.

3. There is a real problem that emerges from reading Black feminist thought as the exclusive or only established reflection on Black women in the academy. In La France Rodgers-Rose's introduction to *The Black Woman* (1980), an edited collection commissioned by Sage Focus edition to understand the empirical situation of Black women, she argues that Black social sciences, Black men included, have sought to refute white supremacist scholarship on Black women, but none of this "social science" literature got the public attention that Black feminism as presented by Michelle Wallace did during the time (p.11).

4. Today there is a tendency to read any and all reflections on Black women as being unified with the Black feminist thesis. This is not only a historical revisionism, but also overlooks the concrete refutations and motivations by Black women authors to not be associated with the Black feminist movement and its emergent analysis. Paula Giddings (1979) "The Lessons of History will Shape the 1980's—Black Macho and the Myth of the Superwoman Won't" is an excellent example of the now largely ignored academic contingent seeking to refute the account of Wallace's story. Ultimately, Giddings concludes that Wallace's work bastardizes history, and repeats the error of Sojourner Truth, overlooking the manipulation of Black women by white feminists as a means to de-radicalize and destroy the political progress of Black people, which has recently been reflected on in Ronald E. Hall's "Woman: Better [w]hite than Male," in *An Historical Analysis of Skin Color Discrimination in America* (2010).

5. Thomas Foster's "The Sexual Abuse of Black Men under American Slavery," agrees with Greg Thomas's analysis. He too argues that, "The rape of slave men has also gone unacknowledged because of the current and historical tendency to define rape along gendered lines, making both victims and perpetrators reluctant to discuss male rape. The sexual assault of men dangerously points out cracks in the marble base of patriarchy that asserts men as penetrators in opposition to the penetrable, whether homosexuals, children, or adult women" (2011, p. 448).

However, there is an additional danger articulated by perpetuating this ignorance about slavery. "Without recognizing male sexual abuse, we run the risk of reinscribing the very stereotypes used by white slave owners and others who reduced black men to bestial sexual predators and white women to passionless and passive vessels." (Foster, 2011, p. 464).

6. For a history of white women's Klu Klux Klan organizations, see Kathleen Blee (1991), *Women of the Klan: Racism and Gender in the 1920's*, and Nancy Maclean (1994), *Behind the Mask of Chivalry: The Making of the Second Ku Klux Klan.*

7. Shannon Shird (2013) has argued that this lyric concerning the Hampton spouse perpetuates the myth of the Black rapist and rape culture. She says, "Knowing his complicity in perpetuating these harmful ideas about Black sexuality certainly doesn't make it better. Regardless of whatever artistic license anyone is willing to give, he uses his platform to describe the mythical Black rapist and contributes to a very real rape culture." Shird's claim suggests an ignorance of how this myth of the Black male rapist actually functions. The myth of the Black rapist is an unaddressed part of rape culture. It's a viewing of sexual assault that over-represents, or solely presents Black men, as the only men that commit rape. According to Davis (1983), "The myth of the Black rapist continues to carry out the insidious work of racist ideology. As long as their analyses focus on accused rapists who are reported and arrested, thus on only a fraction of the rapes actually committed, Black men—and other men of color—will inevitably be viewed as the villains responsible for the current epidemic of sexual violence" (p.199).

As Davis points out, the myth of the Black rapist is not simply a perpetuation of the stereotype that Black men commit rape. This myth is about whom in a racist society gets incarcerated for and then publicly unveiled as "the rapist." In no way does West have the ability or power as a Black man (victim) to perpetuate rape culture through the myth of the Black rapist as Shird suggests, because he is already seen as an integral and necessary part of rape culture, since he—as the Black man—is the rapist. The symbols, ideas, and beliefs that would victimize women, especially white women, and suggest to the public that rape is permissible, are the same symbols, ideas, and beliefs that criminalize and present Black men to the world as the "only" rapist, or the deviant image/thought that all people imagine when they think of "rape." In short, Black men do not "possess the social or economic authority guaranteeing them immunity from prosecution" (Davis, 1983, p. 200), so they do not have the privilege of not being convicted of and identified as a rapist. Here again, feminism contrives Black men's power as creating actual threats to white women without any serious analysis of the integral role white women's allegedly sexual vulnerabilities have in sustaining white supremacy and anti-Black violence against men, or how a consideration of the history of sexual assault against Black men would complicate the picture of Black male and white female sex.

Part III

Theorizing the Aesthetic, the Political, and the Existential

Chapter 10

When Apollo and Dionysus Clash: A Nietzschean Perspective on the Work of Kanye West

Julius Bailey

The problem with philosophy is the ease with which it devolves into abstraction. Looking into a philosophy book replete with arcane words such as "epistemology" and "dialethicism," and with the author holding forth on esoteric matters that apparently live only in the mind, the uninformed or rather uninitiated reader can be forgiven for assuming that philosophers are the very definition of "ivory tower" academics, utterly dissociated from real life and elitists in the worst sense of that much-maligned word. How can one answer the question "What's the point of philosophy" when there are so few examples of how philosophy can be applied to today's everyday life?

One possible answer is to demonstrate the ways in which philosophical concepts *can* be applied to the task of gaining a broader understanding of something. This is what this essay sets out to accomplish. There can be few things more familiar in popular culture than music videos, and this essay demonstrates how Nietzschean concepts can help illuminate the multifaceted meanings of Kanye West and Jay-Z's video "No Church in the Wild."[1] In doing so, we will provide an example of how a philosophical framework can assist in unpacking all that is contained in the taut few minutes of this video.

A work of art, however "high-brow" or "low-brow," always contains within it the seeds of two reactions: the instinctive/emotional, and the intellectual; in classical and Nietzschean terms, the Dionysian and the Apollonian.[2] It is the difference between the felt reaction and the thought reaction that defines our views of art and allows for a discussion of esthetic effects. It can also be played with by artists: as an example, a song, composed of the two elements of music and lyrics, can produce an ironic effect by placing together seemingly contradictory elements. Sarcastic lyrics set to a syrupy melody, for instance, will cause a form of cognitive dissonance in the listener, who is left to piece together the *why* behind this choice. This effect is heightened in the world of the music video. Adding the third element of the visual complicates the audience's reactions even further. The dynamic illustration of music and lyrics can be used with as much inventiveness as the director wishes, from a simple shot of a singer performing to a meta-narrative whose link to the song is left to the audience to determine. The viewer-listener is faced with basic questions of esthetics: What is the artist trying to do? How do the images relate to the song? What is being said, or trying to be said? Does the artist succeed in saying it? Does it fit? Does the intention matter? Through this questioning the audience enters into a dialogue with the work, and through it, with the artist.

These questions do not, however, necessarily offer a framework for looking more deeply at what a work of art suggests. By taking a philosophical concept as a starting point, it is possible to organize one's thoughts, to choose a vantage point from which to look at the work and see what it is doing, and perhaps determine whether that is what the artist intended it to do. Let us look at an example.

The opening sequence of the video is one of silent menace. A black clad, black-skinned man grips a simple glass bottle, a rag inserted into its neck. There is no need for explanations or exegesis. In this time and in this place, most of us have a visual vocabulary that tells us that the combination of these two simple items, the rag and the bottle, come together as something far more deadly than the sum of their parts. It is a visual signifier that tells us that this is a Molotov cocktail, an infamous incendiary device that first saw use during the Spanish Civil War[3] and that was perfected during the Winter War between Finland and the Soviet Union, when the Finns gave it the derisive name of Molotov, an insult aimed at the Soviet foreign minister.[4] As the weapon of the David-like Finns against the Soviet Goliath, with soldiers on foot stopping tanks with the simple expedient of a bottle, this cheap and easily made device became noted as a weapon of choice for a minority struggling against overwhelming force and repression. In the years since the Second World War it has come to be intimately associated with ideas of upheaval. It is the symbol of the riot, the rebellion. In our modern world, it is the anarchist's sigil, evoking in us a host of images and words from the moment it appears, whether in life or, as here, on screen.

While the looming specter of explicit violence confronts us in the image of the unignited Molotov cocktail, its threat yet to be actualized, a more implicit threat of violence is also present, in the form of that black-clad, black-skinned male body. In his work on the philosophy of race, particularly in the existentially grounded *Black Bodies, White Gazes* (2008), philosopher George Yancy discusses the ways in which the black body, particularly the black male body, is read as a threat by white society.[5] As such the Heideggerian *Dasein* of blackness, its very beingness, posits withinthe white gaze, without immediate provocation, the possibility of imminent violence, the threat of social decay. This is a coding that never leaves it even in such innocent act as stepping into an elevator. Because the black body is automatically read as driven by passion rather than by thought, of being bestial rather than fully human, the Black man is a threat, because he has not been, and possibly cannot ever fully be tamed. For much of the first minute of the video that this black body is just that, only a body, featureless, decapitated by the frame that cuts off at the man's neck.

Thus the opening image of the music video for "No Church in the Wild" confronts us with a doubled image of violence, one the explicit threat of the man holding a weapon, the other the implicit threat of this man's blackness. This opening message warns the viewer that we are ready to move beyond the boundaries of the map, passing into those uncharted areas once marked with the ominous warning that *hic svnt dracones*, Latin for here be dragons. With their implications of descent from the empyrean realm of civilization into the bloody conflict of an urban jungle, this image provides us with a fitting point from which to begin an examination of the visual and lyrical message of "No Church in the Wild" within the context of the work of Friedrich Nietzsche, who more than once found himself wrongly accused of spreading a plague of nihilistic thought.

Nietzsche did not advocate of nihilism but was as a careful, patient examiner of the phenomenon. To view Nietzsche as a nihilist would be incorrect and to trivialize his thought. In many ways he did not see nihilism as a valid response to the world, but considered it a decadent response to the world[6] and saw it as a problem to be overcome. It simply wasn't a problem that could be overcome by moral preaching however, rather the proper response had to be grounded in the body and it had to be aesthetic.

Concluding that previous systems of belief had reached their end point, Nietzsche could only follow that logic to its relentless end, nihilism, but he sought also a way forward from it. Thus he created the concept of amor fati, allowing him to affirm a love of life despite what might seem its emptiness:

> I do not want to wage war against ugliness. I do not want to accuse; I do not even want to accuse the accusers. Let looking away be my only negation! And, all in all and on the whole: someday I want only to be a Yes-sayer! (*The Gay Science*, 276)

This is not the most enduring image of Nietzsche. Much more famous, or perhaps more correctly infamous, is the brooding man with the oversized mustache, the Nietzsche who pronounced Theothanatos, "Gott ist tot," the declaration of the death of God.[7] Yet for all that this herald of funerary tidings was one man in the physical sense. In philosophical spirit, it might be said that there were two men named Friedrich Nietzsche, the intellectual nihilist and the relentless life-lover. Reading the early writings of Nietzsche, we find that at the very beginning of his career as a philosopher, Nietzsche was still in the grip of what he would later call a sickness. This sickness, this fever of the mind, was the result of the influence of such men as Wagner, Schopenhauer, and even Kant. It was a sickness of transcendence, in which the world was thought to be still divided into the high and low.

The central focus of Nietzsche's first work, *The Birth of Tragedy*, is art, particularly the dramatic tragedies of ancient Greece. Nietzsche conceives of art neither as the simple pursuit of a group of dilettante craftsmen, nor as the lofty pursuit of an "enlightened" caste of philosopher-artistes. Rather, art is something much greater, something that cannot be confined to these elites classes. It is nothing less than the highest pursuit of man and the metaphysical goal toward which all men should strive. This is contrary, however, to generally accepted Judeo-Christian morality, for which the search for virtue held pride of place and art was a frivolous distraction, if not downright sinful. The young Nietzsche rejected this view. For him, morality was the symbol of a dead god, a debilitating poison that we are tricked into thinking the sweetest of wines, deluding us into believing we are slaking our thirst even as it weakens us. Only through art can we hope to achieve perfection or fulfillment as it is art that allows us to lay title to that contentious claim of authenticity. He did, however, deem art, aesthetic value as it were, as the antidote to nihilism and morality.

The Birth of Tragedy is the epitome of a young man's book; in later years, even Nietzsche himself denounced it, at times savagely. Despite this, it earns a place in our study for its introduction of Nietzsche's concept of art and life being separated into the Dionysian and the

Apollonian. It is the conflict of these two states, named after the wild god of wine and the stately god of poetry and light, respectively, that makes life three-dimensional. And it is also, as we saw earlier, the conflict that informs our view of any given work of art.

In Judeo-Christian morality, influenced by Plato's view of the world of the mind, or the spirit, being truer and more relevant than that of the mere five senses, the Dionysian elements of life were repressed. The enjoyment of the physical world was held to be a sin; fallen humanity should aspire only to abnegation and spiritual enlightenment, ignoring the desires of the body as wiles of the devil. But Nietzsche rejects the view that the physical is inherently inferior or sinful, or that enjoyment is. Mikhail Bakhtin pointed out that the medieval church had to allow Carnival, the eruption of all that was repressed in everyday life. Nietzsche argues that such Saturnalian revelry is not merely steam that has to be occasionally let out from a boiling pot. It is an integral part of humanity, the celebration of the joy of living. Christianity, fixated on the idea of what happens after death, has lost sight of this. What's more, Dionysian revelry is not merely a wild, drunken party: It is a creative act, the source of art. Theatre in Ancient Greece was not, after all, just a pleasant evening out. It was a sacred ritual dedicated to Dionysus.

Despite what Christianity preaches, then, the Dionysian spirit is not an assault on God or an outbreak of atheistic anarchy but rather it is a manifestation of the divine spirit. As the foundation of art, it is at the base of what we have noted is the highest aspiration of humanity.

But Dionysus alone cannot fully create art, because anarchy is formless and shapeless. It is the influence of Apollo that allows art to become something more and enduring. Apollo's realm is that of abstraction, of pure thought, removed and divorced from base physical needs or desires, or for that matter from the threat of the physical. The latter are in the domain Dionysus's, and as such are dangerous. In Ancient Greece, the female followers of Dionysus who slipped the bounds of the deeply repressive patriarchy to run riot through the hills. Men never knew quite what they did, but there were rumors of strange orgies and bloody feasts of goats torn to pieces and eaten raw. It was these Maenads who were responsible for the death of Apollo's son Orpheus, who still mourning his loss of Eurydice, for a second time refused to sleep with them, and they ripped him limb from limb. The Apollonian is thus left both afraid and disgusted by the Dionysian impulse, willing to acknowledge it only under the condition of repressing it.

For all that we are fleshy things and therefore creatures rooted in the Dionysian although we are often educated in the Apollonian mode and taught that the physical is the lesser of the two realms.[8] Certainly Plato, at least in the fictional guise of Socrates leading us through the pages of his *Republic*, thought so. As Plato's famous allegory of the cave suggests, the realm of the Dionysian is the realm of appearance, of shadow, of opinion. So long as we remain bound in the sensual chains of Dionysus we shall be unable to know the light of truth.[9] Even Augustine of Hippo, whose prayer for chastity was tempered by the request that it come not quite yet, held the Neoplatonic conviction that the goodness to be found in the material world was but a pale reflection of the light of God. Thus it would be sinful and foolish to become enamored of the goodness here while becoming blinded to the transcendent goodness of the divine. That is, no matter how wonderful something in this world might be, the divine offers so much more that there is no purpose in contemplating the material. Aristotle, as is well known, considered contemplation the highest form of pleasure, because it brought man closer to the divine spirit, and helped to perfect the soul.

This then is the conclusion of the dominant Classical philosophy that was subsumed in Christianity, that it is to the realm of the Apollonian we should turn our eyes, whether we call it Heaven, the realm of forms, or something else entirely. The ultimate goal is to transcended the limits of our flesh and become something more. Morality, the set of guidelines by which we might engage in right-living, is the primary tool that enables us to do so. Yet Nietzsche felt that it was art, and specifically art contra morality, that should be the guiding principle of humanity. As such, the Apollonian realm should not be the focus of our striving.

Yet the solution is not, according to Nietzsche, to dive more fully into the Dionysian world, which would be as one-sided and misguided as the perpetual focus on the transcendent. It would be more accurate to say that the Apollonian realm should not stand in isolation as the focus of our striving.

Nietzsche believed that the clash between these two realms and their subsequent melding, the forming of a symbiotic whole that was greater than the sum of its parts, not only gave strength to Greek tragedy, but was also a powerful influence on the character of the ancient Greeks as they engaged in the daily performance that we call life. To reject the Dionysian is to deny an essential part of ourselves, yet to cast aside the Apollonian and its "higher" impulses is equally a denial of a part of our nature. Casting either one aside leads to a life-negating mode of being. To be life-affirming, one must embrace the totality of life. Only by joining our highest aspirations to our lowest impulses can one begin to hold a life-affirming stance.

This contrast between life-negating and life-affirming ways of being would continue to be a theme in Nietzsche's work even after he cast aside all thoughts of transcendence. As Deleuze points out in *Nietzsche and Philosophy*, Nietzsche was not a nihilist, because the root of nihilism is "nihil," which means zero, nothingness, the absence of any positivity. "Nihil"-ism is antithetical to any life-affirming ethos, and therefore Nietzsche's "will to power," which is a way of affirming life, is the opposite of a death-drive. It is the will toward life and its intensification.

The above has all been rather abstract. In fact, for the last few paragraphs, we have been working firmly in the Apollonian realm, which can be that ivory tower we previously noted that turns most people off philosophy. Let us bring in Dionysus, then, by returning to the contemplation of a worldly artifact, the video of "No Church in the Wild." This video is especially suited to a discussion of Nietzsche's view because it can not only be discussed in terms of the differences between Apollonian and Dionysian, but also illustrates them.

It is instructive to watch this video with the sound off, to see what is being said in the visual realm alone. We noted earlier how the multidimensionality of the music video complicates the audience's response to it. By separating the visual elements from the audio ones, we can perhaps achieve a closer reading. And so we return to that black body holding the Molotov cocktail and, in light of Nietzsche, another layer is added to our discussion. The fear the black body produces is a very specific type of fear, because in the common white imagining of the world, black humans are purely Dionysian creatures. Colonialism was founded on the assumption that whites were not merely more "civilized," but inherently more capable of civilization. The theoretical benevolence of the "white man's burden," the paternalistic impulse to improve the black man's moral standing, was tempered by the fact that it was understood that the black man could never actually reach the same level as the white man. Blacks were by nature incapable of truly inhabiting Apollo's realm, though they might be instructed in it enough to keep them from being a danger. This view has not entirely disappeared. The black body is still visualized as rampantly physical, as can be seen in the clichés of the black instinctively having "rhythm in their souls," always dancing like the demonic Africans on the shores of the Congo in Joseph Conrad's *Heart of Darkness*, and being a perpetual sexual threat to the white man, assumed to be oversexed, ithyphallic lovers.

So, for example, in the case of a riot, despite the multiple ethnicities of the participants, the event itself is personified by a black man

seen against the background of white policemen. In many instances
the police in America appear to be protecting neoclassical monu-
ments and buildings of power—capital buildings and courthouses—
symbols of Apollonian state rationalism, from the Dionysian rioters.

We have already confronted these threats from the first image of
the video, the contained menace of the unlit cocktail. Now, the sub-
dued scritch of a disposable lighter and the *whomph* of an accelerant-
soaked rag bursting to life presage the birth of a sonorous beat, as our
ears follow our eyes and we are pulled into the dual-exegesis of video
and song. The scenario is one that we've increasingly seen delivered
in the media, from Egypt to Brazil to Europe and America with rioters, of multiple ethnicities, filling the street, and preparing to rush
police as the first Molotov cocktail is let fly. Dionysus is unleashed,
his lack of restraint as visible in the uncontrolled spread of the flames
as in the black man's two upraised middle fingers. There will be no
manners here.

Remaining for a moment only with what we see, not what we hear,
what follows is fascinatingly ambiguous: There is no way to know
what side we should be on. The general ethos of rap makes us suspect
that the rioters are automatically the "good guys," rising up against
an oppressive society represented by the riot police with their clubs
and shields, but the violence demonstrated by both sides suggests
something closer to equality. History provides no guide, while insur-
rections such as these have been as explicable as, say, the Rodney King
riots or as justified as the recent spate of revolutions again dictatorships in the Middle East, others have been as morally bankrupt as the
explosion of anger in Vancouver in 2011 over a lost hockey game. In
the video both sides brought their weapons to the fight, and after all,
the rioters, so far as we can see, fire the first shot. The ethical equality of the two sides is particularly demonstrated toward the middle of
the video, with the juxtaposition of the rioter standing on top of a car
having his feet knocked from under him by a policeman's nightstick,
and a mounted officer being pushed off his horse by a rioter's pole.
The stomach clenches with the same horror at what happens to one
as to the other. Lovers of ancient art will be nervous to see the statuary taken over by the mob, and everyday shoppers will worry as the
rioters attack the mall, throwing rocks at the mannequins—yet more
white statues under threat by an out-of-control destructive force.

The violence of the unleashed Dionysus would appear to justify
its repression. It is the classic argument against anarchism, that without the strictures and taboos of society, people will be too irrational
to look out for anything but what they perceive as their immediate

self-interest, and society will devolve into permanent chaos. Yet transgressions occur even with the existence of moral codes and laws that cannot be absolute. At what point does it become acceptable to riot against current authority? Most people will agree that destructive riots because of the outcome of a sports event lack any sort of morality, what of riots following a clearly unjust verdict in a court case? What of riots against an authority that refuses to listen, as in June 2013 in Turkey? What of riots that bring down dictatorships, as in the Arab Spring? At what point does one change sides? How do we respond to authority using brutality to put down a riot when we agree that the riot needed to be put down? What can we do when protests we agree with begin attacking innocent targets? There can be no clear answer, because life is not cut-and-dried or, dare we say it, black and white. There is a constant ambiguity in how we respond to events, because morality itself is ambiguous, often dependent on circumstances and so connected to the rest of the world that it is impossible to truly measure what effect a decision will have. This ambiguity of morality was the theme of Nietzsche's later *Beyond Good and Evil (1886)*, and it is an ambiguity that pervades much of Kanye West's body of work.

What we see in the video, then, is ambiguous, because we have no guidelines to tell us on which side morality lies. Viewers are likely to decide based on their preexisting concepts of society and the law. In terms of the actions we see, there seems to be nothing to decide between. Both sides seem only to offer violence: Our choice is between agreeing to oppression and beating up rioters, while risking being set on fire, or rebelling, destroying everything we come across, and facing the tear gas, the dogs, and the billyclub. There seems to be no middle ground. The only thing both sides can agree on is causing the other as much pain as possible.

The ambiguity of the visual element is clear. Apollonian order is presented as brutal and repressive, Dionysian riot as violent and destructive. Neither is morally superior option. What happens, then, when we turn the sound back on and consider the artistic ambiguity we touched upon earlier, the relationship of song to image? Apollo and Dionysus clash on screen; Will our intellectual and emotional response to the combination of song and video clash as well?

Ushered in on the pulsing throb of the song's beat after that initial flare of flame, and the mirrored image of bared teeth in the mouth of a riot-control dog and an angry rioter, we are thrust fully into the song. The opening chorus, provided by Frank Ocean, seems to issue a challenge, ending with the line, "What's a god to a non-believer/Who don't believe in anything?" Jay-Z's verse also adopts a similar stance, challenging both secular and religious authority, while at the same time maintaining the stance of someone not necessarily seeking to overthrow, but to find an authentic authority; one that exists beyond the venal corruption of those who currently hold power in the world.

While there is a sensation of disparity between word and image, the relationship between the two in the early parts of the song is clear. Just as Frank Ocean and Jay-Z have issued their challenge, have announced their desire to find a truer way of being in the world, the rioters can be read as fighting against an authority they view as corrupt. They rebel against the system not because they seek to destroy it, but because they wish to forge it into something better.[10] Ocean's line "What's a mob to a king" puts the rioters in their place. A rioting mob is nothing to a king, represented here by the police. This is chiefly due to the ease to which the nation-state can repress such uprisings. We have seen this constant refrain used by authority against rebellions and riots both in America and abroad. The heavy-handed, highly weaponized force by dictators such as Bull Connor (Alabama), Daryl Gates (California), Muammar Gaddafi (Libya), Hosni Mubarak (Egypt), Bashar al-Assad (Syria), and democratically elected authoritarian leaders such as Recep Tayyip Erdogan (Turkey) and Vladimir Putin (Russia), all insisting that protests against their rule was the work of animalistic thugs, anarchists, and foreign agents. Once the rioters are thus dehumanized, it becomes acceptable to use force against them, even though they are as much a part of the society as those who support the rulers. Instead of allowing a dialogue between contradictory ways of seeing the world, searching for common ground, violence is used as an answer—much as in our Nietzschean reading of how the Dionysian is violently denied and repressed by the Apollonian.

Viewing the video less literally, associating the mob on screen to the one in the lyrics, the police, the representatives of authority signify the repressive Apollonian intellect keeping the base impulses of a Dionysian rabble in check. Yet clearly they are failing, for this rioting mob clearly denies the authority of the police, just as Ocean's nonbeliever denies the existence and hence the authority of a god. As the battle rages, Jay-Z, our unseen narrator of this riot of the mind, urges us not to overthrow thought for emotion, but to unify the two.

Taken in isolation, the first half of "No Church in the Wild" certainly resonates with early Nietzsche. Yet as the song moves into its bridge, moving toward Kanye's verse, there is a marked shift both visually and lyrically. During the first half of the video, the police, the Apollonian forces, are clearly in control of the situation. Yet as

The-Dream sings to us of desire, the tide begins to shift, with the rioters becoming the dominant force in the confrontation, reflected not only through the action in the video, but also through shifts in lighting, and even in the image of the statue. Whereas before the selection of statuary suggested a man hiding his face in pain, shame, or impotent rage, or a Herculean figure whose raised club reflects the baton of a police officer bludgeoning a rioter, the statues shown in the second half of the video symbolize power and victory.

This is where the question of whether the video's powerful imagery is at odds with the song's content. Many critics have suggested that Kanye's paean to polyamory, his ode to the joys of sniffing cocaine from her "black skin" (once again we note the black/white dichotomy) conflicts with the visualization of a society in the grips of chaotic discordance. But a closer analysis suggests that this is not so. The rioters stand, as mentioned, as a Dionysian presence. They are the primal force of intoxication, of uncontrolled passion unbound. Kanye's verse stands at odds with traditional strictures; it preaches against those things we are taught are "right" and "normal." Monogamy, Kanye tells us, is not normal. It is imposed on us, and we must reject it if we are to find a better way of being. It is a Dionysian sermon, harkening back to those drunken orgies that the Maenads instigated millennia ago in praise of their god.

Thus there is no dichotomy between word and image. Kanye may sing of threesomes while police officers are set on fire, but the same language is being spoken. It is the language of Dionysus unbound, and the old order swept aside in favor of an unbridled way of being. Yet it is this very unity of word and image that causes Kanye West to fail as a Nietzschean artist. The tentative seeking with which the song opens is cast aside as West announces that we have found our new, more authentic way of being, the Dionysian way. There is no room for the Apollonian in this creed of abandon and upheaval. The Apollonian has been rejected, leaving us no better than half-alive, thus never able to find completion. The Dionysian and its excesses have eclipsed the passionless balance of the Apollonian spirit and any attempt to find a middle ground between the two. For all its passionate embrace of the physical experience, then, in the eyes of early Nietzsche West's verse is merely life-denying.

If "No Church in the Wild" leaves us only damned, half-alive things, how might we fare in the gaze of the man who pronounced theothanatos? The Nietzsche who wrote *The Gay Science* would, at first glance, seem sympathetic to the thoughts expressed in "No Church in the Wild," particularly Ocean's question about the nonbeliever.

In expressing the death of God, Nietzsche announces the downfall of all order; ethics, metaphysics, faith, science, these things have all failed us. Our foundational assumptions are all deeply flawed, and our Nietzschean project is thus to forge a new way, a way that is life-affirming rather than life-denying. In this later Nietzsche we still find the recurring image of the Dionysian, though now he represents the figure of the completed man, the man who walks the life-affirming path free of the life-denying course forced on us by the death of God on the cross.[11] The death of God is the end of transcendence. God died, and was not resurrected. There are no miracles, no enchantment of the world, no divine mystery. God died and stayed dead, the result of violence was permanent.

Unfortunately, too often this Nietzsche is read as espousing mere inversion, a replacement of all current values with their polar opposites. Yet what Nietzsche proposes is not in fact a wholesale rejection of our current way of being so much as a wholesale rejection of the reasons behind our way of being. For instance, Western morality preaches that life is sacred, and that to take life is therefore a sin. It would be easy, sloppily simple even, to thus presume that a Nietzschean way of being would then tell us that if life is sacred in the old order, and the old order is wrong, then life is no longer sacred and there is no meaningful prohibition in place that prevents the taking of life. This simplistic view assumes Nietzsche to be in favor of wholesale murder. In fact, such simplistic and censored views of his philosophy did find its way into the tenets of Nazism.

Living in such a way is failing to make the move Nietzsche desired, which as he so often put it, was a move beyond good and evil, a shift to something other than morality. Merely replacing morality with anti-morality does not accomplish this, because the two are still defined by the same dichotomy, rather than leaving it behind. Deciding that since, in the old view, life was held as sacred; in the new, we must hold ourselves above any stricture (legal, transcendent, or otherwise) on taking life, is to still define ourselves solely in relation to a view of the world that regards life as sacred. Rather than seeking a new way of being, rather than confronting the horrors of freedom, we have simply fooled ourselves into believing that we cannot see our chains.

A more accurate interpretation of Nietzsche, then, that what we must seek is a rejection that results in a revaluation, not an inversion, of values. In choosing to walk a Nietzschean path there is nothing that tells us we must reject life as valuable. Rather, we are told that if we are to value life then we must value life for the right reasons— reasons that call to the transcendent, relying on the orders of a being whose existence Nietzsche did not acknowledge, are clearly insufficient. After all, "What's a god to a non-believer?" Any reason emerging from a teleological narrative is likewise worthless. To explain this Apollonian, ivory-tower word, the teleological, or "goal-seeking," narrative is one that essentially guides us to live our lives for something other than living our lives. The Eden story, though it is by no means the only example, is among the archetypal forms of the teleological narrative. To wit: humans once lived in paradise, they were expelled from Eden; so, we must now spend our lives rejecting sin in the hopes of regaining entrance into paradise or heaven. If we live according to the Edenic narrative, then we are living our lives not for the purpose of living our lives, but solely to secure for ourselves a place in paradise after our deaths. The danger in this is that it can cause us to turn away from the lived reality of existence, not living our lives for ourselves, and subjecting ourselves to someone, or something, else's plan. Insisting on the existence of an idea that cannot be proven, based on revelation we are admonished to live purely for an Apollonian idea, that is something better and transcendent. Thus we must reject the Dionysian, that is, all the pleasures of life—food, comfort, sex—because, as we mentioned earlier, they are irrelevant in the quest for the glorious realities of the next world, and indulging in them may prevent us from reaching it. The teleological view of life does not make us behave well for the right reasons. We will behave in a moral way for the reward of entering heaven, or out of fear of going to hell, rather than because it is right to do so. Our moral actions will not necessarily mean that we are moral beings.

Even if one is to reject Nietzsche's atheism and presume that the divine exists in some form or another, to live in this way is still unhealthy. We can find this sentiment in the work of Kierkegaard, who despite his many criticisms of the church as institution still maintained his faith. Though his reasons for doing so were somewhat different from Nietzsche's, Kierkegaard too insisted that living our lives for the promise of heavenly reward was not only unhealthy, but actually the demonstration of a lack of faith.

Whether one sides with Kierkegaard or Nietzsche on the position of faith in the divine, at the heart of the matter is the idea that life is to be lived for the sake of life itself, and not for the sake of future reward, and not in a fashion that objectifies us. If we hold to the principle that life is of value, and thus must not be taken from another, then the source of that value can only come from within us. It is thus subjective if we wish for this value to be a healthy one. We cannot decide not to kill only out of fear of the divine's riot policemen.

In light of the later work of Nietzsche, then, there is no need of an immediate rejection either of Jay-Z's questioning position, or of Kanye's embrace of hedonism. Yet we are left with a tension that must be resolved. The hedonism espoused by the song, particularly during Kanye's verse, stands in direct opposition to what we are typically taught as good and right. As such, it is not difficult to see it less as a rejection of morality than as an inversion. As discussed, this does not move us beyond good and evil, but leaves us chained to conventional morality. West answers Ocean's question "What's a god to a nonbeliever?" by arguing that the proper response is to indulge in everything the nonexistent god prohibited, rather than bypass these taboos and find one's own morality.

There is a latent linguistic ambiguity in Ocean's question that sheds further light on this point. Ocean says "nonbeliever," but it is unclear exactly what this means. It might have the sense either of "unbeliever" or of "atheist." That is, if a person speaks the phrase "I believe in God," it implies that the speaker believes in the existence of a god. But it also powerfully implies that the speaker worships this God. The two are not identical. It is possible to believe in the existence of a God and yet reject him as unjust, or choose to ignore his strictures, or deliberately invert them as a way of, essentially, giving him the finger. The latter type of nonbeliever, however, has not moved beyond God; those rules are still the defining guidelines, and like the pure hedonist we have been looking at, is therefore not free from God. The nonbeliever who simply denies the existence of any divinity, on the other hand, has the ability to find a new basis for morality. This does not necessarily mean that an atheist will do so, merely that it is possible to. So, Ocean's question has a double answer, depending on how we define his term. To a nonbeliever, God is either something to be fought against, or something to be left entirely out of mind. Only the latter can truly be said to have moved beyond good and evil. West, however, appears to be the former. His hedonism is based on negation rather than creation; his embrace of the Dionysian is not life-affirming, because it is not a search for something new but a mirror image of the old. He rejects common morality but can offer nothing in its place except denying it.

Though morality can be repressive, it cannot be confidently asserted that it is invariably so. As we noted, Nietzsche concluded that morality is ambiguous. Thus we may conclude that monogamy may well be as life-affirming as any other option, depending on circumstance and on those involved. Why should we value polyamory? Because it lets us fuck whomever we want? Why should we value that?

What is the value of promiscuity over monogamy? Should we value it solely because it is the opposite of what those who keep us in chains insist that we do, and thus is a path to freeing ourselves from oppression? We already know that this particular answer is a trap that not only keeps us firmly under the yoke of another, but also, as Foucault says, makes us a tool of oppression in and of ourselves. In our overt act of what we think is rejection and rebellion, we provide the systems of oppression with a tool to show the people what happens when they step out of line.

The ways in which we as a society, particularly in the modern West, consume stories of the flaws and failures of the famous, the ways in which we continue to consume their lives even while holding ourselves as morally, intellectually, or otherwise superior to the celebrity scapegoat of the minute, suggest that this sort of thing is a far more effective tool of control than we might like to admit.

Reactive hedonism does nothing to enrich us. It does not liberate or enlighten us. In order to be considered life-affirming in a Nietzschean perspective, some hedonistic behavior would have to arise from the right place. While the later Nietzsche might seem to suggest that the manner of being articulated in "No Church in the Wild" is a good one, in the context of the rest of the song these hopes seem doomed to be dashed on reality's rock. Without a firmer grounding in *why* we should value the trappings of hedonism, the song ultimately seems nothing more than an inversion of received values. There is no freedom, Nietzschean or otherwise, to be found in the message it brings to us. After all, the video seems to portray an orgy of violence in which the distinctions between right/ wrong and police/ rioters and order/ rebellion are swept away by the anger and rage of both sides. In their violence, they are equal and no longer distinct. There seems to be a need, then, for a new creative response that will result in life-affirming, life-sustaining forms—an Apollonian response. Inasmuch as artists serve as harbingers and visionaries, Jay-Z and West are lacking.

Yet despite his popular reputation, there is more to Kanye West than this. In his song "Through the Wire," he takes an extraordinary risk for an artist immersed in the hyper-masculinized, braggadocio-ridden world of hip-hop. After surviving a car accident that shattered, West recorded a song about his recovery. This willingness to embrace risk and celebrate his survival by rapping with a shattered jaw can be seen as a truly life-affirming act. In tragedy, in music, the walls that delineate individual existence shatter and we experience a loss of ego, of individuality, of self. It is a kind of death. In tragedy, we share in the death of the tragic hero. In the procreative act, we experience the little death of rapture. But the Dionysian brings us to the brink of the abyss and shows us that our individual existence is but a fleeting illusion in the eternity of the universe. And so perhaps West is more of a Nietzschean than "Church in the Wild" makes him seem. On the positive side, through loss we experience, according to Nietzsche, unity with all being and with our fellow human beings in the orgiastic experience of loss of self. But we also run the danger of insight into the illusion of being and thus could collapse into madness. At this moment, according to Nietzsche, the Apollonian resurfaces and restores the beautiful illusion of life and meaning, which we need to survive. Beauty is, according to Nietzsche, the survival instinct's response to the enormity of the Dionysian insight. "Through the Wire" does not reject the stereotyped strictures of the rapping lifestyle, it merely ignores them. It moves, that is, beyond good and evil; and praises life, not for morality or lack of morality, but simply for being life, and for being able to live.

Notes

1. Video directed by Romain Gavras was released on May 29, 2012. It can be seen at http://www.youtube.com/watch?v=FJt7gNi3Nr4
2. Dionysian and Apollian views of art were popularized in *The Birth of Tragedy* (1872) as a juxtaposition or dichotomy of a rational and perfect self (Apollo) and the more irrational or emotive self (Dionysian). This is not unlike a Freudian Id and SuperEgo. But Nietzsche does not see them as hierarchical but rather as natural tension that causes the tragic to develop through is unity.
3. Hugh Thomas (2001). *The Spanish Civil War*. Modern Library Paperback Edition, 454.
4. Arto Bendicken, (2010). "A Thousand Lakes of Red Blood on White Snow." http://ar.to/2010/08/red-blood-white-snow (accessed June 27, 2013).
5. George Yancy (2008) *Black Bodies White Gazes*. Lanham, MD: Roman and Littlefield Publishers Inc.
6. We must remember that he opposed Christianity because of its life-negating, that is, nihilistic morality.
7. The Gay Science (1882), trans. Walter Kaufman Vintage Books (1974), 279.
8. For Nietzsche, the Dionysian represents the underlying "will" of which Schopenhauer speaks—it is a formless wanting, desire, motion. Out of this will, through the principium individuations, the illusory image of myriad individual existences is formed. This is the veil of Maya to which Schopenhauer refers. It is also the Apollonian.

9. With regard to this cave analogy, Nietzsche would read the realm of the Apollonian as the realm of appearances but necessary appearances. This, in part, is because he would reject the platonic ideal forms as true forms, other than their rising from the will's need to populate the universe with images/ illusions. This also has a Schopenhauer quality to it.

10. When discussing this matter in an interview with a colleague, Dr. Timothy Bennett, Wittenberg University, he pushed me further with this claim by asserting "I think the desire 'to forge' something better is a good Apollonian impulse and wonder if this suggests the necessary partnership of both Apollonian and Dionysian (a necessary partnership according to Nietzsche as well). If so, then it might be necessary not to see the Apollonian as repressing the Dionysian. In fact, by challenging moribund forms, the Dionysian might be liberating energies which begin destructively but could empower a newer, more vital set of forms, i.e. they would revitalize the Apollonian."

11. Nietzsche's Madman also asks what new sacred games and rituals need to be invented now that God has been murdered by our scientific culture and challenges us to become God-like, to become creative, to give birth to a new humanity in response to this crime of deceit. According to my colleague Timothy Bennett, "Nothing seems to have disturbed Nietzsche more than modern culture's inability to give rise to a new religion adequate to its challenges. One could read much of his work as an attempt to develop a new sense of the sacred."

Chapter 11

God of the New Slaves *or* Slave to the Ideas of Religion and God?*

Monica R. Miller

Religion, when dethroned from sacrality and the illusion of morality and affirmativeness, is just as ordinary as cherry pie. That talk of religion makes its way into the culture that we call hip-hop is of no surprise—after all, religion becomes just another (linguistic) way in which the social world is often discussed. In the same way, what some see as culture might be considered to hold "religious" weight and value for others and what holds "religious" weight and value for others might simply be referred to as culture. That is to say, there's nothing intrinsic or of inherent value within these words that marks and delineates them as irreducibly different and distinct. What marks race or religion, for example, as "separate" domains is simply the constructed significance placed upon these terms across groups and communities. In other words, a term, or phrase like "religion in hip-hop" is in and of itself, empty of meaning and value. What they come to mean in time and space speaks to the contestation over ideas and values in the larger publics.

A wide variety of uses of religion in rap music, such as references to god, often induce disdain and criticism. They often surprise, cause eyebrows to raise, and elicit charges of blasphemy from the listening public. Take, for example, the controversy surrounding Kanye West's comparison of himself to god on his track "I am A God." Much of the public discussion assumes that the theological signifier god belongs in a womb of protection culminating in a conversation leading some to wonder whether or not hip-hop suffers from a "God Complex."[1] That a figure like Kanye (assumed secular) can liken himself to (a pure, and unchanging) concept like god (assumed sacred) is inconceivable for many.

Religionists often draw a metaphysical line in the sand between ideas of what is classified as sacred and what is considered profane.[2] In other words, a separation is often constructed between that which is seen as and understood to be religious or holy and that which is assumed to be utterly void of religious content and meaning. It is not surprising that much of the discourse on religion in hip-hop, and popular culture for that matter, has relied upon a bifurcation between these two ideas. Earlier works that put hip-hop and rap music in the domain of religious studies began with asking what might be of "religious" value in such cultural data.[3] This query, while holding much utility for earlier debates over whether hip-hop deserved a rightful place in religious and theological studies and analysis, ultimately furthered the divide between what counts as proper data for the study of religion. In recent years, this question, which relies upon a stark division between the sacred and profane, has come under criticism and deconstruction, with newer works advancing and complicating earlier questions to trouble such an existing divide.[4]

At times, the analyst working from the position of a religionist, for example, makes such divisions consciously apparent and stark. In other instances, the slippage between personal faith commitments and our objects of study become blurred, and this manufactured divide (between what is sacred and profane) emerges as a product of the scholar's own fabrication.[5] If we take this methodological critique as a way forward, then the question of "what *is* religious about hip-hop?" seems to hold little to no weight.

New questions brought to bear on old problems must advance with theoretical and methodological developments in the academic study of religion. No divide, I believe, has been more apparent than that evidenced in the ways in which ideas of religion have been intellectually and publically treated in the study of supposed "deviant" cultural forms, like rap music. This divide and debate constructed in the imagination of the analyst has ultimately constrained the development of rigorous scholarship in and around this burgeoning area of study.

The examples in this constructed "deviance" are countless. From Meek Mill being pressured to publicly apologize for his song "Amen," Rick Ross receiving flack over his sixth album titled *God Forgives I Don't*, to the album art of The Game's *Jesus Piece*, and to Kanye West's latest album, *Yeezus*, which includes self-referential claims of being god, the religious references in rap music are both increasing and continue to be fodder for religious controversy in the public sphere. These examples, among many, are not exhaustive, rather, they're representative of a particular sort of respectability and skewed positionality that seem to arise when we misrecognize and conflate the category and function of religion as meaningful, sacred, or what is or should be morally appropriate in culture and society.

A close consideration of the varying ways in which West makes use of religious language not only highlights the brevity and density of religious rhetoric in hip-hop, but likewise, requires, I believe, a more rigorous approach to the category of religion that posits religion as ordinary (not sui generis) talk about the social world and simply something reflective of the contest between social and cultural interests. With such an approach in hand, we can bypass unnecessary debates about moralism and the rightful place of religion (that keep religion arrested to and confined within erroneously fabricated normative notions of "good," "truth," and "value") and begin to see such ideas as products in the competing marketplace of human interests. The former and more traditional approach to such data that privileges and protects the category of religion tells us more about the classifier (the analyst) than the classified (the artists and their cultural productions) and relies upon a flawed view of the social actor, in this case, the rap artist, as fully conscious and aware of why they do what they do. Stated more simply, when people stop worrying about whether or not what Kanye does is right or wrong, they end up in a better position to study his work.

Based on West's songs "No Church in the Wild," "New Slaves," and "I Am a God," this essay considers the interplay between, and proclamations about, race and religion in an effort to examine the social interests at play in some of West's most "controversial" claims.

No Church in the Wild: Constructing a Cosmology of Pleasure

Hip-hop and hip-hoppers like West seem to emerge with a distaste and reticence for institutions because they understand these spaces to have failed, abandoned, and exploited the most marginal and wanting in society (those that West once claimed "Jesus Walks" with in the 'hood). His popular "Jesus Walks" gave rap music a liberation theological facelift, reminding the public of what Jesus of Nazareth was *really* up to in the Gospels, which in West's terms was "the Son of God kickin' it with those defined by society as criminal and deviant." Flipping dominant narratives on their head, Kanye humanizes Jesus and reminds us that he *walked* and continues to *walk* with the oppressed. For those working at the intersections of various sorts of liberation theologies, the "message" of this song was easy to digest and coincided with their radical theology.

While West received public praise for "Jesus Walks," he was not so lucky with his use of religion in "No Church in the Wild," a collaborative effort with Jay Z featuring Frank Ocean from 2011's *Watch the Throne*. Many viewed this song as irreverent, seemingly atheistic, and too closely tying together religious themes with carnal pleasure, lewdness, sex, money, drugs, and an overall scene of chaos and nihilism. Such sentiments are not surprising, considering that religion is often assumed to provide coherence, stability, and order.[6] The popular image of Jesus as the brown liberator and radical might be protected from censure in "Jesus Walks," but god, depicted as a totalitarian overseer, proxy for the law, and ruler in "No Church in the Wild" doesn't engender nor receive a welcomed embrace.

Throughout totalitarian "No Church in the Wild," god talk is metonymically used as a means of talking about prowess in the rap game while also pushing against institutional parameters and confines. This song was assumed to reflect an existential rejection of organized religion, a certain sort of anxiety fraught with concern about the quickly diminishing value of institutional religion in public life. This interpretation finds support in recent Pew surveys that suggest one in five Americans claim no religious affiliation and that young people—the demographic commonly referred to as the Millennial generation—are attending faith institutions far less than they once were. Those rushing to publically defend the song overwhelmingly suggested that the hook of "No Church in the Wild" reflects the divergent ways in which young people are finding "cathartic release and social transformation"[7] in music today—especially hip-hop. Those in this camp might agree with rapper KRS ONE's recent claim that hip-hop is sure to be a new religion on earth in the next 100 years.[8] This positionality operates through a replacement-like logic. If something like institutional religion is failing and faltering then something is sure to take its place. This type of thinking, which influences many social scientific surveys about the changing patterns of religion in public life and fuels the moral panic over hip-hop's religious claims, assumes that the ecology of social actors' lives are not multiplicative. That is, that one might participate in faith institutions out of personal belief, habit, familial inheritance, or social/cultural expectations, while finding cultural products and forms to be simultaneously similarly significant is seldom taken into account. This scenario highlights the reality and brevity of multiple conceptions of belonging.[9] What seems too difficult an idea for many to embrace is that "deviant" rap music might hold similar, if not more, symbolic value in the lives of young people than traditionally defined institutions of religion.

Beyond an institutional critique of religion, "No Church in the Wild" suggests something of the power and authority of god as a metaphor for the nation-state and those who reside under, or become victims of, this authority. Consider, for instance, philosophical questions raised throughout the song that seemingly use questions to and about god to function and figure as questions to and about society and the nation-state. Under ordinary circumstances, the day-to-day critical outbursts against society, the government, and so on, are encouraged and welcomed by many, and they would normally be celebrated as a lawful right in voicing one's concern in the well-being of the world and those that inhabit it. "Malign" talk of and comparisons involving god often invoke in adherents a protectionist stance, thus obscuring the multiple uses and functions of such terms in the data under study. Those who might want to protect the use of god in the song might be surprised to find that they would more likely embrace such views expressed had a more socially acceptable signifier, like "society," replaced the word "God."

"No Church in the Wild" makes a case for choosing carnal pleasure over domination by god, constricting laws, society, normativity, and institutions, which achieves effect through religious and philosophical language. In fact, one could argue that such interests are galvanized through one's adherence and devotion to any one of these things or spaces. In verse one, Jay Z likens the work of Jesus as a metaphorical carpenter building a kingdom and a following to Yeezy's laying of beats, building knowledge through art, and reminding his listeners that Hova's lyrical flow is "Holy Ghost," that is, life changing, transformational, and powerful. Here, both Jay Z and West are not so much making personal claims about religion, rather, they are using the weight and capital of religious language to say something about themselves as artists and the quality of their craft.

Their seemingly rebellious pleasure principle ("I live by you, desire") carried forth and through ideas of religion is advanced in verse two, where, West states that "the threesome" will *not* be controlled despite society's and institutions attempts to do so, because they're forming a new religion where there exists no idea of sin or depravity to judge the best and worst of society. Rather, the rule of this lyrical world constructed by West and Jay Z is "permission" and freedom among all humans, living outside the control of hegemonic regimes like god or the law. After all, the song proposes that the only practice that will be seen as a transgression, a felony, in this domain of pleasure and pain, is "deception." With "No apologies" and a disdain for "monogamy" tattooed and etched into this fleshly cosmology, listeners are told again that this is something that figures of authority, like pastors and teachers, don't preach and teach. In other words, churches, educational institutions, and the like function to help society mask the pain of the masses. As the song goes, the pain ain't cheap. No longer under the watchful eye of god and the state, ideas of religion become useful and clever ways of waxing philosophical about moralism and traditional social conventions that fail to respect the many ways of being and living, even when such practices run counter to what is deemed normative and acceptable.

Yeezus: One Can Be a Slave but not a God

In a cyclical-like fashion, West is put on, taken off, and put back on the hot seat of public scrutiny depending on just how far he lyrically challenges highly contested ideas. West's sixth solo album, which is named after a combinative play between his name and Jesus's, has engendered both praise, in terms of race, and fierce criticism, in terms of religion. Overwhelmingly, the masses have spoken, and they've seemed to conclude that West is better off ranting about race than likening himself to god. Such diametrically opposed opinions, that clearly serve to protect religion and "speak the truth" about the new realities of race, fail to realize that the same strategies and interests at work in West's dealing with race are also evident in his tactical use of religion.

June 18, 2013, was the day, the second coming of the savior, in the sonic form of *Yeezus*, an album that had everyone talking, criticizing, buzzing, praising, and even worshipping, arrived. Like the figure Jesus, Kanye is a master rhetorician, so one need not worry about his lyrics becoming flesh. He takes words, and twists and bends them into pliable strategies that, more often than not, work well for his market. He commands power and authority, not by virtue of *what* he claims, confesses, and professes, but, rather, by capitalizing on the prepackaged worth and value that society has already granted to particular words and ideas like "slave" and "god." Social theorist Bruce Lincoln reminds us that things such as authority are not entities unto themselves. Rather, they are effects that have to be authorized in particular ways across time and space.[10] So what was all the controversy about? Could it be that Kanye has tapped into, yet again, the logic of authority?

Already considered nearly blasphemous for naming his album after the figure of Jesus, West goes even farther by claiming to be god himself in "I Am a God." Here, West capitalizes on the weight of god-language in order to situate *himself* as the Most High in the rap game, letting the listening public know that like god, he too sits on a public throne and deserves similar respect. While this song caused a flurry of outrage in those wanting to protect their idea of god, others were interested in knowing what Kanye really believes. He packages his stardom in a god-complex and quickly reminds his listeners that he is a man of god, drawing another of those metaphysical lines in the sand between his material self and a higher power, meaning he falls below god in power and worth. But as far as the rap game goes, he considers himself the Most High. He also raps that his whole life is in the hands of god but quickly puts himself back on the throne as god; a word of caution for those who have yet to give Kanye the respect he thinks he deserves. Can we assume that such a distinction signals something about Kanye's own religious belief in an actual god? More importantly, does it matter one way or another?

Kanye's use of god is a lyrical interplay, where the concept of god is simply used as a stand-in for claims about the artist's own hubris and power. Despite claims and conspiracies about his religious commitments, here, Kanye is not trying to state his belief in god. Rather, he knows that god is an idea that easily translates something of power, authority, and omniscience. That is not to say that West doesn't actually believe in god. His claims to belief cannot be extracted based on his rhetorical use of god. Thus, the question over god's existence is, ironically, a matter of little to no consequence in a song like "I Am a God." Belief is not as important as what this idea of god can do for West. What matters most is that West is aware that this term carries a social and cultural weight, regardless whether this "thing" is, in fact, real or not. The significance of using god-language will have the intended effect whether god actually exists or not. With West, the question over his belief gives way to the question "What can this idea of god do for him?"

At a listening party held in NYC on June 10, 2013, West tackled the hype over his "blasphemous" album title head on, saying, "I wanna explain something about the title *Yeezus*, simply put, West was my slave name and Yeezus is my god name,"[11] and there you have it, new name, new identity, same old problems. Rather than searching for religious meaning here, perhaps it's more productive to consider what type of social work his claims to identity as slave and as god accomplish? The heated public conversation over "New Slaves" and "I am a God" suggests something about the push and pull between the two signifiers slave and god. I personally find both songs to be interesting and appreciate the crafty, witty, and different way in which West first presented the song "New Slaves" in particular. More than a rhetorician, he's a good illusionist, too, creating social magic by projecting his image on 66 buildings around the world to debut the much talked about song. Quite fitting for a god I'd say, appearing in different places, around the world, around the same time, pretty close to turning water into wine and walking on water. West is living up to his self-given name, *Yeezus*.

Despite the public's concern over blasphemy, West understands that music exists in a marketplace and the artist, like any other social actor, must cultivate strategies that work to shop the best product possible. At the listening party, he reminded his audience that, "We just wanted to make the best product possible..."[12] further stating, "I have a new strategy, it's called 'no strategy.' I have a plan to sell more music it's called 'make better music.'"[13]

This is not West's first go-round with god talk, calling himself Jesus, and playing with religion. West's work and style seem to keep us on our toes—waiting for an event—for something to actually happen. He is good at coloring outside of the lines, which theoretically creates new lines not different from the lines "originally" transgressed. Online articles, tweets, and Facebook posts laud "New Slaves" for being socially conscious and calling out the racism and capitalism of American society, in particular, the prison–industrial complex and the culpability of the Drug Enforcement Agency (DEA) and the Correctional Corporation of America (CCA) for targeting "niggas" specifically. Above all, this song places race on a pedestal with Kanye reminding the public that despite his social status, he still experiences "broke nigga racism" and "rich nigga racism." What's more, West lyrically time travels by referencing the widely cited protest song, "Strange Fruit (1937)," made famous by Billie Holiday which mourns and protests the practice of lynching in the segregated South. In and through this strategic maneuver, an appearance of no change over time in terms of race is portrayed effectively. West executes a powerful illusion of historical stasis and continuity of social ills, racialized in nature, so that his claim of "New Slaves" and his newly proclaimed status of being a slave will be accepted and honored. The public response to this song was affirmative and positive with overwhelming consensus of agreement with the many points made about the unchanging status of blacks in American society today. This type of historical illusion, pulling from the (unchanged) past, to make claims about an (un/changed) present largely goes unquestioned and serves to create a powerful effect in the public imagination, one that is not so easily achieved when talking about religion or god. After all, ideas like god have commonly been understood as static, timeless, and unchanging.

In question is not whether or not West makes an accurate assessment and portrayal of "new nigga racism" and "broke nigga racism" in the twenty-first century but rather, what kind of work does West's essentializing and romanticizing of the black condition seek to accomplish? What types of strategies of identification might be at work here? And does it suggest anything about the difficulty West experiences trying to be free from religion or god in a society where those concepts matter so much to so many?

On race, blackness in particular, Kanye is applauded for wielding his national platform in the service of calling out, and speaking to, racialized oppression, producing his authority through a synchronic appeal to history. After all, this is one of the ways an artist can earn a gold sticker for consciousness and maintain positive and prosocial attention, which is not a bad market to have on your side. In fact, some of the sexist and misogynistic aspects of "New Slaves," which would usually be the subject of severe criticism, go largely unnoticed in the face of racial certainty, consciousness, and awareness.

West might have scored some big points on race, but in terms of the other slippery signifiers he wittingly plays with like the title *Yeezus* and the song "I am a God," for some, he seems to have gone too far. West's presentation of synchronic blackness cuts against his diachronic manipulation of god. The greater public disdain has more to do with West's artistic ineffectiveness of synchronic history qua god. Kanye is still a slave because he's still black; but he's not a god because his personal "history" and life is too in flux. Consulting the netizen fans on this issue yields a plethora of positions. One tumblr site stated:

> Ever since his mom passed [*sic*]& he broke up with his finance before he dropped his 4th album, Kanye West has had an increasingly WARPED relationship with GOD. We've been saying that West comes off as a notorious egomaniac at times, but I think it's way beyond that. From his verse proclaiming that he's 'formed a new religion' & that 'love is cursed by monogamy' on "No Church In The Wild" to "I Am A God" on "Yeezus", Kanye for some reason writes from an idea that he's on equal footing with GOD or maybe he's examining how fame can fool people into thinking that they're 'gods' to the point of absurdity. Is he critical of a mentality that has celebrities 'demanding' that God bless their *menage-a-trois* along with their croissants on "I Am A God" or is he being literal?[14]

This type of moral policing is certainly not a new occurrence for, nor unique to, rap music. Many artists have experienced similar blasts of opposition over the years. I'm less interested in what West purports to mean both personally and confessionally through his use of and play with such religious ideas and symbols as much as I am interested in how the spinning of invisible threads of identity claims (whether racialized or religioned) serve the interests of the weaver.[15]

Might many of the same people who embraced West's claims to twenty-first-century new slave status now be turning their back on him in the face of *his heretical* claim to both *Yeezus* and god? Does West's play with god spark a crisis of faith on behalf some of his fans and listeners? This may be so—but his "controversial" stance is also a slick move, nothing more than a common strategy, that we scholars also make possible by our own uses of certain categories and terms like race and religion. In fact, the very protection we afford certain categories, and not others, is curious in and of itself and serves as a way to make private and personal what is, in fact, a social product up for debate and contestation. Do not the same rhetorical strategies and effects that allow West to be a "new slave" also allow him to be "a god?" In other words, is the category god utterly that unique, different, and distinct from the term slave? But categories are merely human constructs and not immutable. It occurs to me, that on *Yeezus*, West gets to be a modern-day apostle Paul—all things to all people. He can play the slave role and remain "on the ground" and "with the people" showing off his knowledge of history on the underside and also still retain his hubris and omnipotence by claiming god status.

But could he really be a savior or a slave? And if so, from what and for whom? Not only is Kanye's new material pushing the musical boundaries of rap forward, but his lyrics take us back, offering a stark reminder that no level of riches can put an end to racism. Kanye's lyrics achieve effectiveness through tapping into the weight of history, with prophetic zeal. In typical prophet-like fashion, his lyrical tomes are sure to be just as contradictory as other sacred texts. They are garbled with other social problems that only add to the difficulties of his prophecies. In terms of West's power-wielding abilities, his lyrical illusion went off without a hitch, and through it, he secures the right dose of oppression (e.g., "New Slaves") needed to "keep it real" and enough hectoring (e.g., "I am a God") to prove what sacred texts often suggest, that prophets and gods are rarely accepted in their own country.

In the end, Kanye's efforts and the public conversation surrounding them leaves a tension unresolved between "slave" and "god"— two terms, or claims to identity that do a great deal of heavy-lifting for West. On the one hand, producing enough authority to cultivate more positive effects for oneself, and on the other, producing so much authority that it turns on the producer and he ends up crucified by his own tactics on the Golgotha of public opinion. The nails through these two rhetorical "hands," of course, are the authority already held by the terms "slave" and "god," standing ready to make everyone a slave or a god if the right linguistic combination emerges. Kanye might have found part of that recipe.

What Does Kanye (Really) Believe?

The assumed theological incoherence and dizziness concerning the use of god in popular culture, rap music in particular, is quite reflective of the ordinary ways in which most people make use of religious grammar. Attempts to protect the image of god and safeguard religion in popular culture, or to ask what Kanye really believes, involve a methodological confusion that obscures our objects of study. That is, assuming religion to manifest in, and be reflective of, inner essences, intentions, intuition, consciousness, and "natures," all of which need to be somehow hermeneutically decoded by the analyst. The problem with such thinking is that it arrests the category of religion to something that is inward (personal and private) rather than outward (public and observable) thereby protecting whatever "it" is from external scrutiny thus rendering it incontestable (Kanye is wrong and blasphemous). This type of reasoning assumes there is a "thing" called religion (rather than dynamic processes that come to be understood as religion) and this "thing," sometimes called x, y, and z, can be intuitively analyzed from the inside out and assumed to be examined from the outside in.

It is for this reason that I am often flummoxed when asked in interviews to say more about what rappers mean and believe when they use words like "god." My answer that (a) "belief" is of no consequence in answering the question and that (b) uses of such language say nothing about belief itself usually draws unnerving silence. Many "believers" grow uneasy at the idea that god is in of itself a social construction. Many "nonbelievers" and "believers" dislike the idea that though the question of god's existence might matter to them on a personal level, such a "belief" has little bearing on what others believe or on the social circumstances "believers" or "nonbelievers" encounter each day, even if some of the beliefs held might suggest otherwise. Rather than focusing on what a group might believe based on what they say (which seems to be grounded in an erroneous perspective that we are always conscious of why we do what we do), perhaps an exploration of what uses of such language accomplish might better serve our curiosities in more productive ways.

Asking if god or belief exists in x, y, or z is like asking if race exists. Whether you believe your race to be real (to the extent that it matters) or not (as a socially constructed label) does not change the manner in which such ideas are used to accomplish a wide variety of social and cultural interests. So to ask if god exists in hip-hop is to ask if race exists in hip-hop. God is to the world what race is to culture and society. The use of god in society, as discussed here, says less about belief and more about what we can do with the weight and authority that certain words carry.

For hip-hop to be so grounded and centered on words, lyrics, and wordplay, then, the question of Kanye's god-complex and slave status answers itself.

Notes

*This essay is expanded and revised from previous commentaries written for *Culture on the Edge*, BET.com, and *Huffington Post*. These earlier writings can be found at: http://www.huffingtonpost.com/monica-r-miller-phd/no -church-in-the-wild-spirituality-between-beats-and-rhymes_b_1756187. html, http://edge.ua.edu/monica-miller/god-of-the-new-slaves/, http:// www.bet.com/news/national/2013/05/30/commentary-kanye-west-s -most-important-social-critique.html, and http://edge.ua.edu/monica-miller /no-culture-in-the-cockpit-please/

1. http://www.cnn.com/2013/06/20/showbiz/music/kanye-west -god-complex-yeezus
2. For an extended conversation on the manufacturing of the dis- tinction between these two terms, see William Arnal and Russell McCutcheon, *The Sacred Is the Profane* (Oxford: Oxford University Press, 2012).
3. See for example, Anthony B. Pinn, *Noise and Spirit: The Religious and Spiritual Sensibilities of Rap Music* (New York: New York University Press, 2003).
4. Monica R. Miller, *Religion and Hip Hop* (New York: Routledge, 2012).
5. See Jonathan Z. Smith, *Imagining Religion* (Chicago: University of Chicago Press, 1988).
6. See Peter Berger, *The Sacred Canopy* (Anchor, 1990) and Peter Berger and Thomas Luckmann, *The Social Construction of Reality* (Anchor, 1967).
7. http://www.huffingtonpost.com/monica-r-miller-phd/no-church -in-the-wild-spiritualitybetween-beats-and-rhymes_b_1756187.html

8. KRS-One, *The Gospel of Hip Hop* (New York: PowerHouse Books, 2009).
9. See Abby Day, *Believing in Belonging* (Oxford: Oxford University Press, 2011).
10. Bruce Lincoln, *Authority* (Chicago: University of Chicago Press, 1994), 10–11.
11. http://global.christianpost.com/news/kanye-west-reveals-meaning-of-yeezus-album-title
12. http://global.christianpost.com/news/kanye-west-reveals-meaning-of-yeezus-album-title
13. http://www.huffingtonpost.com/2013/06/11/kanye-listening-party-yeezus-track
14. http://radicalexposure.tumblr.com/post/53037846253/yeezus-for-sale
15. http://edge.ua.edu/craig-martin/imagining-identity/ (accessed October 11, 2013)

Chapter 12

Trimalchio from Chicago*: Flashing Lights and The Great Kanye in West Egg

A. D. Carson

There is an axiom that says all books are about other books. This proposition is supported by the fact that the archetypes found in the earliest of recorded literature continue to (re)appear in contemporary literature. Following the supposition that music lyrics, when read through a literary lens, also fall into the contemporary literature category, it is safe to posit that many of the archetypes of classical literature appear in contemporary music. Further, it can be assumed that there exist many songs, as there exist many poems (and other artworks in other forms), "about" classical literature, intentionally or otherwise, that can be used as a tool to make the canonized works more accessible to many students if we open our eyes to the existent possibilities. The popularity (and co-optation in many instances) of hip-hop culture in pop culture places rap music lyrics at the forefront of youthful preoccupation. The storied career of Kanye West places him in great company with moguls such as Jay-Z and Sean Combs not only as a hip-hop tastemaker, but also as a cultural icon with the ability to affect other areas of art and "everyday" living. West has been responsible, almost single-handedly, for cultural movements (progressions, even) in hip-hop and popular culture over the span of his career. Arguably one of the more controversial popular culture icons, Kanye West's life and career can provide interesting background and analysis for comparison (and contrasting) to one of literature's most famous characters, Jay Gatsby.[1]

As Gatsby's quest for Daisy represents the American Dream, so can Kanye West's quest (personal and professional) be similarly viewed. West's fascinating life story, highlighted by his debut album,

College Dropout, is phenomenal, and set his trajectory to the highest of heights, ultimately garnering 10 Grammy nominations, and winning the Best Rap Album Grammy for "Jesus Walks."

Jay Gatsby usually fascinates students even if they don't particularly enjoy or understand F. Scott Fitzgerald's novel. *The Great Gatsby* is probably one of my favorite works to teach because of the time period—the flourishing of the Arts, The Jazz Age, and The Harlem Renaissance—The Roaring Twenties. The Great Depression plays a part in my love of the era as well, but only to symbolize that all good things come to an end, so to speak, as did the run of Jay Gatsby (and those of his ilk). The version of *The Great Gatsby* taught at my high school, "The Authorized Text," has a preface written by Matthew J. Bruccoli (1992) that states, regarding *The Great Gatsby* being "the great American novel":

> If this phrase means anything, it means that the novel is the great work of fiction with defining American thematic qualities and that James Gatz/Jay Gatsby is the great American character. He believes in the American Dream of success ("the orgastic future"); he fulfills it; he confuses it with Daisy; he is betrayed by it. The appellation *great* as applied to Gatsby reverberates with irony. He is truly great by virtue of his capacity to commit himself to his aspirations. (xi)

I agree that Jay Gatsby has come to symbolize "the great American character" much more than I believe *The Great Gatsby* to be "the great American novel," but my arrival at this opinion of Gatsby has come slowly, unfolding as a great narrative itself, told by a narrator with a bit of distance from its central subject, yet close enough to be privy to details so intimate as to captivate a reader. Bruccoli (1992) refers to Nick Carraway as "the partially involved narrator" (xii). I would say such a storyteller narrates this tale.

Much as some people fall in love with the grand concepts of idealism and romanticism, fuelling their love for literature, I am simply in love with the hip-hop love story, which fuels my love for music. It's become an archetype of its own: A kid, somewhere in the world, hears something said in between a kick and a snare drum that evokes a visceral feeling and, at that moment, is struck by H.E.R.—Hip Hop in its Essence and Real, as described by Common Sense (1994). Every person who professes a love for hip-hop knows the moment, and can recall, in vivid detail, their first meeting, courtship, love affair, and heartbreak[s] due to the relationship. I compare the love for literature and music because one of my primary methods of teaching literature has been not only through my love for music, particularly rap lyrics, but also through ideas, expressions, themes, concepts, and characters in hip-hop culture. In *Book of Rhymes: The Poetics of Hip Hop*, Adam Bradley (2009) makes the case for Rap's literary merits:

> Between the street life and the good life is a broad expanse of human experience. Rap has its screenwriters, making Hollywood blockbusters in rhyme with sharp cuts, vivid characters, and intricate plotlines. It has its investigative reporters and conspiracy theorists, its biographers and memoirists, its True Crime authors and its mystery writers. It even has its comics and its sportswriters, its children's authors and its spiritualists. It is high concept and low brow; it has literary hacks and bona fide masters. It has all of these and more, extending an oral tradition as fundamental to human experience, as ancient and as essential, as most anything we have. (158)

Even before I had words to clarify this notion of rap as literature, much of my academic education had been informed by it. I would read a piece of literature and automatically make a connection to it somewhere in the realm of hip-hop culture. Bradley (2009) goes a step further to clarify, "To tell a familiar narrative in a new way is the motivating impulse behind a lot of rap storytelling" (159). As a reader of literature, I always found myself discovering the "familiar narrative" while listening to the "new way" it's being told through hip-hop. With *The Great Gatsby* being taught in high schools across the world, and the renewed interest in F. Scott Fitzgerald and his novel because of Baz Luhrmann's 2013 movie adaptation (arguably a Hollywood blockbuster), I've come to see, more and more, Jay Gatsby's life as a possible parallel to Kanye West's.[2]

I will venture to say that my students' interest in Kanye West is much like their interest in Jay Gatsby—even if they don't particularly enjoy or understand his musical or lyrical intentions, they are interested in him as a person, as a character in the world of pop culture. I will also state that Kanye West, as an artist has, at some point or another in his storied career, worn all of the writerly hats Adam Bradley describes. He has been the screenwriter (his 2010 song, "Runaway," became a short film collaboration with Hype Williams), the investigative reporter and conspiracy theorist (the 2005 song "Diamonds from Sierra Leone," among others), the biographer and memoirist (the 2007 song "Big Brother," a tribute to Jay-Z and his debut single, "Through the Wire," respectively), True Crime author and mystery author (the 2011 collaboration with Jay-Z, "Murder to Excellence" and the 2007 song, "Homecoming," respectively), comic (much of his lyrical content depends on witty, comedic elements) and sports-writer (the 2007 collaboration with Li'l Wayne, "Barry Bonds"), and his lyrical and musical content ranges from low brow to high brow, all of which can be argued to be very intentional on the part of the artist.

By way of analogy, this is where I begin my *The Great Gatsby* lessons with my high school students—with Kanye West. Not only Kanye, but also the world in which he operates that has heralded and hated him, admired and despised him, created and destroyed him. Of course, I would not just give the students Kanye and hip-hop/pop culture as a backdrop and set them loose. There's historical prece-dent for this comparison that the students should know about. Along with abundant information on the "Jazz Age," I present Langston Hughes's 1926 essay, "The Negro Artist and the Racial Mountain." Hughes writes of the plight of "Negro artists" creating in America in the 1920s—the Harlem Renaissance—and some artists' aspirations to create art that is, somehow, not representative of their race or cul-ture, for instance, "a poet—not a Negro poet" (1). This essay begins a discussion about the "responsibility" of artists regarding their lives and their art. I ask, "Can an artist simply be an artist without any consciousness of race and/or culture?" and "If so, are his message and meaning likely to be misinterpreted or misjudged because of the titles we, as students, teachers, appreciators, consumers and critics, place on the artist, whether it's African-American, female, young, old?"[3] This always leads to an interesting discussion, especially because of the correlation to the same questions being asked about current trends and artists in pop culture. Hughes (1926) sums up his perspective in the closing of his essay:

> We younger Negro artists who create now intend to express our indi-vidual dark-skinned selves without fear or shame. If white people are pleased we are glad. If they are not, it doesn't matter. We know we are beautiful. And ugly too. The tom-tom cries and the tom-tom laughs. If colored people are pleased we are glad. If they are not, their displea-sure doesn't matter either. We build our temples for tomorrow, strong as we know how, and we stand on top of the mountain, free within ourselves. (1)

Of course, this is only one of many perspectives on the obligation of artists, specifically "Negro" artists, but raises the question of "keep-ing it real," so to speak, and also makes for a perfect connection to the conversation about hip-hop culture, pop culture, and the responsibility of popular artists to be "good" representatives of what it means to be black in America. It opens up conversations about mainstream v. underground, the business of music (or art, in general)[4] and artistic integrity.

After a bit of conversation about the era in which the work was created, I like to discuss the author of the work, to see if the students can gain any valuable information about the work from the life of the person who created it. In his *Gatsby* introduction, Bruccoli (1992) recalls an F. Scott Fitzgerald quote from 1922, before *The Great Gatsby* was written, in which he declares, "I want to write something *new*—something extraordinary and beautiful and simple + intricately patterned" (vii). Similarly Kanye West, in an interview with the *New York Times*'s Jon Caramanica (2013), preceding the release of his album *Yeezus*, heralds it as a project on which Kanye strives for "aspirational minimalism," stating, "I want to break glass ceilings" (n.p.).[5] Mr. West's previous solo album is interestingly, in this context, titled *My Beautiful Dark Twisted Fantasy* (2010). No author, no artist, is so independent of his work that his craft, his brushstrokes, his personality, some degree of his being is not recognizable in the stories he tells. As Fitzgerald wrote Gatsby, Kanye writes *KANYE*. It is a well-known fact that much of what Fitzgerald wrote was inspired by people he'd known (or knew, as is the case with his wife Zelda, and the pages of her diary that inspired some of his stories). As much as they write about the worlds in which they live, both write about themselves. My comparison of Kanye West as a personality—a character—presented in his music and to the music and pop culture–consuming public to Jay Gatsby, therefore, also operates as a comparison of Kanye West as an author and architect to F. Scott Fitzgerald as well. Both men, to varying degrees of achievement, create great American success stories, just as Kanye West's life follows the archetype embodied by Fitzgerald's Jay Gatsby.

With the groundwork laid, the discussion of the archetypes can commence. It's at this point that I digress a bit, but only to help illustrate my greater point. I start, as one should, at the beginning of the novel.

"In my younger and more vulnerable years," begins the narrator in the opening lines of *The Great Gatsby*, "my father gave me some advice that I've been turning over in my mind ever since.

'Whenever you feel like criticizing any one,' he told me, 'just remember that all the people in this world haven't had the advantages that you've had.'"

In the version of the story I'm always the Nick Carraway character, reserving my judgment, allowing my audience—my students—to come to their own conclusions. I merely state the facts for them:

I met Kanye West in 1999. We both performed at a music festival at Columbia College in Chicago, and I had just killed what was one of the biggest shows of my short "professional" rap career. The year leading up to that show I had struggled. I had given up an academic scholarship, dropped out of college, lived in my car, and wrote songs I felt represented a struggle that needed to be shared with the masses.

I walked offstage, proud, through the crowd of aspiring rappers and R&B singers, and greeted him with a compliment, as I assumed many people had in the past (and I'm certain did in the future).

A simple, "That was dope." He returned the compliment.

I told him my name, and as he made a start to tell me who he was, I interjected, "Oh yeah, I know who you are. You did the tracks on the Infamous Syndicate album. Dope album."

I even quoted a few lines from "What You Do to Me" to prove I actually was a fan. I gave him a copy of my demo, and we exchanged information. There was a follow-up call the next day—he liked two tracks (there were 17 on the tape), and even offered production for an exceptionally reasonable price. I thanked him for the feedback and the offer of a businesslike relationship—I passed on the beats. I prided myself on the fact that I had relationships with producers who worked pro bono, because they liked the rhymes I wrote to their music, and I was the epitome of a struggling artist, so I didn't have the money, even if I wanted to purchase tracks. But I was on my way to stardom and figured our paths would cross again somewhere beyond the atmosphere. My assuredness was only secured by the fact that I had met him—one of my heroes—on an even playing field. We were doing the same thing. We performed on the same stage.

The next year I would release my album, do more shows, and eventually lose all of that optimistic ambition about my rap career. In that same year Kanye West would go on to become *KANYE WEST*, rapper/producer extraordinaire, hip-hop/pop culture icon. When his debut album, *The College Dropout*, dropped in 2004, I was fresh out of school, having finished my Bachelor's degree in English Education and Creative Writing. I was right back where I started, I thought, in those classrooms that helped shape my rap dreams, the same city that fueled those hip-hop ambitions. I became an English teacher because rap didn't work out. I don't think it was because I'm not skilled at it; I just don't think I could commit fully to the idea of venturing out so far with no guarantees and no backup plan.

I would continue to write and rap, releasing several music projects, a multimedia novel, and a collection of poetry, stories, and essays.[6] I would eventually come to understand that Mr. West and I were (and possibly still are) flipsides to the same coin. Hip-hop never stopped being my outlet, and I would argue having the experiences that led to my reentry to academia and my career as an educator made me more studious, more industrious, and more driven to "make it." I felt his debut album lampooned what I was doing, and felt it was not only a slight on me and people like me, but also a dangerous message to anyone who listened and thought it might be just *that* easy to become a celebrity overnight.

I've made it my duty to follow West's career, if for no other reason than to remain aware of how he attempts to move hip-hop culture forward, to see what possibly could have been. I am aware of the fact that his career and mine are different roads traveled from that fateful (for me) meeting in 1999. I am also aware of the fact that it has made all the difference in the world that the road he is traveling has informed mine, and in many ways, mine his. I set out to prove, despite his lampooning, a man could graduate from college, love hip-hop, produce, create, excel, and be fulfilled. I imagine that he has spent his career answering to fans like me, the ones who know about the Infamous Syndicate work and the Bad Boy work—the people who were (and still are) fans, and want to know what's next.

Not only do I continue writing verses and songs, I have found a bit of contentment in writing about hip-hop. In that way, I like to fancy myself Nick Carraway. Carraway moves from the Midwest to New York to learn the bond business; I wanted to learn the business of hip-hop. Nick meets Jay Gatsby, the epitome of the American Dream—successful, flashy, host of the best parties. In my imagination, Jay Gatsby is Kanye West. West has not been able to find peace in the limelight, rather, it seems the more attention he receives, the more he balks at the very idea of "fame"—it could be argued that Kanye West, much like F. Scott Fitzgerald's titular character, is somehow standing in a vast wilderness—perhaps pop culture—the darkness that is the current state of hip-hop (music and culture)—looking out over the ocean at the ever-elusive flashing lights. It's my job to narrate the story and try my best not to judge, simply state facts as I know them to be.

Interestingly enough, the Kanye comparison works in this archetypical fashion, and brings many parallels with it. Reality television has given Kim Kardashian a platform to flaunt the excesses of celebrity for the sake of celebrity. She is one of the highest earning reality television stars, and is involved in many business ventures as a result of her reality television fame—quite an ascension from being the daughter of O. J. Simpson's defense attorney and step-daughter of an American Olympic gold medalist. If Kanye is Gatsby, then one could easily make a very basic case for Kim Kardashian being Daisy Buchanan, the self-absorbed party girl/flapper from "old money" with whom Gatsby becomes enamored and who sets him on course to create a fantasy in which she can live and he can have her to himself, forever reliving those wonderful moments they shared in their youth; her (ex) husband, Kris Humphries, would perhaps be Tom Buchanan, Daisy's husband, who represents "old money" as well, and is a former athlete. Tom could very easily be paralleled to Reggie Bush as well, and perhaps more appropriately so since Kanye's former friend and collaborator, Consequence (2013), revealed (with Jen "The Pen" Bayer, the mother of his child), in a January 21, 2013, interview on New York's Power 105.1 Breakfast Club Show, that he'd facilitated meetings between Kim and Kanye while she was dating the NFL star (YouTube video[7]). Consequence, then, would understand Nick Carraway's discomfort when asked to do the very same for Gatsby and Daisy in chapter 4 of the novel, which he eventually does in chapter 5. This is a pivotal moment for Gatsby, because it seems it is the realization of his dream, to have Daisy. His life's work is complete because he has obtained what it is that he has worked so hard to get; whether it's genuinely the love of his life, or if she is a symbol of status, Gatsby has Daisy, and the charade, it seems, is over. He has proven himself, perhaps only to himself. Gatsby calls off his lavish parties, preoccupied with his new "life" with Daisy, and Nick, during a visit to the Buchanan home where Gatsby and Jordan Baker are also present, becomes acutely aware of Daisy's disinterest in her and Tom's young child. This is the point at which the reader comes to learn the defining aspects and true nature of all the principal characters in the novel. This is also the beginning of Gatsby's great fall. At this point, the comparison of Gatsby to Kanye becomes more the work of the student than anything, leaving room for contrast and speculation regarding Mr. West's ultimate fate or whether his life can be seen as wholly comparable to that of Gatsby. Nick ultimately becomes aware that the Buchanans are careless people who recklessly go through life doing whatever they please, only to retreat behind their money when anything goes awry. Whatever your opinion of the world and the people who occupy the world in which Kanye West lives, there exists a viable correlation, and if not, at least room for a meaningful discussion on the topic.

As previously stated, I find great interest in the hip-hop love story—
Hip Hop in its Essence and Real—and how this love sets many artists on the same course as Gatsby after he met Daisy in 1917. And,
like Gatsby with Daisy, the artist finds H.E.R. "excitingly desirable,"
perhaps because the meeting is "a colossal accident," but he still takes
"what he can get, ravenously and unscrupulously," and ultimately,
after having her finds that he has "committed himself to the following of a grail," feeling "married to her" (155–157). The artist finds
that he is in love with H.E.R. and will do most anything to have
H.E.R. the way that he had H.E.R. when they first met. Common is
disillusioned and despises that he sees H.E.R. commercialized, used,
and abused, and vows to "take her back" much as Gatsby aims to take
Daisy back from Tom. Whereas in Gatsby's case, "It excited him too
that many men had already loved Daisy—it increased her value in
his eyes," Common feels a bit different (156). Common is obviously
displeased with H.E.R. dalliances with other artists because he wants
H.E.R. all to himself.

Kanye West, on his 2008 album *Graduation*, pays homage to
Common's "I Used to Love H.E.R." with "Homecoming," an ode
to a "girl" he met when he was three years old named "Wendy." His
lyrics formulate a well-hidden conceit much like Common's, only to
reveal that instead of being a story about "Hip Hop," this is homage to "Chi-Town." Hip-hop, by connecting the past to the present,
creates for future artists a story that merits repeating, remixing, and
retelling. If the axiom is true, and all books are indeed about other
books, perhaps all songs are about other songs, or, more fittingly, all
lyrics are about other lyrics. And maybe, then, the journey of Kanye's
to reclaim a "lost love" has much less to do with Kim Kardashian as
an emblematic status symbol or a reminder of the promise of times
past like Daisy,[8] and more to do with Hip Hop in its Essence and
Real. And perhaps that "aspirational sparseness" that he is now test-
ing out is his telling us, as the passage in *The Great Gatsby* in which
Gatsby says to Nick, who cautions him not to get his hopes up about
Daisy because their past can't be repeated, "'Can't repeat the past?'
he cried incredulously. 'Why of course you can!'" (116). Kanye constantly speaks about his duty as an artist to aspire to purity. This, it
seems, is the true essence of art for him, and is perhaps what drives
him to not only be a fascinating cultural figure, but also solidifies his
comparison to Jay Gatsby—the reaching out toward the metaphorical green light at the end of the Buchanan's dock, the willingness to
risk all of his successes and accomplishments to push forward and to
push back, the need to say and do what he feels needs to be said and

done to maintain that purity, the essence of what he sees as H.E.R. In a *Rolling Stone* (2010) interview about *My Beautiful Dark Twisted Fantasy* he states:

> I forget the word, but there's [sic] people throughout history that [sic] their responsibility is to be conveyors of truth on to next generations. There's a word for that type of person. And I feel like I'm that type of person that [sic] has to carry on the truth and tell 'The Story' not 'His Story.' Tell the story, where it's like Raphael's painting Jesus' wife, knowing the pope would have his head but he died before the pope got the piece. But as a [sic] artist he said, "Yo, I need to express this or I'll die, I'll die inside. This is what I saw, this is what I want to paint as a [sic] artist." I feel like artists take their lives to serious or not serious enough. Where, you know, who would really put their life on the line for what they really, really believe in? Who would make a sacrifice? (Video Interview[9])

Kanye goes on in the interview to explain that he believes many of his contemporaries to be "scared," saying they "run away from popular culture," and because of this, he sees them as "falling short of the greatness of Rock 'n' Roll" (Video Interview[10]). From his humble, anonymous beginnings in the world of hip-hop, producing music he was barely credited for doing, to his production work on one of the defining albums in hip-hop history, Jay-Z's *Blueprint*, Kanye West has aspired to see hip-hop created and performed in its purest essence. In an interview about his debut album, *The College Dropout*, with *Associated Press* writer Nekesa Mumbi Moody (2004), West states that his hip-hop aspirations started early, first convincing his mother to loan him money to buy his first keyboard, believing so much in himself and his musical potential that he says, "I thought I was going to get signed back when I was 13 years old, and come out with a record and take Kris Kross out" (1).

That moment created by Kanye West in 2004, when he experienced H.E.R., the essence of hip-hop, and brought the world his view of what hip-hop could be—*The College Dropout*— created a moment he's been striving to recreate since, as Gatsby did all he could, throwing his lavish weekly parties and befriending her cousin Nick, to create the circumstance in which he could again have a chance encounter with Daisy. Feeling "married" in those moments to their respective dreams, both set on a course forward, by going backward, propelled toward an ideal future by a "perfect moment" from their pasts. Nick narrates to readers at the close of the novel, "Gatsby believed in the green light, the orgastic future that year by year recedes before us" (189). To Gatsby, the green light is a symbol of Daisy, of old money, perhaps of wealth in general, of simpler times, of happiness—all ideas associated with the American Dream. As Kanye West has written and recorded songs such as "All of the Lights," "Flashing Lights," and "Street Lights," on topics that could easily be aligned with the ideals of Life, Liberty, and the Pursuit of Happiness—"The Good Life," to use his own words, but also being sure to shine as much light on the "bad" as the "good," embracing Langston Hughes's challenge, "express[ing] [his] individual dark-skinned [self] without fear or shame," baring his soul for the sake of art—the dream of any artist (1). Gatsby's fate is sealed, as he is consumed by the world he creates and in which he participates. It's not the implied illegal activities in which he is rumored to be involved, but the fantasy he creates, of picking up from that moment they met and continuing his life with Daisy. Reporter Chris Campion (2011) asks Kanye if he feels as though the success of his debut album is because he "brought something different back to hip hop" (1). Kanye replies, "Well, I don't know how you can bring something different back. You can either bring something that's done back or else bring something different" (1). The brand of different created by Kanye with H.E.R. has been his aspiration since *The College Dropout*, to what levels of success he has achieved it is debatable. He has not met Gatsby's fate, though some fans and critics believe the "old" Kanye to be no more. To date, Kanye's is a happier tale than Gatsby's: he's both got his dream girl in Kim Kardashian and he's doing his dream job, receiving much critical acclaim for his latest musical contribution, *Yeezus*. He goes on to tell Campion, "I guess [I'm] bringing something different. Hip hop is fixated on fantasy" (1). Unlike Gatsby, Kanye's fantasy has worked out, and he has found a way to successfully live in it.

As for my part as the "partially involved narrator," I, as Nick, am "inclined to reserve all judgments" (5). Maybe, in the end, we will all come to see Kanye in the same light Nick saw Gatsby:

> ...who represented everything for which I have an unaffected scorn. If personality is an unbroken series of successful gestures, then there was something gorgeous about him, some heightened sensitivity to the promises of life, as if he were related to one of those machines that register earthquakes ten thousand miles away. This responsiveness had nothing to do with that flabby impressionability which is dignified under the name of the "creative temperament"—it was his extraordinary gift for hope, a romantic readiness such as I have never found in any other person and which it is not likely I shall ever find again (6).

Kanye may very well be hip-hop's Gatsby, representing everything I loathe about the culture while simultaneously embodying everything that is beautiful about it as well, because the recognition of those loathsome attributes are simply a reflection—a yin to a yang—of what *is* beautiful. Perhaps Kanye's life, as Gatsby's could likewise easily be described, is evolving into a beautiful, dark, twisted fantasy into which his sensitivity provides an outlook we consumers, mere outsiders peeking in at (or, through), only register through the binary of "genius" or "crazy" "Creative temperament" is what we tend to call it, because we have—even if he hasn't, and has no reason to—given up hope, and rather than recognize it as the extraordinary gift it is, we mistakenly overlook it in search of something else. We look for another angle: a controversy, a quarrel, a personality flaw, or something even less significant, when we could simply try to view Kanye as Nick saw Gatsby.

Eventually, we may come to say "No—Kanye turned out all right in the end; it was what preyed on Kanye, what foul dust floated in the wake of his dreams that temporarily closed out our interest in the abortive sorrows and short-winded elations of men." (7) And we will realize that he was "worth the whole damn bunch put together," Nick's words to Gatsby at the end of their last meeting, letting Gatsby know that Nick sees him for who he is: A great man who believes in his dream and is willing to sacrifice everything in his quest to reach it.

Notes

*Trimalchio is a character who is known for throwing lavish parties in the early Latin work of fiction, *The Satyricon*, by Gaius Petronius. Jay Gatsby is compared to Trimalchio early in chapter 7 of *The Great Gatsby*. *Trimalchio* and *Trimalchio in West Egg* were also proposed titles for *The Great Gatsby*.

1. Interestingly enough, the Rap Genius website has a F. Scott Fitzgerald page, rife with annotations about his seminal text, as it does with rap lyrics—a fitting place for students to gain perspective about a text and an author who embodied, at the very least, the spirit of hip-hop in both his most famous text and one of America's most beloved characters, who starts from the bottom, so to speak, and soars to great heights, only to be felled by the very ambition that precipitates his ascension to the ranks of greatness.

2. The film's trailer actually features music co-written and co-produced by Kanye West, particularly "No Church in the Wild," and the film features more music from West and Jay-Z's album, *Watch The Throne* (2012).

3. My follow-up questions to this are: "What about an artist who happens to be female in a male-dominated field?" and "What about

African-American artists in a predominantly white environment?" I also make sure to point out, through inquiry, "What happens when the artist wants to just be known for the art, but the consumers and critics continue to bring race and culture into the conversation? Can the artist be 'simply' an artist in this case?"

4. More directly, the idea that some ideas, images, and concepts are promoted simply because they will make more money, so regardless of an artist's intentions or desires, the art (product) will be marketed in the most effective method to move it from the shelves to consumers.

5. In the same interview, Kanye discusses learning from Dead Prez how to "make raps with a message sound cool" and how, because he was able to "slip past," he has "a responsibility at all times," which echoes Langston Hughes's sentiment in "The Negro Artist and the Racial Mountain."

6. *COLD* (2011), and *The City* (2012), respectively; Mayhaven Publishing, Inc.

7. HipHipWired.com Interview: January 21, 2013, http://hiphopwired.com/2013/01/21/consequence-jen-the-pen-slander-kanye-west-q-tip-love-hip-hop-cast-video/ (accessed June 29, 2013).

8. I don't mean to imply Kim is a "lost love," but that what it is that Kanye is chasing may not be her at all, and H.E.R.... something that he has actually always been in pursuit of.

9. *Rolling Stone* (Website) Video Interview. November 21, 2010, http://www.rollingstone.com/music/albumreviews/my-beautiful-dark-twisted-fantasy-20101109 (accessed July 1, 2013).

10. *Rolling Stone* (Website) Video Interview. November 21, 2010, http://www.rollingstone.com/music/albumreviews/my-beautiful-dark-twisted- (accessed July 1, 2013).

Chapter 13

Confidently (Non)cognizant of Neoliberalism: Kanye West and the Interruption of Taylor Swift

Nicholas D. Krebs

Born alongside neoliberalism during the late twentieth century, hip-hop exemplifies capitalist interactions involving stigmatized bodies and success. Kanye West's interruption of Taylor Swift at the 2009 MTV Video Music Awards (VMAs) reveals modern manifestations of privilege hidden behind the ease of consumption allocated by competition in a meritocratic free market system. Regardless of the race of the interrupter, outrage at the obvious rudeness would have resulted in societal castigation. Race came in to play because West's gesture broke a multitude of social conventions. Swift—the first country singer to win a Video Music Award—was interrupted by West, a musical laborer engaged in traditional forms of black critique. [1] West's actions, albeit rude, can be understood as a defensive reaction to covert and overt messages of racial privilege evidenced by the selection of Taylor Swift as the award recipient. Championing Beyoncé Knowles, West seized power over the cultural/musical productions under review and interjected a critically conscious discourse of resistance into the neoliberal cultural celebration at hand. Despite being lynched by society at large for his act, West's aspirations for equity and power were not crushed. [2] Cognizant of the rules of meritocracy and consumer culture, West continues to master the meritocratic merry-go-round with a pragmatic and relative form of humanism predicated on a simple premise: Neoliberalism is incongruent with democratic enfranchisement, and meritocracy is nothing more than a fantastic lie obscuring the oppressive social realities of the United States.

From Running This Town, to Running from This Town

Crafted by powerful whites in the 1980s as the next iteration of control, neoliberalism and meritocracy intended to reinforce class distinctions and white supremacy, rather than enable minorities to claim equal economic and cultural status through commercial victory. Sticking to the rules of the neoliberal system—using his raps as labor—Kanye West produces an exclusive manifesto of pride aimed at disturbing the dominant narrative. This is explicitly demonstrated by the fifth track off his 2011 collaboration with Jay-Z, a record aptly titled *Watch the Throne*. In "Gotta Have It," West (2011a) directly addresses the media lynching that followed his interruption of Taylor Swift as an assassination attempt against his character that also sought to enact a divorce upon his "money matrimony." Referencing a tendency to "hate ballers these days," West links his portrayal and treatment in the media to stereotypical societal tropes affecting black superstars such as LeBron James and Dorothy Dandridge. The media firestorm surrounding the success or demise of black superstars reveals a racially charged ethic reminiscent of the "bad nigger" syndrome originally posited by Frantz Fanon (1952) in *Black Skin, White Masks*, and discussed by Edward Bruce Bynum (1999) in *The African Unconscious*. Confidence and pride in trade-craft is at once a sign of disrespect toward capital and society at large. The schadenfreude experienced by many whites watching confident black men and women fail is highlighted in the obsessive attention garnered to Tiger Woods and Kanye West in their most recent debacles, not to mention the automatic assumption that Whitney Houston died of a drug-related death. Similar attention was not given to Tom Brady and his out-of-wedlock child, or Ben Roethlisberger and his multiple allegations/instances of rape.

In his investigation of the late twentieth century as a "revolutionary turning-point in the world's social and economic history," anthropologist David Harvey (2005) described how neoliberalism became the dominating sociopolitical and cultural force by revamping democratic and socialist societies alike around market-driven values:

Neoliberalism is in the first instance a theory of political economic practices that proposes that human well-being can best be advanced by liberating individual entrepreneurial freedoms and skills within an institutional framework characterized by strong private property rights, free markets, and free trade. The role of the state is to create and preserve an institutional framework appropriate to such practices...But beyond these tasks the state should not venture[3] (Harvey, 2005: 1–2).

Neoliberalism encroaches upon all manner of beliefs, instilling meritocracy as the primary conditioning agent, resulting in an invisible barrier to social parity for America's masses. Meritocracy is a method of social control rooted in the guise of greater freedom and prosperity for all. Harvey (2005) succinctly documents the resulting effects of neoliberalism: "Deregulation, privatization, and withdrawal of the state from many areas of social provision...neoliberalism has, in short, become hegemonic as a mode of discourse. It has pervasive effects on ways of thought to the point where it has become incorporated into the common-sense way many of us interpret, live in, and understand the world" (Harvey, 2005: 2–3). The idea of equality garnered by opportunity and market participation does not change the status quo; instead, it leaves minorities in a disadvantaged position. Pretending to extend full equality to nonwhite citizens in exchange for their labor and consumer power, whites are able to maintain their privileged position by continuing to occupy and protect the increasingly privatized spaces of production. Therein lay the roots of West's interruption of Taylor Swift. West mistook his labor power for full equality. Believing he was a full member of the producing bourgeois, West confidently stood up and interjected his opinion into the public forum of live television.

What was West's outburst really about? His public statements, apology to Swift, and resulting musical productions speak one story. The media and social lynching highlighting his arrogant use of the "race card" encompassed by Swift's response speak another. Swift, who is known for public revelations of artistic motivation, linked West and his outburst to her song "Innocent" when she performed at the 2010 MTV VMAs. Using the interruption as an introduction, Swift screened a clip from the prior year's show where she was infamously interrupted while accepting the VMA for Best Female Video of the Year. In the clip, West interrupts Swift and indirectly insults her by exclaiming that Beyoncé had "one of the best videos of all time."[4] West never directly attacks Swift; indeed, he begins by congratulating her and expressing his happiness for her win. However, while the audience shares in Swift's embarrassment, West inadvertently and publicly attacks Swift's socially constructed image. A pretty little white girl in a pearl-white sequin dress is upstaged by a confident black male. "Innocent," a track off Swift's 2010 album *Speak Now*, dismisses the issue outright and provides a politically correct escape route claiming colorblindness and post-racial existence. In "Innocent," Swift (2010) sings of memories of the easier times of childhood complete with "bed[s] to crawl into...and everybody believ[ing] in you." Perhaps

Swift enjoyed her "fire-fly catchin' days," as a privileged child such as herself had every reason too. A comparison between her childhood and West's upbringing, however, cannot fly. The offspring of a college professor and a Black Panther, West's intuitive capabilities and conscious awareness are a direct result of that union, and span his entire discography. Despite his economic and educationally privileged background, West did not, and does not, have everyone believing in him in the way Swift, a product of white privilege, suggests.

Believing he ran this town, West confidently interrupted Swift. Seduced by commercial success that enabled him to go wherever he pleased, West forgot a very important lesson. Neoliberal trade policies such as the North American Free Trade Agreement implemented in 1994 allow capital to move freely, but prevent bodies—especially nonwhite bodies—from doing likewise.[5] A confident black male secured by market success, West's entrepreneurial focus crystallized during the summer before the VMAs. On "Run This Town," a track off Jay-Z's 2009 album *The Blueprint 3*, West emphasizes the priority of his economic motives by reminding the audience he is in the business to reap rewards, not just "to push a fucking Rav 4."[6] Obsessed with success, West forgot he was himself the commodity, an artist in a commoditized industry, the capital so easily allowed to traverse neoliberal-controlled time and space. Ergo, the interruption worked in two ways: (1) it reinforced Kanye West's confident cognition of our neoliberal racist reality, and (2) revealed Taylor Swift's failure to recognize the theoretical post-racialism of meritocracy as a fantasy. Remaining innocently noncognizant of neoliberal control, Swift forgot that the color of West's skin still matters.

Reenlistment of the Selfless Preacher

West's interruption of Swift, an iconic young white female enshrined in the authority of sales, skin, and sex, tore away the post-racial veil to reveal a well-oiled machine hard at work. Publicly and directly insulting the dominant sociocultural system of white patriarchy that produced Swift, West crossed lines of labor and personhood that remain thin at best. Rather than coding his critique in the language of labor—his music—West stood up and interjected a stream of critical consciousness into the comfortable intellectual poverty established by the selection of Swift as the award's recipient. It is important here to remember that West's focus was on Beyoncé and her success as a black woman in an industry still hegemonically controlled by white men. Conflating his labor with his reality as a black male, Kanye West

confidently disrupted Taylor Swift's symbolic representation, consequently striking a tender nerve as he failed to participate in idolatry.

Following the interruption, West fled the country on fellow
MC Mos Def's recommendation, and sought refuge in Japan and
Italy before settling in Hawaii to record *My Beautiful Dark Twisted
Fantasy*.[7] In an interview with Ellen DeGeneres, West (2010) explained
the motivation behind his projects following the interruption: "I feel
like, in some ways like I'm a soldier of culture, and I realize that no
one wants that to be my job ... will I feel convicted about things that
really meant stuff to culture that constantly get denied for years and
years and years and years, I'm sorry, I will. I cannot lie about it in
order to sell records." This theme, which reverberates throughout
My Beautiful Dark Twisted Fantasy, manifests concretely in the third
track "Power" wherein West (2010b) describes his "superhero" theme
music as "screams from the haters" that "got a nice ring to it." West's
power comes from commercial success, the consumer limelight provides a double-edged sword; West can attempt to destroy certain stereotypes at the same time that he personifies others.

Speaking about the incident on Hot 97 radio (97.1 FM, New York),
West (Itzkoff, 2010) stresses publicly that the incident was bigger
than his commentary about George W. Bush's inadequate response to
Hurricane Katrina.[8] West further elaborates on the complexity of the
situation by noting the attached social responsibility as a successful
black artist:

> There's just so few black men make it that far. That's a responsibility,
> that's why so many fans of mine were upset because they're like: "Man,
> you've got a powerful situation where you can put your music out like
> that and do award shows and everything. You can't be so reckless with
> your opinion. Like, we can agree with you but you've got to play it in
> another type of way, because you can't throw away the opportunity."
> (Itzkoff, 2010)

The opportunity West references relates to the documentation of continued racial exploitation. By ensuring the voices of others are heard
through his, West aligns himself with the needs of his fan-base while
staying true to his roots. This frames the interruption as a selfless
act focused on the need to celebrate the impact of a successful artist
at the time of inception instead of posthumously. In West's opinion,
Beyoncé had one of the best music videos of all time and the world
needed to recognize that in the moment at hand.

Reporting on West's first comments following the incident for *OK!
Magazine*, Nicole Eggenberger (2010) focused on West's insistence

that "the incident wasn't about Taylor personally, and it definitely wasn't about race…Where I messed up is, at the end of the day, it's your show, Taylor. It's your show, MTV." This astonishing admission highlights West's labeling of the incident as selfless and focused on recognition of Beyoncé. West did not act on race because he knows that racism is alive and real. West simply mismanaged his social and cultural capital through his attempt to act with charity in support of a fellow artist he felt was robbed of adequate recognition. West also expressed this sentiment in the Hot 97 interview:

> It's not my show, but you've got to realize with Jordan—Jordan, Kobe, whoever—if you're that important in the game, you can make that much of a difference. At a certain point, they're going to say, we need instant replay clocks or we're going to scream. Jordan used to be able to scream at the refs, because he's Jordan. With us, when I see it happen, year after year after year—one of the things I really want to stress is it's not a black or a white thing, even though it usually falls like that. It's not. Because when Justin [Timberlake] lost to the Dixie Chicks, it affected me, because I give so much of everything I am to music, and this is our only Super Bowl. This is something that matters, the documentation. (Itzkoff, 2010)

The music industry and the sociocultural system at large still view West as a laboring black male, a body entrenched in physical and visceral signifiers primarily understood through the coincidentally ignored history of chattel slavery. West commented on the industry as if he ran the industry. By doing so, not only did he anger the dominant perspective, but he also demonstrated recognition of his commercial success and the cultural capital he controls.

Positioning himself in concert with a deep understanding of the stereotypes he embodies daily—his phenotype labeling him a monstrous beast to be gawked at—West (2010c) embraces the menacing moniker in "Monster," the sixth track off *My Beautiful Dark Twisted Fantasy*. Confidently claiming power over himself through his labor of rapping and producing, West awards himself a "triple-double, no assist" in the beginning of the verse for "doing the rap and the track."[9] West then describes the legacy of his economic prowess, establishing his ability to secure women and money, material possessions symbolic of power in a white patriarchal society.[10] Finishing the track, West (2010c) establishes control over his place and space by suggesting his very presence in the present is itself a gift for which the listener should be thankful. Claiming the façade of a monster as a contested space for strategic satire, West cracks pun after pun to discursively disarm the mass-media–controlled image surrounding his interruption of Swift. The penultimate joke, it seems, is on neoliberals, as their agenda commodified hip-hop, producing the right conditions for West and other artists to safely criticize the system while reaping profitable rewards. West's embodiment of every characteristic of the egotistic is a pun at the system for freely giving him his power. West openly thanks critics for pointing out his flaws, as they remind him of his success. Critics are the theme music for his superstardom, the cheerleading of haters who would not hate if he was not great.

Enlisting the vocal talents of Kid Cudi on "Gorgeous," the third track from his 2010 solo album *My Beautiful Dark Twisted Fantasy*, West (2010a) expresses the angst he felt post-interruption as he fled the country. Serving as the hook, Cudi croons a twofold tale of dialogic exchange between West and society at large that reminds the listener of the interruption and resulting aftermath. Secured by market success, West (2010a) claims the ability to rise above the social mayhem because he "chose a field where they couldn't sack me." In the second verse, West's discussion of religion, hip-hop, and soul music encapsulates his role as a modern-day preacher willing to take up the reins of his forebears in a tradition hallowed within the black community.[11] Constantly deferring to his consumer base, West establishes himself as a conscious commodity aware of the market, stuck in a liminal position between racial recognition and commercial success. Rounding out his bases in the third verse, West expresses his continued desire to never let white America live the interruption down by reminding the listener of the impossibility for West to be "black balled" since his phenotype spreads uniformly across his epidermis. The rampant masculine imagery and expressive egotism is a performance of the very things West knows will inflame his opponents and enlist his own: braggadocio, swagger, and critically conscious confidence that connects him to the lineage of linguistic resistance in the experiences of American black folk.

The Twenty-First-Century Schizoid Man

Without an appropriate foreground, epistemologies become nothing more than obfuscated lenses of ignorance and control. In neoliberal politics, control often comes in the form of synthesizing master narratives that censor all other perspectives. Master narratives enforce dominant ideas, limiting the voices of marginalized peoples and the issues they face. As a commodified industry in a consumer market governed by neoliberal values, the rap game is a contested battle ground.[12] Lyricism has always been a weapon of resistance used by MC's to express collective experience, similar to the field songs of slavery and singing the Blues. Like any other form of popular cultural resistance, the capitalist bourgeois managed to subvert the hip-hop narrative into a surplus producing package of transpositional control. Once hip-hop entered the mainstream as rap, it lost some, but not all, of its revolutionary potential due to subjective audience reception. While *My Beautiful Dark Twisted Fantasy, Watch the Throne,* and *Cruel Summer* maintain ties to neoliberalism in the quest for monetary success and continued power, West (2010d)—who self-identifies as a modern-day Socrates with "skin more chocolatey" in "See Me Now," the bonus track from *My Beautiful Dark Twisted Fantasy*— enlists multiple like-minded soldiers of culture, such as Jay-Z and Kid Cudi, to defend the diaspora and "kill the hypocrisy" that surrounds our aristocracy.

According to curriculum theorist Gloria Ladson-Billings (2005), "Critical Race Theory sees the official knowledge . . . of the school curriculum as a culturally specific artifact designed to maintain the current social order which 'erases' or 'sanitizes' people of color, women and anyone else who challenge the master script" (Ladson-Billings, 2005: 59). Neoliberal curricula reinforce the stigmas attached to certain social signifiers such as race, class, sexuality, and gender, by labeling them as losers of the meritocratic system. Hip-hop exemplifies the praxis and tenants of Critical Race Theory (CRT) in its attempt to combat all forms of oppression championed by neoliberalism. In the 2002 article "Counter-Storytelling as an Analytical Framework for Educational Research," Daniel Solórzano and Taylor Yosso described the tenants of CRT as "the intercentricity of race and racism with other forms of subordination, the challenge to dominant ideology, commitment to social justice, and the centrality of experiential knowledge" (132–133). With its counter-narrative chronicle of marginalized voices, hip-hop places race and oppression at the center of its discourse, challenging the dominant neoliberal ideology of white supremacy. Hip-hop contains methodological elements enabling labored civic spaces to amplify the voices of all marginalized experiences. Having played the consumer game and amassed commercial success, West (2012a, 2012) reflects on his own ascendance by asking two prominent and provocative questions: (1) "Can't a young nigga get money anymore?" and (2) "What makes you think an Illuminati would ever let some niggas in?"[13]

As the "21st century schizoid man," West (2010b, 2010a) explicitly exacerbates neoliberal control "treat[ing] the cash the way

the government treats AIDS," relinquishing his satisfaction until "all my niggas get it, get it?" One steady theme in West's music post-interruption has been a pathological—almost Janus-like—attachment to society. From labeling himself a monster on *My Beautiful Dark Twisted Fantasy* to his exclamation that he is the illest because he suffers from realness on *Watch the Throne*, West (2010c, 2011) has frequently blamed society for intoxicating him with its polluted racial stereotypes. On *Cruel Summer*, West (2012a) continues this theme in the track "Cold.1" where he accuses society of being infected with intolerance and in need of some medicine, specifically TheraFlu. TheraFlu, a brand of over-the-counter cough syrup produced by multinational pharmaceutical giant Novartis, is known to contain the psycho-hallucinogenic drug dextromethorphan (DXM) as a cough suppressant. At high doses, DXM causes dissociative psycho-hallucinogenic states.[14] West's commercial success has provided a platform enabling double-conscious dictation to his audience, suggesting the ingestion of a drug that would cause them to experience what he does every waking moment: a state where time is lost, and separation between mind and body occurs; the conscious struggle over one's authentic and aesthetic representation of racialized identity.

When West explained how race was not a factor behind his interruption of Taylor Swift, society at large continued to use race as an excuse for its vilification. The virtual lynching West received planted the seeds for his subsequent manifesto. Neoliberalism succeeded in the United States due to its market profitability: Racism still sells well. Neoliberalism's hegemony relies on claims of meritocratic uplift because theoretically and empirically it allows any individual to reach high levels of material success. Individual victories by minorities do not disturb the meritocratic myth; they reinforce the system by guaranteeing a competitive market of marginalized cultural collectives vying for second place. Our persistent investment in the neoliberal system requires no truncated rationale, but rather a straightforward admission of our addiction to an oppressive reality. The frequent opportunities for minority and marginalized cultures to seize worldwide attention is greater now than ever, providing spaces for insurgent resistance that can widen the fissures of global white supremacy currently rooted in the clutches of neoliberalism.

Neoliberal capitalism attempts to save one's soul through free-market access. West's experiences demonstrate that such a goal is, in effect, an empty promise. Historian David Roediger (2008) reveals why: "Looking at the world today we might better argue...that capital prefers varying degrees of freedom and bondage, and a full set of opportunities to exploit the differences in social position among workers" (Roediger, 2008: 71–72). Competition creates a demand that needs to be supplied. Maintaining profitability requires predict-able outcomes and sustainable growth. Humans are nothing more than necessary variables in business equations. Interrupting the busi-ness model deemed most worthy—a young, white, female country singer—West attacked capital directly. West's interruption of Swift revealed the socially constructed basis for capitalist exchanges in a post-racial United States posited by Roediger: "Race will vanish—but whiteness will persist." (Roediger, 2008: 214). West is far from white, something that Swift—blonde and wearing a pearl-sequin out-fit highlighting her whiteness—fully embodied when he made his interjection in favor of Beyoncé.

How can West possibly fulfill the role of a preacher uplifting his community if he simultaneously fulfills stereotypical roles to suc-cessfully market his commodified image of black labor? Philosopher Alison Bailey (2007) provides one distinct possibility through a loop-hole within the epistemic ignorance of the racial contract. Building on Charles Mills's *The Racial Contract* (1997), Bailey focuses on neoliber-alism's control over identities. The racial contract perpetuated by neo-liberalism not only creates assimilationist policies of whiteness, but also enables active spaces for minority collaboration in perpetuating white supremacy. Suggesting that ignorance can be used strategically to pro-vide individual and collective benefit, Alison Bailey defines "strategic ignorance" as "a way of expediently working with a dominant group's tendency to see wrongly. It is a form of knowing that uses dominant misconceptions as a basis for active creative responses to oppression" (Bailey, 2007: 88). Admitting that this can require direct pandering to racist stereotypes, Bailey suggests that strategic ignorance comes "at an enormous psychological cost...almost always involv[ing] some degree of dissemblance, or masking" (Bailey, 2007: 89). Following his interruption of Taylor Swift, Kanye West embraced society's super-imposed masks as both a monster and paranoid schizophrenic, fulfill-ing Bailey's criteria for strategic insurgency.

Literary critic Stephany Rose (2011) suggests that outside of the obvious "social, economic, and political benefits whites in the United States have due to the existence of race...what is left out of the conversation is the roles racialized minorities have played in the flourishing of whiteness" (Rose 2011: 117). According to Rose, the pejorative characteristics of hip-hop common to its commercial dis-course, namely, rampant materialism, continued sexism, and wearing of the master's wardrobe, are not unique characteristics of hip-hop culture; they are fundamental qualities of American culture. Because they are, it is unjust to merely single out the behavior of some within the hip-hop community as anomalies when the concern is complicated by one's interaction and existence inside a matrix shaped by principles of whiteness—capitalism, Protestantism, patriarchy, and heterosexism. However, one cannot be uncritical of such actualities within hip hop if the ultimate objective is the deconstruction of white supremacy and the development of truly libratory practices. We must address critical questions in order to foreground revolutionary objectives. How can and/or do hip hop artists speak against the structure of white supremacy while representing the structure and still be accountable to both community and institution within their labor system? And, how possible is it to destroy the master's house while living in it and utilizing the master's tools?[15] (Rose, 2011: 122)

For Rose, West's attachment and subsequent fascination with mastering the capitalist system is an inherent function of his black masculinity and subsequent critique. Perhaps West assumes his economic dominance will eventually allow him to rewrite the sociocultural contracts that dominate society? Unfortunately for West, Rose points out that "what is misconstrued by many blacks in guerrilla pursuit of full enfranchisement in American nationalism is the impossibility of the task because race and the master signifier of whiteness demands difference and exclusion" (Rose 2011: 124). Despite active awareness and constant cognition of our reified racial reality, neoliberalism has ensured the persistence of white supremacy and its nefarious forms of affirmative reaction.[16] As Rose notes, "Everything is alright: business as usual remains as racism, sexism, and elitism continues to keep the nation oppressed despite four decades of hip hop" (Rose, 2011: 126). Hip-hop, even under exposed epistemologies, double-conscious strategies, and paranoid delusions, remains a predictable market product controlled by the bourgeoisie. Not until the bourgeoisie reflects the demographics and interests of the legions of hip-hop fandom, will our desert of the real have any hope of blooming into an oasis of opportunity for all.

Summation

As human beings, our identities are fundamentally shaped by the social and cultural reference systems within which we exist. Reference systems constitute valuation differently, providing for a natural variety of preferential normalization. Neoliberalism is simply the latest iteration of a constantly remodeled mechanism of social control designed to produce racial privilege. Although neoliberalism offers a meritocratic strategy enabling minority and marginalized populations' personal uplift, it prevents anything contrary to white heteronormative masculinity from gaining collective traction. As soon as any cultural fad emerges, neoliberalism controls its commodification into a consumer product flaunted with ease by the elite, reducing revolutionary potential to another form of privileged access or stereotypical public performance.

Kanye West exemplifies capitalist interactions involving stigmatized bodies and success. Interrupting Taylor Swift at the 2009 MTV Video Music Awards, West revealed the modern iterations of our pathological post-racial state. Cognizant of meritocratic policies, West continues his attempt to navigate our consumer culture, blazing the trail for future generations. Favoring a pragmatic and relative view allows West to slip between value modes, maintaining aesthetic standards of racial authenticity and tolerant uplift. After repeated interruptions of the dominant narrative, West has seemingly dedicated himself to using his position of power and privilege to help uplift other aspiring artists he sees as pushing blacks forward. This does not prevent whiteness from affirmatively reacting to insurgent efforts in order to maintain cultural control. Majority of modes of production are still situated within the grasp of white supremacy. This hegemonic capitalistic bloc must be disturbed through market collaboration to introduce a new form of American equity based on true democratic practices of civic equality.

Notes

1. In her interview on ABC's *The View* (September 15, 2009) following the awards ceremony, the hostesses note that Taylor Swift was the first country artist to ever win a Video Music Award. http://www .iviewtube.com.
2. I am referring to the common media phenomenon where coverage predominantly rushes to a quick judgment, highlighting typical xenophobic racialized stereotypes such as "pulling the race card."
3. According to Harvey, neoliberals believe that "State interventions in markets (once created) must be kept to a bare minimum because, according to the theory, the state cannot possibly possess enough information to second-guess market signals (prices) and because powerful interest groups will inevitably distort and bias state interventions (particularly democracies) for their own benefit."
4. Quoting West verbatim. http://www.youtube.com.

5. See Stephanie Black's 2001 documentary film *Life + Debt* for a detailed look at so-called free trade agreements.

6. The *Blueprint 3* was released on September 8, 2009, five days before the Video Music Awards occurred. "Run This Town," had been released as a radio single surfing the airwaves since July 24, 2009. Also see the track "Hate," off the same album.

7. West describes the ordeal as a "bugged out situation" where Mos Def suggested he flee to escape the media mobs in an interview with Ellen DeGeneres. See West (2010).

8. West specifically said: "It's an amazing, compelling situation. The situation is bigger to me than the Bush moment. It's bigger than a lot of things."

9. West also states that he is "getting high on his own supply," in "Made in America," the eleventh track off his 2011 collaboration with Jay-Z, Watch the Throne.

10. Kanye's explicit use of gendered terms, homoerotic, and sexually misogynistic themes are too dense for full analysis in this paper. It is as equally possible that it is part of the performance, as that it is a character trait. I leave this to the reader and further researchers to discern.

11. Religious themes flow throughout Kanye's discography. His attachment to religion in recent works appears as a transcendent approach towards neoliberal capital reminiscent of Joel Osteen—pastor and televangelist of Lakewood Church in Houston, Texas—and other mainstream Christian mega-churches preaching a gospel of wealth and prosperity.

12. Coincidentally, a black–white binary exists between artists supporting Kanye or Taylor. With those supporting Kanye, a strong appeal to his ability to "tell the truth consistently" is mentioned. Eminem's support of Taylor focuses on his definition of her being "a little girl" who needs protection similar to his own daughters. See Langhorne (2010).

13. The Illuminati, according to conspiracy theories, is a group of ultra-rich capitalists who control society through manipulation. Some critics of Jay-Z and Kanye West suggest that subtle motifs, such as diamond-shaped hand-gestures at concerts, imply direct appeal to the Illuminati who have secured their commercial fame. Realistically, the Illuminati represent the controlling hegemony of white supremacy, and therefore remain completely antithetical to minority success.

14. See the Erowid vault: http://www.erowid.org/chemicals/dxm/.

15. Rose reflects on the hustler mentality that arose as a by-product of black critique's during the 1960s and 1970s. This "militant ruthless critique, coupled with limited job opportunities and an ever-present sense of patriarchal masculinity that required access to money and power, calcified sentiments of nihilism among many black men. It did not settle into an abdication of capitalism, but fortified even

greater desires to become major players within the dominant capitalist structure...As much as the hustler and hustler's mentality is a newer phenomenon in black communities, it is a much older practice in larger white American society. It particularly reflects a combined ethos of the capitalist economic structure and the mythos of the self-made man...born in the infancy of the independent U.S. republic and...a direct result of volatile masculinities constructed in a racialized and marketplace-driven society...the history of citizenship in the United States is built upon a history of race, gender, and class—one could not enjoy the fullness of citizenship unless one were white, male, and a property owner."

16. For a detailed discussion of reactant neoliberal cultural phenomena, see Carroll (2011).

Chapter 14

Kanye Omari West: Visions of Modernity

Dawn Boeck

Kanye West's album, *Yeezus* (2013), marks a divisive point within West's career because of its raw and minimalistic sound as well as its unapologetic and antagonistic message. Although West has pushed the boundaries within his previous artistic work and public life, his creation of *Yeezus* as well as his media-magnified life defiantly operates outside societal expectations and boundaries (Caramanica, 2013; Makarechi, 2013). Through his career as a producer, rapper, singer, director, writer, artist, designer, celebrity, and social critic, West has solidified his position as a facet of American culture. As a black male living in the twenty-first century, West additionally reflects the complex race relations that continue to exist. Following Gilroy (1993), West creates "routes/roots" through his artistic work that map his own relationship to modernity as he makes connections between the past and present to construct his individual and collective identity as a black male. West's artistic work utilizes his individual agency to create a critical message that envisions possibilities for societal transformation. The power of West's artistic work comes from his ability to unite aesthetic creations with the cognitive and pragmatic capabilities of his audience. Tyrangiel (2005) makes the point that "In music, West's juxtapositions make your head nod. In life, they can sometimes make it spin" (Tyrangiel, 2005: 35). West's innovation has continually set him apart from other hip-hop artists as he has continued to grow and push the boundaries throughout his career, utilizing postmodern artistic techniques such as renewed historicism, sampling, and pragmatism. West's position as a postmodern artist enables him to envision alternative models of modernity that seek to transform society through dialectical understanding. The progression of West's career,

as seen through three distinct artistic periods, exemplifies various
visions or models of modernity. In viewing West's career through the
lens of modernity, we are able to explore West's historical foundations, his processes of transition, and the future visions he continually
seeks to elucidate.

Modernity

Modernity, in its earliest conception, was a European concept that
excluded difference, most notably racial and ethnic difference.
Gilroy's (1993) concept of the black Atlantic offers an understanding
of the hybridity and double-consciousness experienced by individuals of the African diaspora as a "counterculture of modernity." More
contemporary understandings of modernity seek to include multiple
and interacting modernities, or visions of the future, that are founded
on inclusivity, a critical awareness of the past and a cognitive and
pragmatic preparation for the future. This conception of modernity
is founded in the ability of human agency to envision and participate in processes of social transformation (Delanty, 2004; Therborn,
2003). Stripped to its most basic definition, modernity is the capacity
for human awareness, imagination, and aspiration. Therborn (2003)
defines modernity as "a time conception looking forward to this
worldly future, open, novel, reachable or constructable, a conception
seeing the present as a possible preparation for a future, and the past
either as something to leave behind or as a heap of ruins, pieces of
which might be used for building a new future" (Therborn, 2003:
294). Defined as a "time conception," this view of modernity supports social change that is rooted in an awareness and understanding
of the past that envisions and prepares for the future. This view of
modernity also emphasizes the potential of human agency in both
imagining and constructing these future visions.
    Hip-hop is founded on an awareness of the past, the power of indi-
vidual autonomy, and the freedom to express one's own perspective to
inform and inspire others. Although an individual's agency to think
critically is powerful, the implications of this critical awareness can
extend beyond the individual to influence larger structures and systems of society in profound ways. Hip-hop offers the potential space
for artists to conceive, construct, and convey visions of modernity to
individuals, thereby creating the potential for transformative change
in the future. To account for the individualized nature and plural-
ity within these models of modernity, Delanty (2006) explores the
concept of the cosmopolitan imagination in connection to multiple

modernities, as they interact dialogically to transform social worlds. Delanty (2006) explains that while modernity can take a multitude of forms within society, "fundamental to it is the movement toward self-transformation, the belief that human agency can radically transform the present in the image of an imagined future" (Delanty, 2006: 38). In viewing West's career through the lens of modernity, we are able to explore West's historical foundations, his processes of transition, and the future visions he continually seeks to elucidate.

Models of Modernity: Engaging Past, Present, Future

Within his career, West has constructed multiple models of visions of modernity that challenge the past, engage the present, and envision a future. In each of these visions of modernity, West grapples with a critical awareness of his historical ancestry as a black male, a fatalistic understanding of his own lived reality as a commodity, and a genuine confidence in his capacity to be an agent for social change. West challenges the past in his work through historical examples of black exploitation and insurgency, including slavery and the exploitative systems that it perpetuates, the struggle for Civil Rights, the Black Power Movement, and the involvement of the US government in the purposeful subjugation of black communities. West engages the present by drawing parallels between these historical allusions and contemporary structures, such as consumerism and social mobility, but he also recognizes his own involvement in these structures. West imagines a future that is constructed through this critical awareness of the past and engagement with the present, a future that transcends the traditional and limiting perceptions of class, race, education, and consumption.

The experiences of West's upbringing play a vital role in the visions of modernity he has constructed throughout his career as he has continually drawn from his individual and collective past to create his work. Although his mother most heavily influenced his upbringing, West's identity has been shaped by the family lineage of both his mother, Donda (Williams) West, and his father, Ray West. Although there were differences in the childhood experiences of Donda and Ray, they were both raised with a critical awareness of their shared history as African Americans as well as a pride in their heritage that they passed on to their only son.[1] Ray West and Donda Williams married in 1973 and on June 8, 1977, Kanye Omari West[2] was born in Atlanta, Georgia. Following the divorce of his parents when he was three years old, Kanye spent the majority of his childhood with his mother in Chicago and spent summers with his father in Atlanta (Tyrangiel, 2005; D. West, 2004). As a college professor of English at Chicago State University and a single mother, Donda West worked hard to provide a comfortable upbringing for her son in the middle-class suburb of South Shore in Chicago (D. West, 2004). She empha-sized the importance of education to her son, nurtured his creative interests, and exposed him to different cultures through travel.[3] This access and exposure to education, creative expression, and varying cul-tures afforded West experiences historically denied to many African Americans. Ciccariello-Maher (2006) argues that West's "double-privilege of being raised middle-class and with the firm educational impetus of his mother" created in him a "double-consciousness" comparable to that of W. E. B. Du Bois's (1903) depiction of the concept in *Souls of Black Folk* (385). In experiencing both sides of the veil,[4] Ciccariello-Maher (2006) asserts that West is able to not only "rise above" or move between the sides of the veil, but also to chal-lenge the institutions and social structures that perpetuate the veil's existence. Throughout West's career, he has continually highlighted these institutions and structures as a means to deconstruct them and envision new possibilities for the future.

Artistic Periods

Now spanning over a decade, West's career spans multiple artistic periods. Each of these artistic periods include the artistic products that West creates as well as his lived reality as a commodity that is consumed and constructed by a media-obsessed society. The progression of West's work in each artistic period exemplifies various visions or models of modernity that, as a whole, seek to inspire individuals to educate and enlighten themselves, to think outside imposed social structures, and to enact change in their own lives and communities. Although a uni-fied vision of modernity is constructed over the span of West's career, each artistic period constructs its own vision of modernity.

Period One: Dropout Bear (2004–2007)

The first period of West's career is characterized by the critical themes and narrative techniques exemplified in his first three albums, *The College Dropout* (2004), *Late Registration* (2005), and *Graduation* (2007). These albums explore themes that are critical of historical foundations, social structures, and economic systems. In addition, these albums utilize narrative techniques, such as historical allusions and sampling, to make tangible connections between past, present, and future. West's first artistic period establishes his foundation as a hip-hop artist, musically, stylistically, and ideologically. The vision of modernity constructed within West's first artistic period offers a recognition of his individual and communal past as a black male subject, an awareness of the limitations of his individual agency, and a confidence in his ability to acquire and maintain his status as an influential artist.

The changes undergone by Dropout Bear, the mascot featured on the cover of each of West's first three albums, emphasize this shared vision of modernity while also reflecting the progression and development of West's career during his first artistic period. Making his debut on the cover of West's 2004 *The College Dropout*, Dropout Bear is portrayed as a mascot for college dropouts; dressed in jeans and a t-shirt, he is slouched on wooden bleachers, conveying an air of indifference. West's visual construction of this persona is grounded in the lived reality of many college dropouts (and students) in contemporary American society as they continue to grow more disillusioned with the empty promises of higher education. As a college dropout himself, West identifies with the persona of Dropout Bear and utilizes him to extend his message and vision of modernity in *The College Dropout* (2004), *Late Registration* (2005), and *Graduation* (2007). As West progressed and grew more influential as an artist, the visual portrayal of Dropout Bear similarly evolved. On *Late Registration*, Dropout Bear slips into the hallowed halls of an institution, wearing a private school jacket and standing defiantly against the formidable wooden doors—in spite of his status as a college dropout. In *Graduation*, Dropout Bear is launched into outer space, literally graduating himself and leaving behind worldly constructions, most explicitly institutions of higher education. The evolution of Dropout Bear, from a college dropout in a bear suit to a futuristic cartoon character,[5] emphasizes the continuity of West's vision of modernity within his first artistic period. Within this vision, West draws on a critical awareness of his past, offers his own perspective on the present, and constructs a vision of the future that seeks to expand beyond limiting social constraints. In challenging the value of social structures, West hopes to open up the possibility of social awareness and social transformation.

Transition One (2008–2009)

West's fourth album, *808s & Heartbreak* (2009), represents a transition between the first and second periods of his career. The synthesized sounds of the album as well as its themes of isolation and disillusionment separate it from West's first and second artistic movements. The album's creation and release coincide with a difficult time in West's personal life as he struggled with the death of his mother and the dissolution of personal and professional relationships. This transition period is visualized in *We Were Once a Fairytale* (2009), a short film written and directed by Spike Jonze[6]. The vision created within this period of transition in West's career reveals the inadequacy of wealth and celebrity in the face of tragedy and isolation.

Period Two: Constructing a Fantasy (2010–2011)

West's fifth album, *My Beautiful Dark Twisted Fantasy* (2010c), represents a rebirth of West's career following his self-imposed exile in 2009.[7] *My Beautiful Dark Twisted Fantasy* and West's 35-minute short film *Runaway* (2011) embody the second artistic period of West's career. The album explores themes of excess and celebrity while continuing an emphasis on West's own contradictory involvement in these structures. The film, written by Hype Williams and directed by West, constructs a visual representation of West's subjective fantasy, one that is fictional yet saturated in the reality of West's experiences and visions. The vision of modernity constructed within West's second artistic period continues a reliance on West's individual and communal history as a black male subject but draws more heavily on West's individual experiences as an artist and a commodity. The vision reflects contradictions within American society and envisions a future that embraces rather than represses difference. This vision of modernity also recognizes the constraints of West's ability to express himself through music and words alone, as he immerses himself in the medium of film to visually manifest his fantasy.

Period Three: Commander of Culture (2011–2013 and beyond)

West's third artistic period includes his collaborative ventures on *Watch the Throne* (2011) and *Cruel Summer* (2012) as well as his sixth solo album, *Yeezus* (2013). During this period, West has developed as a collaborative artist, sharpened his individual style and message, and expanded his influence as a powerful agent of social change. West's third artistic period is grounded in the power that West commands, not only as a producer, creator, and artist, but also as a commodity that is consumed and constructed by society. The vision constructed within this period is critical of society's continued dependence on value systems that maintain inequality and injustice within contemporary society. This vision additionally seeks to rearticulate the perceptions of the black community as well as their contributions to contemporary understandings of modernity.

Analysis of Artistic Periods

To understand each of West's artistic periods and their visions of modernity, the postmodern aesthetics West embodies through his artistic practice will be analyzed. Shusterman (2004) discusses the "aesthetics of rap, or 'hip hop,'" arguing these postmodern aesthetics challenge traditional notions of aesthetic, cognitive, and practical value within society (p. 459). In challenging these traditional notions, the artistic practice of hip-hop music and art enables individuals and communities to gain a critical awareness of history and their connections to it, acknowledge the limitations of their present circumstances, and envision future possibilities. In his own artistic work, West utilizes the postmodern artistic practices of renewed historicism, sampling, and pragmatism to construct his visions of modernity.

West's explicit connection to the past within his artistic work exists as the foundation for each of his visions of modernity. West utilizes the historical past "as a heap of ruins, pieces of which might be used for building a new future" (Therborn, 2003:294). Throughout his career, West has referenced elements of his individual and shared history to illuminate the contradictions within his present reality. Dyson (2004) discusses the significance of "renewed historicism" within hip-hop music and culture, arguing that it "permits young blacks to discern links between the past and their present circumstances, using the past as a fertile source of social reflection, cultural creation, and political resistance" (Dyson, 2004: 67). West has utilized this "renewed historicism" throughout his career to engage his audience with a critical awareness of their own realities. In doing so, West is able to utilize the past and present to inspire a future, or a vision of modernity, that is tangible through human agency and social transformation.

West also utilizes sampling to create literal and abstract connections between the past and present. Sampling enables the hip-hop artist to utilize elements of previous works to construct their own original work, with an explicit emphasis on the postmodern act of borrowing and recreation. Schloss (2004) asserts that it is the relationship created between these previously recorded sounds "that represents the producers' art, and it is this relationship that reveals the producers' aesthetic goals" (Schloss, 2004: 150). Therefore, understanding this relationship between the sample(s) used within a song contributes to understanding the overall theme, message, and purpose of the song as an aesthetic production. Sampling also builds a connection between artist and audience in its creation of a multilayered product. The artist pulls in outside musical texts that have their own emotions, associations, and memories and melds them with their own vision and purpose. West's experiences as a producer prior to his solo debut in 2004 enable him to recognize the historical, artistic, and rhetorical value of using samples within his own work as he appropriates them to create his own unique aesthetic products.

West infuses his artistic work with critical themes and opportunities for pragmatic action. The purpose of "knowledge rap" or "message rap" is to unite the aesthetic with the cognitive and practical through the exposure of realities and truths within society, most notably those that have been relegated to the periphery (Shusterman, 2004). In creating music that entertains, informs, and inspires, West is able to construct and deliver his visions of modernity to his audience and engage individuals in the pragmatic construction of an imagined future.

Period One: Dropout Bear

Within West's first artistic period (2004–2007), he explores critical themes and utilizes sampling to establish his identity as a hip-hop artist. Within this first period, West challenges romanticized notions of wealth and consumerism, questions traditional notions of power, and compares the discriminatory experiences of his ancestors to contemporary systems of oppression and exploitation. West additionally establishes himself as "a model for critical thinking," as he seeks to expose systems of oppression while also emphasizing his own involvement in these systems (Richardson, 2011). Through his use of sampling, renewed historicism, and a pragmatic approach, West is able to construct a vision of modernity in his first artistic period that seeks to entertain, inform, and inspire his audience.

Sampling Soul

One salient example of sampling within West's first artistic period is his 2004 song "Through the Wire." To create this song, West pairs a sped-up and auto-tuned version[8] of Chaka Khan's 1984 "Through the Fire" with the backbeat from OutKast's 1993 "Player's Ball." West's sampling in "Through the Wire" manipulates elements from two songs with distinctive, even disparate, sounds to create his own unique product, both stylistically and lyrically. West's lyrics in the song focus on his recovery following a near-fatal collision in his car on October 23, 2002, in Los Angeles and emphasize his determination to overcome this challenge.[9] He plays on the title of the sample track "Through the Fire" by alluding to his injuries in his own title, "Through the Wire." The chorus of Chaka Khan's original song, "Through the fire, to the limit, to the wall / For a chance to be with you, I'd gladly risk it all," articulate the limits she is willing to overcome for the sake of loving someone. West builds on the themes of self-sacrifice that are explored in the original song to emphasize his own determination to overcome his physical limitations to reach his audience through his words and music. In "Through the Wire," West introduces himself and his purpose as a hip-hop artist through a depiction of his own experiences.

West sets himself apart from mainstream hip-hop, while associating himself with the historical African American art form of spoken word as a means to emphasize his authenticity and agency as a hip-hop artist. West's negotiation of his artistic persona through his artistic work reflects the complex negotiations of double consciousness that both constrict and construct his subjectivity as an artist and a social critic.

Coping with Materialism

West's 2004 song "All Falls Down" offers another example of his use of sampling as well as his use of renewed historicism within his first artistic period. West samples the voice of Syleena Johnson performing[10] the hook from Lauryn Hill's 2002 "Mystery of Iniquity." West's use of Hill's words also acts as a sampling of her female perspective and unique artistic persona, as Lauryn Hill represents a powerful female force within hip-hop culture and the black community.[11] Hill's 2002 "Mystery of Inequity" is a scathing and soulful critique of the US legal and political systems, exposing characteristics of manipulation and deceit beneath the façade of power. Hill also exposes the empty and constructed nature of the "American dream" and directly confronts inequality within access to higher education as well as the divisive social structures it maintains, a thematic connection to West's criticism of the education system in "All Falls Down." The hook of "Mystery of Iniquity" emphasizes the constructed nature and assured collapse of these man-made systems.

In sampling Hill's revelatory lyrics in his own song, West alludes to the critical themes expressed by Hill and emphasizes the inevitable collapse of these constructed systems through the creation of his own unique artistic product. West's song explores themes of materialism and racism through the experiences of a young black female and the subjective and self-critical lens of his own experiences. In narrating the experiences of a "single black female addicted to retail," West challenges the assumption that a college degree equates to success and social mobility. In criticizing his own involvement as a consumer obsessed with authenticating his wealth and success through material acquisition, West acknowledges the alluring power of these societal values. His use of the pronouns "they" and "us" throughout the song address the black community and their participation in systems of consumption that perpetuate divisions of inequality within society.

West's exposure of these economic structures and systems is emphasized through their connection to historical examples of inequality and subjugation. West's explicit comparison between contemporary consumption with the era of Reconstruction emphasizes the pervasiveness of oppressive systems within American culture and the inadequacy of efforts to overcome racism and inequality in the twenty-first century. West's play on the word "coupe/coop" connotes both a two-door car as well as a cage, and denotes the constraint experienced by black subjects attempting to gain equality through the pursuit of material gain. Drawing on elements of renewed historicism, West seeks to challenge romanticized notions of wealth and consumption within American society by exposing the exclusionary reality of these structures.

Creating Truth

In his 2005 song "Crack Music," West continues his use of renewed historicism to make connections between past and present and emphasizes the pragmatic elements of his message and visions of modernity. In "Crack Music," West takes on the exploitative systems created and perpetuated by the US government's "war" on drugs. Ciccariello-Maher (2009) emphasizes the significance of this concept within the black community, "as it effectively binds together counterinsurgency and pacification of radical thoughts, the economic and social destruction of communities and of course, the booming prison-industrial complex, a monster that feeds exceedingly heavily on Black bodies" (Ciccariello-Maher, 2009: 394). West builds on these historical foundations of institutionalized racism and his words highlight the fact that hip-hop music is both a product of, and coping mechanism for, the unequal systems that are perpetuated by the drug trade. The song draws explicit parallels between the manufacture and consumption of crack and the creation and consumption of hip-hop, or "crack music." In both instances, black subjects are exploited by systems controlled by privileged whites. In making these comparisons, West unites the aesthetic production of "Crack Music" with the practical reality of inequality, corruption, and injustice within American society. The song requires the listener to acknowledge the powerful assertions being made and demands active and critical thinking that has the potential to extend beyond simple entertainment.

Exposing Systems

West's 2005 collaboration with Jay Z on "Diamonds from Sierra Leone (Remix)" extends West's recognition of historical and contemporary systems of oppression within the United States to the global and interconnected system of blood diamonds.[12] West samples the theme song from the 1971 James Bond film, *Diamonds Are Forever.* While the sultry sample of Shirley Bassey lauds the perfection and permanence of diamonds, West's message unveils the subjugation and violence involved in the global diamond trade. West alludes to the conflict in Sierra Leone and connects it to the consumer culture of American society, thereby emphasizing the shared inequality of these systems and their global connection to the black diaspora[13] (Dyson, 2007). West describes the atrocities associated with the mining and trade of blood diamonds and emphasizes how these horrendous acts of violence are connected to American consumer culture.

The parallel West makes in these words, between drugs, money, and diamonds, highlights the interconnected systems of inequality experienced by black subjects around the world. West's use of "we" emphasizes this parallel through his own participation in the acquisition of diamonds as well as his identification with the black community that values these symbols of success. The message of "Diamonds from Sierra Leone (Remix)" seeks not only to entertain or even inform, but also to inspire critical self-reflection and practical action on a significant contemporary issue. In creating this song and delivering his message, West unites his aesthetic production with pragmatic reflection and application by his audience.

Viewed together as an artistic period, the first three albums represent West's foundation and identity as a hip-hop artist through his use of renewed historicism, sampling, and pragmatism. Within this period, West constructs a vision of modernity that offers recognition of his history as a black male subject, a critical awareness of his individual agency, and a confidence in his influence as a hip-hop artist and social critic.

Intermission

Following the success of West's first artistic period, West was confronted by the untimely death of his mother and mentor, Donda West, in November 2007. This devastating loss forced him to recognize the limitations of success and wealth in the face of mortality. West states, "After my mother passed, I didn't want to deal with the reality that that had happened. I was just a shell of a man. I was in a position where I was bound to crack" (West, 2010b). Out of his loss and pain, West created his fourth album, *808s & Heartbreak* (2009), which represents a transition between periods one and two of his career. The album signals a departure for West on a personal and artistic level, as it explores themes of loss and isolation, emphasizes his disillusionment with the social constructs of fame and celebrity, and relies on a synthesized and distorted manipulation of his voice.[14]

This period of transition within West's career (2008–2009) is visually portrayed in a short film directed and written by Spike Jonze, titled *We Were Once a Fairyale* (2009). The film features West's song "See You in My Nightmares" and utilizes West's persona as the lead role and thematic focus. In spite of West's acting in the film, the film reflects the dominant themes of chaos and isolation within West's life during this period of transition. The final scene of the film finds West in a basement-level bathroom as he violently vomits rose petals into a sink. Finding a bowie knife on the bathroom floor, West gouges the blade into his gut to release a torrential flow of rose petals. He then reaches deep into himself to remove a small, demon-like creature, which he severs from himself. West pulls a miniature blade from the sheath of the bowie knife, hands it to the demon, and nods with a look of nostalgia as the demon kills itself. The scene and the film end with the image of West staring at the dead demon lying on the counter. The film offers a bizarre yet revealing representation of West as it symbolizes the confrontation and symbolic eradication of his inner demons: materialism, fame, and even his own pain. West's collaboration with Jonze to create such an emotionally charged film mirroring his own experiences demonstrates the period of transition that West was experiencing between the first and second periods of his career.

Period Two: Constructing a Fantasy

The creation of West's fifth album, *My Beautiful Dark Twisted Fantasy* (2010c), and the short film he directed titled *Runaway* (2011) embody the entirety of West's second artistic period (2010–2011) through their construction of a second vision of modernity. The second artistic period of West's career grew out of a transitional period, which offered him the opportunity to gain freedom from the public that enslaved him, explore his creativity, and reflect on his own identity and purpose. As a whole, *My Beautiful Dark Twisted Fantasy* (2010c) and *Runaway* (2011) are products of West's self-reflexivity and growth as an artist. As a celebrity and commodity in American and global cultures, West's artistic platform has grown since his debut solo album in 2004. Following the "media massacre" that engulfed West in 2009 following his comments to Taylor Swift, he was forced to look critically at his artistic platform and purpose (West, 2010b). Although West builds on the foundation he constructed in his first four albums, he also uses this foundation to engage with new possibilities that mirror his present reality. The second artistic period within West's career represents his most overt vision of modernity because of its emphasis on narrative through the subjective and temporal lens of fantasy. The vision of modernity that is constructed in West's second artistic period offers new possibilities for societal transformation through his construction of new symbols and values based on inclusivity and dialectical understanding. This vision is visually manifested in West's 35-minute short film, *Runaway* (2011).

Runaway (2011) represents an alternative perspective on the traditional narrative or myth of American history. *Runaway* artfully combines nine songs from *My Beautiful Dark Twisted Fantasy* (2010c) to depict the story of a phoenix-woman fallen to earth, who is subsequently judged and excluded for her otherness. The film begins and ends with samples that emphasize the vision of modernity West is constructing within *Runaway*.[15] The prologue is narrated by the sampled voice of Nicki Minaj and addresses the audience in the second person, deliberately engaging the audience with an alternative perspective. The narrator's words emphasize the fictitious nature of the "story" we think we know—a national narrative or myth that contributes to contemporary understandings of American society. The narrator is critical of this unchallenged representation of history, pronouncing that this accepted narrative has been "watered down" and "made up" into a "twisted fiction." By directly addressing the audience and exposing the constructed nature of this "story," the narrator creates the potential for critical engagement.

The epilogue of the film offers an extension of the prologue through the sampled words of Gil Scott-Heron's 1970 "Comment No. 1." The original recording of Scott-Heron's spoken word piece is set to a drumbeat and was delivered in response to the oppressive conditions he was observing in Harlem in 1970. West's sample of Scott-Heron's piece is a pared-down version of the original; however, Scott-Heron's challenge of the "American dream" remains clear. In sampling the spoken word of Gil Scott-Heron, West pays tribute to the black artists, social critics, and activists who have come before him, utilizing renewed historicism to connect contemporary audiences to the historical legacy of Gil Scott-Heron. Additionally, the message and critical themes expressed by Scott-Heron prevail in twenty-first-century American society.[16] In concluding the film with the words of Scott-Heron, West delivers the message that black individuals and communities continue to experience misrepresentation, inequality, and exclusion within American society.

The experiences of the phoenix, played by supermodel Selita Ebanks, embody West's message in *Runaway*, as she is symbolic of difference within a community that values conformity. The visual representation and musical scores chosen for the formal dinner scene create a distillation of West's message in *Runaway*. The scene opens on a long, white-clothed table placed in the center of a whitewashed hangar. The guests at the table are representative of a unified and homogeneous group, as they are black individuals dressed in outfits of varying white and cream colors and accented with gold jewelry. In contrast to the diners, the servants are white, dressed in matching white gowns with bare feet, and standing silently on the periphery. Discussing his creation of *Runaway*, West posits, "People will think these ideas are racially charged—they're not—they're completely based off color palette" (West, 2010a). In creating this dinner scene, West asks his audience to look beyond the color of the diners and servants and their outer appearance to focus on what is happening between these people as individuals. The conversation between Griffin[17] and another man during the formal dinner scene embodies the experiences of the phoenix as well as West's overall message in the film. The man tells Griffin, "Your girlfriend is really beautiful," to which Griffin proudly replies, "Thank you." The man then asks, "Do you know she's a bird?" to which he responds, pained, "Naw, I never noticed that." The man then tells Griffin, "I mean, like, leave the monkey in the zoo." The brief conversation is representative of the attitude that exists at the root of exclusionary systems within society: conform or be constrained.

Through the creation of *My Beautiful Dark Twisted Fantasy* and *Runaway*, West constructs his second vision of modernity. West explains that his goal in creating *Runaway* was to challenge the accepted cultural symbols of value within contemporary society and "open up the gates for people to just think" (West, 2010a). In "opening up the gates" of thought for his audience, West is constructing a vision of modernity that reflects the larger contradictions within American society. This vision goes beyond criticism to engage with the present to envision a future society that thrives on difference rather than represses it.

Period Three: Commander of Culture

The start of West's third artistic period is marked by his full-length collaborative album with Jay Z titled *Watch the Throne* (2011), an album that celebrates themes of excess and power while also seeking to redefine perceptions of the black community through the upwardly mobile concept of "black excellence." The third artistic period of West's career also includes his collaboration on *Cruel Summer* (2012), an album created by members of West's record label, G.O.O.D. Music,[18] and his sixth solo album, *Yeezus* (2013). Within this artistic period, West continues to utilize the postmodern artistic practices of sampling, renewed historicism, and pragmatism to construct his work. Although each of these albums is distinct in its sound and message, each contributes to the vision of modernity West constructs within his third artistic period. This vision is critical of societal structures while also rearticulating perceptions of the black community and their contributions to contemporary understandings of modernity.

Redefining Black Excellence

West's longtime collaborative partnership with Jay Z culminated in their shared full-length album *Watch the Throne* (2011). Both West and Jay Z have attained a level of wealth and influence that far exceeds the majority of listeners they aim to reach. This disconnection between creator(s) and audience is discussed by Rakim, "the conscience of rap," who is concerned by the "luxury rap" being promoted in albums such as *Watch the Throne* (Samuels, 2012). Rakim asserts, "It's making the listener a little envious of what's going on, and it's almost demeaning" (Samuels, 2012). Although the album does emphasize these themes of excess and power, West and Jay Z acknowledge issues of racism, inequality, and division within American society. The song "Murder to Excellence" makes connections between black on black crime and the potential for redefining black identity to create a more unified and powerful black community. The song "Made in America" establishes West and Jay Z as an extension of the Civil Rights era and envisions the future society and legacy future generations will inherit.

In 2012, West continued his collaborative work with members of his record label, G.O.O.D. Music, with *Cruel Summer* (2012), an album that received lackluster reviews (Golianopoulos, 2012; Greene,

2012; Weiner, 2012). In addition to the album, West also envisioned, wrote, directed, and produced a short film of the same title. To create the 30-minute film, West utilized the "Seven Screen Experience" in his creation and delivery through the use of multiple camera angles and projection screens[19] (Isenberg, 2012). The collaborative ventures at the start of West's third artistic period allowed him to expand his realm of influence and sharpen his individual style and message.

Yeezus Walks

Utilizing the freedom he has gained through his successful career, West utilizes his sixth solo album, *Yeezus* (2013), to speak back to the societal systems that seek to control, construct, and consume him. Although his previous albums challenged social structures, West's work on *Yeezus* operates outside these constraints to construct a searing criticism of contemporary society. In a discussion of West's performance on *Saturday Night Live*, Kelley (2013) observes:

> There are ideas in "New Slaves" and "Black Skinheads' that are echoed in the editorial pages of *The New York Times*, but Kanye's songs give them volume and heart. They are a reminder of what music can do—and the isolation artists feel when they say things we don't want to hear.

As West continues in his third artistic period, he is no longer concerned about fulfilling people's expectations of him; he is only determined to express his perspective of the truth. In an interview discussing the upcoming release his new album, West states, "I don't want to be inside anymore. Like, I uninvited myself" (Caramanica, 2013). The artistic platform that West now inhabits allows him the freedom to express his vision of modernity, but it also alienates him from the public and magnifies his continued involvement in societal structures that perpetuate inequality. West's 2013 song "New Slaves" featuring Frank Ocean draws on renewed historicism and pragmatism to deliver the most aggressive and direct message on *Yeezus*. In titling the song "New Slaves," West makes the statement that contemporary systems of material consumption and incarceration are the new form of slavery. The song is built around a minimal beat, which emphasizes West's voice and the song's ominous tone. West begins the song with a connection to the historical experiences of his family and, by extension, examples of slavery and institutionalized racism within American history. He connects this renewed historicism to contemporary systems of material consumption to emphasize how black individuals continue to experience enslavement. West's words illustrate the spectrum of enslavement and highlight the parallels between both acts of discrimination toward black individuals and challenge the discriminatory voices that perpetuate these beliefs. He further emphasizes his message in "New Slaves" through the pragmatic connection he draws between the DEA (Drug Enforcement Agency) and the CCA (Corrections Corporation of America). West's words call attention to the profits made by corporations (individuals) from the incarceration of black individuals, a message that demands critical reflection. Continuing with the racially charged message of "New Slaves," West's 2013 song "Black Skinhead" exposes the racial divide that continues to permeate American society. The song is built on a looped sample of Marilyn Manson's 1996 song "The Beautiful People," which creates a tone of urgency and anger within the song and builds on the controversial reputation of Manson's persona. West's play on the title, "Black Skinhead," emphasizes his antiestablishment attitude as it reverses the white supremacist attitudes traditionally associated with the term "skinhead." Instead, West is a black man, rapping and screaming into a microphone—spewing *his* perspective unapologetically. West's song acknowledges current social issues connected to racism, most notably his own public persona as a black man perceived as "King Kong[20]" and the comparison he draws between the violence in Iraq and the violence in Chicago with the phrase "Chiraq." In addressing these significant issues within American society, West continues his emphasis on the pragmatic within his music and seeks to inspire critical reflection from his audience.

Societal Implications for West's Modernity

As a self-proclaimed "soldier of culture," Kanye West will continue to create his work without fear (Andersson, 2013). His goal as an artist is to go *beyond* what other artists have achieved to inspire individuals and pave the way for future dreamers and artists. Although his confidence as an artist is frequently perceived as narcissistic, it is this unfailing belief in his own human agency that propels him to express his own perspective of truth and justice. The purpose of West's work in each of his artistic periods is to envision a future that is not only aware of but also liberated from the social structures and systems that continue to oppress and subjugate individuals within contemporary society. The visions of modernity that West constructs are significant because they reflect the challenges of contemporary culture and society. As individuals continue to become more connected through technology and education, it is vital that hip-hop artists maintain their devoted focus on socially significant issues that may be ignored or concealed by the dominant culture.

As a black male living under the microscope of the media, West's art as well as his lived reality as a public commodity represent the complex negotiations of double consciousness that both constrict and construct his subjectivity as an artist, public persona, and social critic. As West continues to grow more accustomed to his life of luxury and power, his critical lens seems to be losing its precise focus. His slide down the slippery slope of consumerism and a life of decadence has disconnected him from the reality in which most of his consumers exist. As an artist who was once applauded for the unique critical consciousness he promoted in his life and work, the question now becomes: Where will Kanye go from here? If he continues to regress into the self-absorbed consumerism that pervades American popular culture, the efforts he achieved within his first two artistic movements are empty and meaningless because they offer no substantial vision of a transformative modernity. However, if West progresses through his third artistic period reflexively and connects to the current context of society, his vision of modernity can succeed in inspiring others to enact transformation in their individual and communal lives.

Notes

1. Ray West was raised in a military family and recalls experiencing discrimination throughout his childhood (D. West, 2007). When Ray entered college at the University of Delaware, he became actively involved in the Black Student Government and later became a member of the Black Panther Party (D. West, 2007; Ciccariello-Maher, 2009). Donda Williams grew up in the Jim Crow south and remembers her mother insisting they use the restrooms and water fountains reserved for whites (D. West, 2007, p. 21). In 1958, Donda and her brother joined the NAACP Youth Council to participate "in the first national sit-in demonstration to acquire public accommodations for people of color" ("Donda C. West", 2007).

2. Donda and her mother selected his name: Kanye, an Ethiopian name meaning "the only one," and Omari, meaning "wise man" (D. West, 2007, p. 46).

3. Donda West fostered her son's early interest in art by taking him to free art lessons at the Chicago Academy for the Arts (D. West, 2004, p. 80). She also took Kanye on trips to Oklahoma City to visit her family, to Washington, DC, and to Florida. When West was 10 years old, he and his mother lived in China for a year while she taught English as part of an exchange program between Nanjing University and Chicago State University (D. West, 2004, p. 86).

4. Du Bois defines the veil in his 1903 *The Souls of Black Folk* as a man-made and socially perpetuated division between the Black and White worlds. Ciccariello-Maher (2006) discusses the veil as "an actual institution—formal and informal racialization and segregation—that creates the 'two worlds,' Black and White, on either side of the color line. It is, one might say, an empirical reality, despite our not being able to point to it" (p. 380).

5. On the cover of *Graduation* (2007), Dropout Bear is animated by Takashi Murakami (b. 1962), a contemporary Japanese artist who founded a postmodern art movement called "superflat," which sought to delineate the aesthetics of postwar culture in Japan. His art commonly blurs the lines between high and low Japanese cultures.

6. Spike Jonze (b. 1969 as Adam Spiegel) is an American photographer and director of music videos, commercials, and films. Jonze is known for his eccentric style and is regarded as a contemporary artist whose art truly reflects lived reality (Smith, 1999). He directed West's 2008 music video "Flashing Lights" as well as West and Jay Z's 2011 music video "Otis."

7. At the 2009 MTV Video Music Awards, West stole the microphone and the stage from Taylor Swift as she attempted to accept her award for best female video. The criticism for his comment, that "Beyoncé had one of the greatest videos *of all time*," reached all the way to the White House, as President Obama called West a "jackass." West made a personal decision to excuse himself from the US mainland and spent the remainder of 2009 traveling and taking time to reflect (Callahan-Bever, 2010; West, 2010b).

8. "Through the Fire" is representative of West's signature sampling style, known as "chipmunk soul," in which he speeds up sections of classic R&B and pop songs and samples them to create his own unique products. West has emphasized that he borrowed this technique from The RZA, member of the Wu-Tang Clan (Tyrangiel, 2005; Serpick, n.d.).

9. Driving to his hotel around 4:00 a.m. following a recording session, West fell asleep at the wheel and collided with an oncoming vehicle (D. West, 2007). West's face was broken in three places and required reconstructive surgery to repair. Following surgery, West's mouth was wired shut and he began to write the lyrics of "Through the Wire," "rapping them through jaws wired shut" (D. West, 2007: 134).

10. Although West sought to sample Hill's original recording of "Mystery of Iniquity," in his own song "All Falls Down," the legal rights were not cleared. West's former manager, John Monopoly, explained, "I was even in communication with Mrs. Hill. I thought we came to terms, but because of what some other people that were in the mix did, it didn't happen" (Reid, 2005).

11. Lauryn Hill's first solo album, *The Miseducation of Lauryn Hill* (1998) won five Grammys, including Album of the Year. Hill is one of the first successful female hip-hop artists to be accepted within hip-hop and mainstream American music.

12. Blood diamonds, or conflict diamonds, are diamonds (or other valuable minerals) that are mined and sold to finance Third World conflicts, most notably in African countries such as Liberia, Angola, and Sierra Leone. The 2006 film *Blood Diamond*, starring Leonardo DiCaprio, is set during the Sierra Leone Civil War (1991–2002) and sheds light on the violent systems behind conflict diamonds.

13. In his discussion of "Diamonds from Sierra Leone (Remix)", Dyson (2007) asserts that it "engage[s] with the black diaspora in one of its more nefarious moments: the appropriation of African labor at the violent cost to life and limb, as African American millionaires across the waters celebrate a gaudily excessive lifestyle fueled by the suffering and death of their kin slaving in caves thousands of miles away" (p. 51).

14. Both the title of West's fourth album and its synthetic sound are a tribute to the Roland TR-808, the programmable drum machine pioneered by Marvin Gaye's 1982 "Sexual Healing" and later utilized by the founders of hip-hop music.

15. Both *Runaway* and *My Beautiful Dark Twisted Fantasy* feature the same prologue and epilogue.

16. Hamilton (2011) discusses West's choice to sample Scott-Heron's 1970 "Comment No. 1," stating, "In wielding this voice West closes at album that drives maximalism to its breaking point with the stirring statement: this is still not enough, we must be still more than this, this business is serious. It is Scott-Heron's voice that says this, not in its words but in its pure sound, grain, its young and ferocious assuredness" (p. 113).

17. Griffin is the character played by West in *Runaway* (2011).

18. G.O.O.D. Music stands for Getting Out Our Dreams, a production company started by West in 2004 that represents artists including Malik Yusef, Mr Hudson, CyHi the Prynce, and Mos Def.

19. West premiered his short film, *Cruel Summer* (2012), in a custom-built theater featuring seven screens that surrounded the periphery of the audience at the Cannes Film Festival. The film was created using a custom-built camera rig with multiple cameras to gain different perspectives ("Kanye West debuts," 2012).

20. In "Black Skinhead," West writes "They see a black man with a white woman at the top floor they gon' come to kill King Kong." Like King Kong, West is perceived by the public as a black "monster," stealing away the white woman from the top floor. West's use of the words "with a white woman at the top floor" express his status as an affluent and influential individual who has taken hold of not only notions of "white" success, but also the "white" woman.

References

Alexander, M. (2013, July 23). "The Zimmerman Mindset: Why Black Men Are a Permanent UnderCaste." *Time*.

Allen, R. (1970). *Black Awakening in Capitalist America*. Garden City, NY: Doubleday Anchor Book.

Althusser, L. (1971) "Ideology and Ideological State Apparatuses: (Notes towards an Investigation)." *Lenin and Philosophy*. New York: Monthly Review P. 127–86. Print. and Def Jam.

Anderson, C. C. (2013). *Where the Lonely Kids Go When the Bell Rings*. [Video File]. Retrieved from https://vimeo.com

Bailey, A. (2007). *Strategic Ignorance. Race and Epistemologies of Ignorance*, edited by Sullivan and Tuana. Albany, New York: SUNY Press, 77–94.

Baldwin, J. (1974). *If Beale Street Could Talk*. New York, NY: Vintage International Press.

Baldwin, J. (1985). *The Evidence of Things Not Seen*. New York: Henry Holt & Company.

Ball, J. (2011). *I Mix What I Like: A Mixtape Manifesto*. Oakland, CA: AK Press.

Baraka, A. (1970). *Technology & Ethos: 2. Book of Life. In Raise, Race, Rays, Raze: Essays Since 1965*. New York: Random House.

Barnett, M. (2004)."A Qualitative Analysis of Family Support and Interaction among Black College Students at an Ivy League University." *The Journal of Negro Education* 73, no. 1 (Winter): 53–68.

Bederman, G. (1995). *Manliness & Civilization: A Cultural History of Gender and Race in the United States 1880–1917*. Chicago: University of Chicago Press.

Bell, D. (1980). "Brown v. Board of Education and the Interest-Convergence Dilemma." *Harvard Law Review* 93: 518–533.

Bell, W. (2002). "A Community of Futurists and the State of the Futures Field." *Futures* 34: 235–247.

Benjamin, W. (1968). "The Work of Art in the Age of Mechanical Reproduction." In *Illuminations*, edited by Arendt H., 214–218. London: Fontana.

Bennett M. (2006). "Theadoxic Adventures of John Henry in the 21st Century." *Socialism and Democracy* 20, no. 3: 245–258.

Berghaus, G. (2005). *Theatre, Performance, and the Historical Avant-garde*. New York, NY: Palgrave Macmillan.

Black, Stephanie. (2001). *Life + Debt.* Tuff Gong Pictures.

Blanco, A. A., (January 21, 2013). *HipHopWired.com.* "Consequence & Jen The Pen Slander Kanye West, Q-Tip & Love & Hip Hop Cast [VIDEO]," http:// hiphopwired.com/2013/01/21/consequence-jen-the-pen-slander -kanye-west-q-tip-love-hip-hop-cast-video/ (accessed June 29, 2013).

Blee, K. (1991). *Women of the Klan: Racism and Gender in the 1920's.* Berkeley: University of California Press.

Bloom, Harold. (1997)*The Anxiety of Influence.* Oxford: Oxford University Press.

Bogues, A. (2003). *Black Heretics, Black Prophets: Radical Political Intellectuals.* New York: Routledge.

Bohte, J. (2001). "School Bureaucracy and Student Performance at the Local Level." *Public Administration Review* 61: 92–99.

Bonilla-S., E. (1996). "Rethinking Racism: Towards a Structural Interpretation." *American Sociological Review* 62, no. 3: 465–480.

Botelho, G. (2013) "What Happened the Night Trayvon Martin Died?" *CNN Justice.* March 23, 2012. Weblog. Entry posted on June 20, 2013.

Bould, M. (2007). "The Ships Landed Long Ago: Afrofuturism and Black SF." *Science Fiction Studies*, 34, no. 2: 177.

Bradley, A. (2009). *Book of Rhymes: The Poetics of Hip Hop.* New York: Basic*Civitas.*

Bruccoli, M. J. (1992). "Introduction." In *The Great Gatsby: The Authorized Text,* edited by F. S. Fitzgerald, i–xvi. New York: Scribner.

Buck-M. S. (1992). "Aesthetics and Anaesthetics: Walter Benjamin's Artwork Essay Reconsidered." *October* 62: 3–41.

Bynum, E. B. (1999). *The African Unconscious.* New York: NY Teacher's College Press.

Callahan-Bever, N. (2010, November 22). Kanye West: Project *Runaway. Complex Music.*

Campion, C. (March 8, 2011). "Kanye West on Break Dancing in China, Self-Esteem Issues, and the KKK." http://sabotagetimes.com/music /kanye-west-on-breakdancing-in-china-self-esteem-issues-and-the-kkk / (accessed July 1, 2013).

Capurro, R. (2010). "Digital Hermeneutics: An Outline." *AI & Society* 35, no. 1: 35–42.

Caramanica, J. (2012, February 13). "Everything Old Is Praised Again." Retrieved May 21, 2013, from http://www.nytimes.com

Caramanica, J. "Behind Kanye's Mask." *The New York Times* (p. AR1). June 16, 2013.

Carroll, Hamilton. (2011). *Affirmative Reaction: New Formations of White Masculinity.* Durham, NC: Duke University Press.

Carter, S, P. Williams, J. Brown, Joseph Roach, T. Pinckney, and F. Wesley. (2011a). "Gotta Have It." Watch the Throne. Roc-a-fella Records.

Carter, Shawn/Jay-Z, Ernest Wilson, Jeff Bhasker, Kanye West, and Robyn Fenty. (2009). "Run This Town (featuring Rihanna and Kanye West)." The Blueprint 3. Roc Nation/Atlantic Records.

Chaka, K. (1984). "Through The Fire." In *I feel for you*. Burbank, CA: Warner Brothers.

Chang, J. (2005). *Can't Stop Won't Stop: A History of the Hip-Hop Generation*. New York: Picador.

Chappell, B. (2010, November 3). "Bush Says Kanye West's Attack Was Low Point of His Presidency; West Agrees." Retrieved May 21, 2013, from http://www.npr.org/blogs/thetwo-way/2010/11/03/131052717

check: *Hip-hop from NPR Music*. Retrieved from http://www.npr.org/

Ciccariello-Maher, G. (2009). "A Critique of Du Boisian Reason: Kanye West and the Fruitfulness." *Journal of Black Studies* 39, no. 3: 371–401.

Cleaver, E. (1968). *Soul on Ice*. New York: McGraw Hill/ Ramparts.

Cole, H. J. (2010). "Kanye West: A Critical Analysis of Mass Media Representation of a Cultural Icon's Rhetoric and Celebrity." In *Rock Brands: Selling Sound in a Media Saturated Culture*, edited by C. Barfoot, 195–212. Lanham, MD: Lexington Books.

Combahee River Collective. "The Combahee River Collective Statement: A Black Feminist Statement." *The Second Wave: A Reader in Feminist Theory*, edited by Linda Nicholson. New York, NY: Routledge, 1997. 63–71.

Combahee River Collective. (n.d.) "Taylor Swift Got Kanyed." Retrieved May 22, 2013, from http://www.time.com/time/specials/packages/article/0,28804,1922188_1922187_192 190,00.html #ixzz2TNgqWqsT

Combahee River Collective. (2013, March 27). "Justin Timberlake, 'The 20/20 Experience': Is There A Visual Preference For Whiteness?." http://www.huffingtonpost.com/2013/03/27

Combahee River Collective. (2005, September 3). "Kanye West's Torrent of Criticism, Live on NBC." Retrieved July 18, 2006, from http://www.washingtonpost.com/

Combahee River Collective. (2005, September 9). "First lady: Charges Racism Slowed Aid 'Disgusting'." *CNN.com*. Retrieved May 15, 2006, from http://www.cnn.com/2005/POLITICS/09/08/katrina.laurabush.

Common, 2 Chainz, Cyhi The Prynce, Kid Cudi and D'Banj. Cruel Summer. G.O.O.D. Music/Def Jam Records.

Crenshaw, Kimberle. (1998). "Demarginalizing the Intersection of Race and Sex: A Black Feminist Critique of Antidiscrimination Doctrine, Feminist Theory, and Antiracist Politics." In *Feminism and Politics*, edited by Anne Phillips, 314–343. Oxford: Oxford University Press.

Crisp, G., and Cruz, I. (2009). "Mentoring College Students: A Critical Review of the Literature between 1990 and 2007." *Research in Higher Education* 50: 525–545.

Crosley, H. (2009, September 14). "Kanye West Apologizes to Taylor Swift for VMA Rant." Retrieved from www.mtv.com/news/articles/1621410/kanye-west-apologizes-taylor-swift-vma-rant.jhtml

Crosley. H. (2013). "Joan Morgan on Black Sex, Identity, and the Politics of Pleasure." *Parlour*.

Cruse, H. (2005). *The Crisis of the Negro Intellectual: A Historical Analysis of the Failure of Black Leadership*. New York: Review Books Classics.

Curry, T. J. (2009). "I'm Too Real For Yah: Krumpin as a Culturalogical Exploration of Black Aesthetic Submergence." *Radical Philosophy Review* 12, no. 1/2: 61–77, 503–532.

David, M. (2007). "Afrofuturism and Post-Soul Possibility in Black Popular" Music. *African American Review* 41, no. 4: 695–707.

Davis, A. Y. (1983). *Woman, Race and Class.* New York: Vintage Books.

Delanty, G. (2006). "The Cosmopolitan Imagination: Critical Cosmopolitanism and Social Theory." *British Journal of Sociology* 57, no. 1: 25–174.

De Moraes, L. (2004, September 14). "Donald Trump: Boycott Kanye!" Retrieved May 22, 2013, from http://www.tmz.com/2009/09/14/donald-trump-boycott-kanye-west-

de Moraes, L. (2005, September 3). "Kanye West's Torrent of Criticism, Live on NBC." Retrieved July 18, 2006, from http://www.washingtonpost.com/wpdyn/content/article/2005/09/03/AR2005090300165.html

Dery, M. (1994). "Flame Wars: The Discourse of Cyberculture." Durham: Duke University Press.

Dinh, James. (October 11, 2010). Taylor Swift on Kanye West: "It Was Important To Write A Song To Him," *MTV News*: http://www.mtv.com/news/articles/1649743/taylor-swift-on-kanye-west-it-was-important-write-song-him.jhtml (accessed May 27, 2012).

Dombai, R. (2010). Power. *Pitchfork.* http://pitchfork.com/reviews/tracks/11905.

Donda C. West obituary. (2007, November 18). *The Oklahoman.*

Du Bois W. E. B. (1903). *The Souls of Black Folk.*

Du Bois, W. E. B. (1901). *The Spawn of Slavery: The Convict Lease System in the South.* In *Race, Crime and Justice: A Reader,* edited by S. Gabbidon and H. T. Greene, 3–8. New York: Routledge.

Du Bois, W. E. B. (1915). *The Negro.* New York: Holt Press.

Du Bois, W. E. B. (1897) "Strivings of the Negro people." *The Atlantic.* http://www.theatlantic.com/magazine/archive/1897/08/strivings-of-the-negro-people/305446/ (accessed July 1, 2013).

Dyson, M. E. (2004). "The Culture of Hip Hop." In *The Michael Eric Dyson Reader,* 401–410. New York, NY: Basic Books.

Dyson, M. E. (2007). *Know What I Mean? Reflections on Hip Hop.* New York, NY: Basic Civitas.

Dyson, M. E. (2006). *Come Hell or High Water: Hurricane Katrina and the Color of Disaster.* New York, NY: Basic Civitas.

Dyson, M. E. (2011, August 5). "5 NOPD Officers Guilty in Post-Katrina Danziger Bridge Shootings, Cover-up." Retrieved August 29, 2013, from http://www.nola.com/crime/index.ssf/2011/08/danziger_bridge_verdict_do_not.html

Dyson, M. E. (2005, September 9). "First lady: Charges Racism Slowed Aid 'Disgusting.'" CNN.com. Retrieved May 15, 2006, from http://www.cnn.com/2005/POLITICS/09/08/katrina.laurabush.

Eagleton, T. (2008). *Literary Theory: An Introduction. Anniversary Edition.* Minneapolis: University of Minnesota Press.

Edelman, P., Holzer, H. J., and Offner, P. (eds.). (2006). *Reconnecting Disadvantaged Young Men.* Washington, DC: The Urban Institute Press.

Eggenberger, Nicole. (September 15, 2010). Kanye West After Taylor Swift Incident: "I Felt Very Alone," *OK*!: http://www.okmagazine.com /news/kanye-west-after-taylor-swift-incident-i-felt-very-alone (accessed May 27, 2012).

Eglash, R. (2002). "Race, Sex, and Nerds: From Black Geeks to Asian American Hipsters." *Social Text* 20, no. 2: 49–64.

Eimers, M. T., and Pike, G. R. (1997). "Minority and Nonminority Adjustment to College: Differences or Similarities?" *Research in Higher Education* 38: 77–97.

Ellison, R. (1995). *The Collected Essays of Ralph Ellison.* New York, NY: Random House.

Ellison, R. (1995). "Change the Joke and Slip the Yoke." In *Shadow and Act.* New York: First Vintage Int. Edition.

Ellison, R. (1947) *Invisible Man.* New York: Vintage International.

Eshun, K. (1998). *More Brilliant than the Sun: Adventures in Sonic Fiction.* London: Quartet Books.

Everett, A. (2009). *Digital Diaspora: A Race for Cyberspace.* Albany: State University of New York Press.

Fanon, F. (1952). *Black Skins, White Masks.* New York: Grove Press.

Fanon, F. (1967) *Black Skin, White Masks.* New York: Grove Press.

Few, A. L., Piercy, F. P., and Stremmel, A. (2004). "Balancing the Passion for Activism with the Demands of Tenure: One Professional's Story from Three Perspectives." *NWSA Journal* 19: 47–66.

Foster, T. (2011). The Sexual Abuse of Black Men under Slavery. *Journal of the History of Sexuality* 20, no. 3: 445–464.

Foucault, M. (1990). *The History of Sexuality: An Introduction.* Translated by Robert Hurley. New York: Vintage.

France, L. R. (2009, September 14). "Anger over West's disruption at MTV awards." Retrieved May 22, 2013, from http://www.cnn.com/2009 /SHOWBIZ/09/14/kanye.west.reaction/

Freire, P. *Pedagogy of the Oppressed.* Translated by Myra Bergman Ramos. New York: Continuum, 2000. Digital File.

G.O.O.D. Music. (2012). *Cruel summer.* New York, NY: G.O.O.D., Def Jam.

Galli, C. (2009). "Hip-Hop Futurism: Remixing Afrofuturism and the Hermeneutics of Identity." Honors Project, Rhode Island College.

George, N. (2001). *Buppies, B-boys, Baps, and Bohos: Notes on Post-Soul Black Culture.* New York: Da Capo Press.

Giddings, P. (1979, March 19). "The Lessons of History will Shape the 1980's—Black Macho and the Myth of the Superwoman Won't." *Encore American* and *Worldwide News* (March 19): 50–51.

Gilroy, P. (1992). *The Black Atlantic: Modernity and Double Consciousness.* Cambridge, MA: Harvard University Press.

Golianopoulos, T. (2012, September 19). "Cruel Summer" Album Review: Kanye West Indulges http://www.vibe.com/article/cruel-summer-album -review-kanye-west-indulges-not-so-good-instincts (accessed July 14, 2013).

Gomery, D. (2000). Interpreting Media Ownership. In *Who Owns the Media: Competition and Concentration in Mass Media Industry,* 3rd ed., edited by B. Compaine and D. Gomery. New York, NY: Routledge.

Hall, R. E. (2010). *An Historical Analysis of Skin Color Discrimination in America: Victimism among Victim Group Populations.* New York: Springer.

Hamilton, J. (2011). "Pieces of a Man: The Meaning of Gil Scott-Heron. *Transition* 106, no. 1: 112–126.

Hamilton, T., Williams, H., and Strong, N. (2005, September)."Katrina: Hip-Hop Reacts and Responds." http://www.allhiphop.com.

Harris, L. (Winter 2012/13). "Against Minstrelsy." *Black Diaspora Review* 3, no. 2:1–13.

Hartman, S. V. (1997). *Scenes of Subjection: Terror, Slavery, and Self-Making in 19th Century America.* New York: Oxford University Press.

Hartmann, H. (1997). "The Unhappy Marriage of Marxism and Feminism: Towards a More Progressive Union." *The Second Wave: A Reader in Feminist Theory,* edited by Linda Nicholson, 97–122. New York: Routledge.

Harvey, D. (1990). *The Condition of Postmodernity.* Cambridge, MA: Wiley-Blackwell.

Harvey, David. (2005). *A Brief History of Neoliberalism.* New York, NY: Oxford University Press.

Hill, L. (2002)." Mystery of Iniquity." On *MTV unplugged No. 2.0.* New York, NY: Columbia.

his not so G.O.O.D instincts. http://www.vibe.com/

Hoffman, N. (2003). "College Credit in High School: Increasing College Attainment Rates For Underrepresented Students." *Change* 35: 42–48.

Hollis, C., J. T. Smith, and M. Lu' Ree Williams. (2012a). "Cold.1 (Kanye West & DJ Khaled)." Cruel Summer. (G.O.O.D. Music/Def Jam Records).

Holmgren, M. (2005, October 27). "Rap Artist Kanye West Censored on NBC." http://freemuse.org/freemuseArchives/freerip/freemuse.org /sw10987.html

Holmgren, M. (2005, September 5). "Interview with George H.W. Bush, Barbara Bush." *Larry King Live.* CNN.

hooks, b. (1992). *Black Looks: Race and Representation.* Cambridge: South End Press.

hooks, b. (2004). *We Real Cool Black Men and Masculinity.* New York, NY: Routledge.

hooks, bell. (2009). "Feminism Inside: Toward a Black Body Politic." *Modern Art Culture: A Reader*, edited by Francis Frascina, 17–25. New York: Routledge.

Hovey, Craig. (2008). *Nietzsche and Theology*. New York, NY: Continuum Press.

http://concreteloop.com/interviews-kanyewest

http://nymag.com

http://pitchfork.com/

http://www.huffingtonpost.com/

http://www.legacy.com/obituaries/oklahoman/obituary

http://www.nytimes.com/

http://www.rollingstone.com

http://www.rollingstone.com/

http://www.rollingstone.com/

http://www.theatlantic.com/magazine

http://www.thefader.com/2012/11/29/kanye-west-im-amazing/

http://www.time.com/time/magazine

Hughes, L. (1926). "The Negro Artist and the Racial Mountain." University of Illinois at Urbana-Champaign. http://www.english.illinois.edu/maps/poets/g_l/hughes/mountain.htm (accessed May 3, 2013).Irvin, D. (2013, June 19). "Kanye West avoids 'Rick Ross treatment' for his misogynistic 'Yeezus' lyrics." Retrieved June 26, 2013, from The Grio: http://thegrio.com/2013/06/19/kanye-west-avoids-rick-ross-treatment-for-his-misogynistic-yeezus-lyrics/

"Is 'Yeezus' the Tipping Point for Rap Misogyny?" (2013, June 28). http://www.spin.com/articles/yeezus-kanye-west-sexism-misogyny-rick-ross/

Itzkoff, Dave. (November 3, 2010). Kanye West Says Taylor Swift Incident Was "Bigger" Than "Bush Moment" After Katrina. *The New York Times*: http://artsbeat.blogs.nytimes.com/2010/11/03/kanye-west-says-taylor-swift-incident-is-bigger-than-bush-moment-after-katrina/ (accessed May 27, 2012).

Jackson, R. (2006). *Scripting the Black Masculine Body: Identity, Discourse, and Racial Politics in Popular Media*. New York: State University of New York Press.

James, J. (2005). "'F**K tha Police [State]': Rap, Warfare, and the Leviathan" In D. Darby, and T. Shelby (eds.), *Hip Hop and Philosophy: Rhyme 2 Reason*, 65–76. Chicago: Open Court.

Jay-Z and K. West. (2011). "Niggas in Paris." In *Watch the Throne*. New York: Def Jam.

Jenkins, T. S. (2006). "Mr. Nigger: The Challenges of Educating Black Males within American Society." *Journal of Black Studies* 37: 127–155.

Jhally, S. (1989). "The Political Economy of Culture." In *Cultural Politics in Contemporary America*, Edited by S. Jhally and I. Augus, 65–81. New York, NY: Routledge.

Johnston, A. (2013, June 17). "Kanye West's Sex Problem." *Salon*: http://www.salon.com/2013/06/17/kanye_wests_sex_problem/

Jones, L. (1964). "Black Dada Nihilismus." In *The Dead Lecturer: Poems* by LeRoi Jones. New York: Grove Press.

Jordan, J. (1995). "A New Politics of Sexuality." In *Words of Fire: An Anthology of African-American Feminist Thought,* edited by Beverly Guy-Sheftall, 407–11. New York: New York Press.

"Kanye West Debuts Short Film *Cruel Summer*" at Cannes. (2012, May 24).

Kanye West, Q-Tip and Love & Hip Hop Cast [VIDEO]". http://hiphop-wired.com/2013/01/21/

"Kanye's Motives, Tastes." *The Huffington Post.*

Kelley, F., and Muhammad, A. S. (2013, May 21). "Kanye West Stands Alone." In *MicrophoneCheck*. Radio interview. http://www.npr.org/blogs/therecord/2013/05/21/185781341/kanye-west-stands-alone (accessed July 1, 2013).

Kelley, R. (2002). *Freedom Dreams*. Boston, MA: Beacon Press.

King, J. (2013, March 22). "The Trouble with Justin Timberlake's Appropriation of Black Music." http://colorlines.com/archives/2013/03

King, J. (2013, March 27). "Justin Timberlake, 'The 20/20 Experience': Is There a Visual Preference for Whiteness?" http://www.huffingtonpost.com/2013/03/27/justin-timberlake-the-2020-experience-is-there-a-visual-preference-for-whiteness_n_2965509.html

Kline, D (2012, March 1). "The Grammys as White Nostalgia?" Retrieved May 21, 2013, from http://www.racialicious.com/2012/03/01/the-grammys-as-white-nostalgia/

Kreeps, D. (2009, September 13). "Kanye West Storms the VMAs Stage during Taylor Swift's Speech." http://www.rollingstone.com/music

Kwan, P. (1997). "Jeffrey Dahmer and the Cosynthesis of Categories." *Hastings Law Journal* 48: 1257–1292.

Ladson-Billings, G. (2005). *New Directions in Multicultural Education: Complexities, Boundaries, and Critical Race Theory. Handbook of Research on Multicultural Education,* edited by J. A. Banks and C. A. M. Banks. San Francisco: Jossey Bass.

Langhorne, Cyrus. (July 23, 2010). Eminem Scolds Kanye West Over Taylor Swift Incident. *SOHH.com*: http://www.sohh.com/2010/07/eminem_scolds_kanye_west_over_taylor_swi.html (accessed May 27, 2012).

Laws, A. (2007). "Exclusive Interview with Kanye West." *Concrete Loop.* Retrieved April 5, 2013, from http://concreteloop.com/interviews-kanyewest

Lennard, Natasha. (2013) "The Truth in Kanye's Anti-Prison Rap." *Salon.* Salon Media Group. Weblog entry posted on May 20, 2013. http://www.salon.com/2013/05/20/the_truth_in_kanyes_anti_prison_rap/ (accessed July 1, 2013).

Levenda, P. (2002). *Unholy Alliance: A History of Nazi Involvement with the Occult*. New York: Continuum.

Lewis, L. (2010, March 04). "Black Male Privilege?" *NPR*: http://www.npr.org/templates/story/story.php?storyId=124320675

Lynn, L. (Common Sense; Common) (1994). "I Used to Love H.E.R." *Resurrection*. New York: Relativity Records.

Macia, P. (2012). "Kanye West: I'm Amazing." http://www.thefader.com/2012/11/29/kanye-west-im-amazing/ (accessed June 1, 2013).

Maclean, N. (1994). *Behind the Mask of Chivalry: The Making of the Second Ku Klux Klan*. New York: Oxford University Press.

Makarechi, K. (2013, June 21). "'Yeezus' Backlash Begins As Second-Day Reviews Question Kanye's Motives, Taste." *Huffington Post*: http://www.huffingtonpost.com/2013/06/21/.

Manovich, L. (2013). *Software Takes Command*. New York: Bloomsbury Academic.

Marsh, W. (2011). "Acknowledging Black Male Privilege." *Harvard Journal of African American Policy*: http://isites.harvard.edu

MartínezAlamán, A. M., and Salkever, K. (2003). "Mission, Multiculturalism, and the Liberal Arts College: A Qualitative Investigation." *The Journal of Higher Education* 74: 563–596.

Mayer, Marc. (2010) *Basquiat*. New York: Merrell Publishers.

McWhorter, J. (2010, November 17). "Pulling the Race Card on George Bush." http://www.cbsnews.com

Mdembe, A. (2003). "Necropolitics." *Public Culture* 15, no. 1: 11–40.

Menyes, C. (2013, June 19). "Kanye West 'Yeezus': Does New Album Treat Women Unfairly? Sexist Lyrics Rampant Despite New Baby Daughter with Kim Kardashian." Retrieved July 17, 2013, from *Mstar News*: http://www.mstarz.com/articles

Miller, M. C. (1997, August 1). Who Controls The Music? *The Nation*, 11–16.

Mills, C. W. (1997). *The Racial Contract*. Ithaca, NY. Cornell University Press.

Mincy, R. B. (Ed.). (2006). *Black Males Left Behind*. Washington, DC: The Urban Institute Press.

Mitchell, M. (2004). *Righteous Propagation: African Americans and the Politics of Racial Destiny after Reconstruction*. Chapel Hill: University of North Carolina Press.

Moody, N. M. (September 11, 2004). *Associated Press*. "Kanye West Doesn't Need Critics to Tell Him He's Good—He Knows It." http://onlineathens.com/stories.

Moser, J. J. (2009, September 16). "Don't Boycott Kanye West because of Taylor Swift Incident." http://blogs.mcall.com/lehighvalleymusic/2009/09/

Myer, L., and Kleck, C. (2007). "From Independent to Corporate: A Political Economic Analysis of Rap Billboard Toppers." *Popular Music and Society* 30, no. 2: 137–148.

Neal, M. (2013). *Looking for Leroy: Illegible Black Masculinities*. New York: New York University.

Neal, M. A. (2004, July 16). "Taking on Politics, Leadership and Hip-Hop Culture." http://www.seeingblack.com/2004/x071604/stand_deliver.shtml.

Neal, M. A. (2004, May 27). "Hip Hop's Gender Problem." http://www
    .alternet.org/story/18811/

Neal, M. A. (2013). *Looking for Leroy: Illegible Black Masculinities.* New
    York: New York University Press.

Neal, M. N. (2005). "White Chocolate Soul: Teena Marie and Lewis Taylor."
    Popular Music 24, no. 3: 369–380.

Negroponte, N. (1995). *Being Digital.* New York. Alfred A. Knopf.

Nelson, A., Tu, T. L., and Headlam-Hines, A. (2001). *Technicolor: Race,
    Technology, and Everyday Life.* New York. New York University Press.

Nietzsche, F. (1998). *Beyond Good and Evil.* Oxford: Oxford World Classics.

Nietzsche, F. (2006). *Thus Spoke Zarathustra.* Cambridge: Cambridge
    University Press.

Nigatu, H. (2013, June 20). "In Defense of Kanye's Vanity: The Politics
    of Black Self-Love." *Buzz Feed* : http://www.buzzfeed.com/hnigatu
    /in-defense-of-kanyes-vanity-the-politics-of-black-self-love

Noble, S (2009, September 14). "Kayne (oops) Kanye West Is a Race-Baiting
    Thug." http://noblethinking.com/2009/09/14/

Nurrudin, Y. (2006). Ancient Black Astronauts and Extraterrestrial Jihads:
    Islamic Science Fiction as Urban Mythology. *Socialism and Democracy* 20,
    no. 3: 127–165.

O'Neil, T. (2009, September 13). "Sorry, MTV VMA Queen Taylor Swift:
    Kanye West Is King of Award-Show Tantrum." http://goldderby.latimes
    .com/awards_goldderby/2009/09/

O'Reilly, B. (2005, September 5). "Keeping the Record Straight on the
    Katrina Story." http://www.foxnews.com/story/0,2933,168552,00.html.

O'Reilly, B. (2006, January 16). "Personal Story Segment 20th Anniversary
    of MLK, Jr. Day." The O'Reilly Factor, *Fox News.*

Olson, D. (2012). "Techno-Utopia and the Search for Saaraba (1989)". In
    The Black Imagination: Science Fiction, Futurism and the Speculative,
    edited by S. Jackson, and J. Moody Freeman. New York. Peter Lang.

Parker, M. (2012, February 13). "Dave Grohl's Grammys speech Tells
    Industry to Learn an Instrument Foos Man Wins TG Award for Best
    Grammys Acceptance." http://www.musicradar.com.

Pearlman, J. (2007). *Love Me Hate Me: Barry Bonds and the Making of an
    Antihero.* New York, NY: Harper Collins.

Perry, I. (2004). *Prophets of the Hood: Politics and Poetics in Hip Hop.* Durham,
    NC: Duke University Press.

Perry, Imani. (2004). *Prophets of the Hood.* Durham, NC: Duke University Press.

Pettit, B. (2012). *Invisible Men: Mass Incarceration and the Myth of Black
    Progress.* New York: Russell Sage Foundation.

Pisters, P. (2012). *The Neuro-Image: A Deleuzian Film Philosophy of Digital
    Screen Culture.* Stanford, CA: Stanford University Press.

Potter, R. (1995). *Spectacular Vernaculars: Hip-Hop and the Politics of
    Postmodernism.* Albany: State University of New York Press.

Powers, A. (2010). "Critic's Notebook: Kanye West's Growing Pains." *Los
    Angeles Times.*

Radano, R.M and Bohlman, P.V., (eds.) (2001). *Music and the Racial Imagination*. Chicago: University of Chicago Press.

Ramirez, C. (2008). "Afrofuturism/ Chicana Futurism: Fictive Kin." *Atzlan: A Journal of Chicano Studies* 33, no. 1: 185–194.

Reid, S. (2005, February 9). Road to the Grammys: The Making of Kanye West's *College Dropout* http://www.mtv.com/news/articles/1496766 /road-grammys-kanye-west.jhtml (accessed June 2013 (n.d.).

Reid, Shaheem. (2007). Kanye's Graduation: Inside the NYC Listening Party for West's So-called 'Comeback'. http://www.mtv.com/news /articles/1568459/inside-listening-party-kanyes-comeback-album.jhtml (accessed May 14, 2013).

Reid-Pharr, Robert. (2007). *Once You Go Black: Choice, Desire, and the Black American Intellectual*. New York: New York University Press.

Richardson, C. (2011). Can't Tell Me Nothing: Symbolic Violence, Education, and Kanye West. *Popular Music and Society* 34, no. 1: 97–112.

Rodriguez, J. (2009, September 13). "Kanye West Crashes VMA Stage during Taylor Swift's Award Speech." http://www.mtv.com/news/articles/1621389.

Roediger, David R. (2008). *How Race Survived U.S. History: From Settlement and Slavery to the Obama Phenomenon*. London: Verso Books.

Rose, Stephany. (2011). Black Marketing Whiteness. *Jay-Z Essays on Hip Hop's Philosopher King*, edited by Julius Bailey, 117–131. Jefferson, NC: McFarland Publishing Company.

Ross, D. (2008). *The Nightmare and the Dream: Nas, Jay-Z and the History of Conflict in African American Culture*. New York: NY: Outside the Box Publishing.

Samuels, D. (2012). "American Mozart." *Atlantic Monthly* 309, no. 4: 72–83.

Sarte, Jean-Paul. *Black Orpheus*. Translated in 1963.

Schloss, J. (2004). *Making Beats: The Art of Sample-Based Hip-Hop*. Middletown, CT: Wesleyan University Press.

Schloss, J. G. (2004). *Making Beats: The Art of Sample-Based Hip-Hop*. Middletown, CT: Wesleyan University Press.

Scholtes, P. (2005, November 11). "Welcome to the Superdome: How Hurricane Katrina made T.I, David Banner get behind Bush's comments." http://mtv.com/news/articles/1509000/20050906/story.jhtml.

Schur, R. (2009). *Parodies of Ownership Hip Hop Aesthetics and Intellectual Property Law*. Ann Arbor, MI: University of Michigan Press.

Scraggs, A. (2007). Kanye West: A Genius in Praise of Himself. *Rolling Stone*.

Serpick, E. (n.d.). Kanye West: Biography. *Rolling Stone*.

Sexton, J. (2010). "People-Of-Color Blindness: Notes on the Afterlife of Slavery." *Social Text 103*. 28, no. 2: 31–56.

Sheffield, R. "Kanye West" (Album Review) (25 November 2010). *Rolling Stone.com*. (Video Interview) http://www.rollingstone.com/music /albumreviews

Shird, S. (2013, June 25). On Yeezus and Black Feminism. *Progressive Pupil*: http://progressivepupil.wordpress.com/2013/06/25/on-yeezus-and -black-feminism/

Shusterman, R. (2004). "Challenging Conventions in the Fine Art of Rap." In M. Forman and M. A.Neal (eds.) *That's The Joint! The Hip-hop Studies Reader,* 61–68. New York, NY: Routledge.

Sites, W. (2012). *Radical Culture in Black Necropolis: Sun Ra, Alton Abraham and Postwar Chicago. Journal of Urban History* 38 (July 2012): 687–719.

Small, C. (1998). *Musicking: The Meanings of Performing and Listening (Music Culture).* Middletown, CT: Wesleyan University Press.

Smith, E. (1999, October 25). *Spike Jonze Unmasked. New York,* October 25, 1999.

Solórzano, Daniel G., and Tara J. Yosso. (2002). "Critical Race Methodology: Counter-Storytelling as an Analytical Framework for Educational Research". In *Foundations of Critical Race Theory in Education,* edited by Taylor et al., 131–147. New York: Routledge.

Spooner, C. (2007) *Contemporary Gothic.* London: Reaktion Books.

St. John, E. P., Hu, S., Simmons, A., Carter, D. F., and Weber, J. (2004). "What Difference Does a Major Make?: The Influence of College Major Field on Persistence by African American and White students." *Research in Higher Education* 45: 209–232.

Stafford, B. (2004). "Visual Pragmatism for a Virtual World." In *Visual Rhetoric in a Digital World: A Critical Sourcebook,* edited by C. Handa. New York: Bedford/St. Martin's.

Standtmiller, M. and Li, D. K. (2009, September 14). "'Drunk' Kanye Steals Show at VMAs. Kanye Grabs Mike from Taylor Swift." http://www .nypost.com/p/news/local/manhattan

Sturken M. and Cartwright L. (2009). *Practices of Looking: An Introduction to Visual Culture.* Oxford: Oxford University Press.

Swift, T. and T Pain, (2009). "Thug Life," Retrieved May 21, 2013, from http://www.metrolyrics.com/

Swift, Taylor. (2010). "Innocent." Speak Now. Big Machine Records.

Swift, Taylor. (September 15, 2009). Interview on ABC's The View: http://www.iviewtube.com/v/86019/.

Syme, R. (2009, September 22). "Beyonce's Moment." Retrieved May 21, 2013, from http://www.thedailybeast.com/articles/2009/09/23 /the-man-behind-single-ladies.html

Szwed, J. (1998). *Space Is The Place: The Life and Times of Sun Ra.* New York. Da Capo P.

Tate, G. (2003). *Everything but the Burden: What White People Are Taking from Black Culture.* New York: Broadway Books.

Tate, G. (n.d.) "Taylor Swift Got Kanyed." Retrieved May 22, 2013. http://www.time.com/time/specials/packages/article/0,28804,1922188 _1922187_1922190,00.html #ixzz2TNgqWqsT

Therborn, G. (2003). "Entangled Modernities." *European Journal of Social Theory* 6, no. 3: 293–305.

Thomas, G. (2009). *Hip Hop Revolution in the Flesh: Power, Knowledge, and Pleasure in Lil Kim's Lyricism.* New York: Palgrave Macmillan.

Tyrangiel, J. (2005, August 21). Why You Can't Ignore Kanye. *Time*, 32–39.

Utley, E. (2013, June 20). "Kanye West's Yeezus May be Sexist, but Is Not Blasphemous." *Huffington Post* http://www.huffingtonpost.com/

Utley, E. (2012). *Rap and Religion: Understanding the Gangsta's God*. Santa Barbara: Praeger.

Van Veen, T. (2004). *Reconstruction and Rhythm Science*. PhD thesis, McGill University.

Vattimo, G. (1991). *The End of Modernity: Nihilism and Hermeneutics in Post-Modern Culture*. Cambridge: Polity Press.

Vozick-Levinson, S. (2009, September 15). "Kanye West and Taylor Swift: Why Do People Care So Much About This Story?" http://musicmix .ew.com/2009/09/15/

Wahneema, L. (2008). "But Compared to What? Reading Realism, Representation, and Essentialisms in School Daze, Do the Right Thing, and the Spike Lee Discourse." In *The Spike Lee Reader*, edited by P. Massood, 30–57. Philadelphia, PA: Temple University Press.

Wallace, M. (1978). *Black Macho* and *the Myth of the Super-Woman*. New York: Dial Press.

Wallace, M. (1978). *Black Macho and the Myth of the Superwoman*. New York: Dial Press.

Weiner, J. (2012, September 20). Review: G.O.O.D. Music, Cruel Summer.

West, Donda. (2007). *Raising Kanye: Life Lessons from the Mother of a Hip-Hop Superstar*. New York: Pocket Books.

West, K. (2004). "All Falls Down." On *College Dropout* [CD.] New York: Roc-A-Fella Records.

West, K. (2004). "Graduation Day." On *College Dropout* [CD.] New York: Roc-A-Fella Records.

West, K. (2004). "Last Call." On *College Dropout* [CD.] New York: Roc-A-Fella Records.

West, K. (2004). Li'l Jimmy Skit. On *College Dropout* [CD.] New York: Roc-A-Fella Records.

West, K. (2004). "School spirit skit #1." On *College Dropout* [CD.] New York: Roc-A-Fella Records.

West, K. (2004). "We don't care." On *College Dropout* [CD.] New York: Roc-A-Fella Records.

West, K. (2005). "Hey Mama." On *Late Registration* [CD.] New York: Roc-A-Fella Records.

West, K. (2005). *Late Registration*. New York, NY: Roc-A-Fella, Def Jam.

West, K. (2005). "Late." On *Late Registration* [CD.] New York: Roc-A-Fella Records.

West, K. (2005). "Wake up, Mr. West Intro." On *Late Registration* [CD.] New York: Roc-A-Fella Records.

West, K. (2005). "We Major." On *Late Registration* [CD.] New York: Roc-A-Fella Records.

West, K. (2007). "Champion." On *Graduation* [CD.] New York: Roc-A-Fella Records.

West, K. (2007). *Graduation*. New York, NY: Roc-A-Fella, Def Jam.

West, K. (2008). *808s & Heartbreak*. New York, NY: Roc-A-Fella, Def Jam.

West, K. (2008). *808s & Heartbreak* [CD]. New York: Island Def Jam.

West, K. (2010a). Interview by S. Calloway [Digital Video Recording]. Retrieved

West, K. (2010b). La dolce vita. *XXL*. Retrieved from http://www.xxlmag .com/

West, K. (Composer). (2004). "All Falls Down." [K. West, Performer] On College Dropout.

West, K. (Composer). (2010). "All of the Lights." [K. West, Performer] On My Beautiful Dark Twisted Fantasy.

West, K. (Composer). (2010). "Gorgeous." [K. West, Performer] On My Beautiful Dark Twisted Fantasy.

West, K. (Composer). (2010). "Hell of a Life." [K. West, Performer] On My Beautiful Dark Twisted Fantasy.

West, K. (Composer). (2010). "Power." [K. West, Performer]

West, K. (Composer). (2013). Black Skinhead. [K. West, Performer] On Yeezus.

West, K. (Composer). (2013). I am a God. [K. West, Performer] On Yeezus.

West, K. (Composer). (2013). New Slaves. [K. West, Performer] On Yeezus.

West, K. (Composer). (2013). On Sight. [K. West, Performer] On Yeezus.

West, K. (Director). (2011). *Runaway*. Retrieved from http://www.vevo .com

West, K., & Jay Z. (2011). *Watch the Throne*. New York, NY: Roc-A-Fella Records, Roc Nation,

West, K., Green, T. K., and Lynn, Jr., L. R. (2004). Get 'em high. On *College dropout* [CD.] New York: Roc-A-Fella Records.

West, K., S. Carter, C. Hollis, W. A. Donaldson, and M. Dean. (2011). "Niggas in Paris." Watch the Throne. Roc-a-fella Records.

West, Kanye, Ernest Wilson, Corey Woods, Scott Mescudi, Gene Clark, Roger McGuinn, Mike Dean, Malik Jones, and Che Smith. (2010a). "Gorgeous (featuring Kid Cudi and Raekwon)." My Beautiful Dark Twisted Fantasy. Roc-a-fella Records.

West, K., B. Knowles, C. Wilson, E. Wilson, M. Dean, S. Anderson, B. Russell, and B. Russell. (2010d). "See Me Now (featuring Beyoncé, Charlie Wilson and Big Sean)." My Beautiful Dark Twisted Fantasy. Roc-a-fella Records; a bonus track on the deluxe edition.

West, K, L. Griffin, A. Gardner, K. Lewis, F. Bernheim, Jean Pierre Lang, Boris Bergman, Mike Dean, Jeff Bhasker, Robert Fripp, Michael Giles, Greg Lake, Ian McDonald, and Peter Sinfield. (2010b). "Power." My Beautiful Dark Twisted Fantasy. Roc-a-fella Records.

West, K., S. Carter, W. Roberts, O. Maraj, J. Vernon, J. Bhasker, P. Reynolds, and M. Dean. (2010c). "Monster (feat. Jay-Z, Rick Ross, Nicki Minaj, and Bon Iver)." My Beautiful Dark Twisted Fantasy. Roc-a-fella Records.

West, Kanye. (2004). *The College Dropout*. Roc-A-Fella Records, Def Jam.

West, Kanye. (2005). *Late Registration*. Roc-A-Fella Records.

West, Kanye. (2007). *Graduation*. Roc-A-Fella Records.

West, Kanye. (2010). *My Beautiful Dark Twisted Fantasy*. Roc-A-Fella.

West, Kanye. (2012). *Cruel Summer*. G.O.O.D Music.

West, Kanye. (2013). *Yeezus*. Roc-A-Fella, Def Jam.

West, Kanye. (October 19, 2010). Interview with Ellen DeGeneres: http://www.youtube.com.

West, K., E. Wilson, C. Woods, S. Mescudi, G. Clark, R. McGuinn, M. Dean, M. Jones, and Che Smith. (2010a). "Gorgeous (feat. Kid Cudi & Raekwon)." My "Beautiful Dark Twisted Fantasy." Roc-a-fella Records.

West, K. "Can't Tell Me Nothing: Symbolic Violence, Education, and Kanye West." *Popular Music and Society* 34, no. 1: 97–112. doi:10.1080/03007766.539831 February 2011.

Wilderson, F. (2010). *Red, White, and Black: Cinema and the Structure of U.S. Antagonisms*. Durham: Duke University Press.

Williams, J. A. (2007). "Kanye West: The Man, the Music, and the Message." *Black Collegian*

Winant, H. (2004). *The New Politics of Race: Globalism, Difference, Justice*. Minneapolis, MN: University of Minnesota Press.

Woodson, J. (2006, June 1). "Hip Hop's Black Political Activism." Retrieved May 25, 2006, from http://www.zmag.org

Wynter, S. (1992). "No Humans Involved: An Open Letter to My Colleagues." *Voices of the African Diaspora: The CAAS Research Review* 8, no. 2: 13–16.

Yaszek, L. (2005). "An Afrofuturist Reading of Ralph Ellison's Invisible Man Rethinking History" *The Journal of Theory and Practice* 9, no. 2/3: 297–313.

Yousman, B. (2003). "Blackophilia and Blackophobia: White youth, The Consumption of Rap Music, and White Supremacy." *Communication Theory* 13, no. 4: 366–391.

Youth Action Project. (2013). In *White Privilege Conference*. http://www.whiteprivilegeconference.com/youth.html

Zirin, D. (2005, September 28). "Etan Thomas Rises to the Occasion." Retrieved May 15, 2006, from http://www.thenation.com/20050926/zirin

Contributors

Reynaldo Anderson, PhD currently serves as assistant professor of Humanities at Harris-Stowe State University in Saint Louis, MO. Dr. Anderson has published articles, book chapters, and has presented extensive research documenting the Africana and/or the Communication Studies experience. Former chair of the Black Caucus of the National Communication Association and still an Executive member of the Missouri Arts Council,

Julius Bailey, PhD, a Christian Existentialist teaching in the Department of Philosophy at Wittenberg University. He is a philosopher, cultural critic, social theorist, and diversity lecturer. Recent publication includes: *Jay-Z: Essays on Hip Hop's Philosopher King* (McFarland, 2011) and *Philosophy and Hip Hop: Ruminations on Postmodern Cultural Form* (Palgrave, 2014) and a host of articles on Hip Hop Pedagogy and Social Justice issues. Can be found at www.juliusbailey.com

Sha' Dawn Battle is in the doctoral program in literature at the University of Cincinnati. In 2009, she earned an MA in English language and literatures from Wright State University. She also graduated from Wright State with a certificate in Women's Studies. She also serves as primary editor for Speaker of the House Publishing Company.

Dawn Boeck is a composition instructor and a writing consultant at Texas A&M University—Corpus Christi (TX). She received her Master of Arts with an emphasis in Rhetoric, Composition, and Borderlands Studies in May 2012 from TAMUCC. As an active member of the TAMUCC community, Dawn focuses her research and writing in diverse fields, both within and outside the academic community.

Regina N. Bradley received her PhD in African American Literature at Florida State University and currently teaches at Kennesaw State University. She writes about post–Civil Rights African American literature, pop culture, race and sound, and Hip Hop. *Current Musicology*. Regina's public scholarship has been featured on AllHipHop, TheLoop21, PopMatters, NewsOne, Racialicious, and her own blog, http://redclayscholar.blogspot.com

A. D. Carson is currently in the doctoral program for Rhetoric at The University of South Carolina. A high school educator, author, and performance artist, he has written hundreds of unpublished poems, stories, songs, and other tangentially related pieces, some of which he shares on his website, AydeeTheGreat.com. Author of *COLD* and essays *The City: [un]poems*, Thoughts, Rhymes and Miscellany (Mayhaven Publishing)

Tommy Curry is an associate professor of philosophy at Texas A&M University. His work spans across the various fields of philosophy, jurisprudence, Africana Studies, and Gender Studies. Though trained in American and Continental philosophical traditions, his primary research interests are in Critical Race Theory and Africana Philosophy.

Akil Houston, PhD is an sssistant professor of Cultural and Media Studies in the Department of African American Studies. A filmmaker, dj, social critic, and one of the nation's most authentic hip-hop scholars, his work includes articles in *Philosophical Studies in Education Journal, The International Journal of Africana Studies*, and *Empathy and the Imagination-Intellect: Writings of Healing and Resistance* (Peter Lang, 2012).

John Jennings, PhD is an associate professor of Graphic Design at the University of Illinois at Urbana-Champaign. An accomplished designer, curator, illustrator, cartoonist, and award-winning graphic novelist, his work includes co-authoring *Black Comix: African American Independent Comics and Culture* (Mark Batty/Random House 2010), *Exploring the Visual Communication in Hip Hop Culture Design Research: Designing Culture* (Princeton Architectural Press, 2007).

Nicholas D. Krebs is a graduate instructor in the Department of African American Studies and Research Center at Purdue University. He holds a Masters in American Studies focuses on the formation and transmission of cultural knowledge.

David J. Leonard, PhD is an associate professor and chair in the Department of Critical Culture, Gender and Race Studies at Washington State University, Pullman. He is author of *After Artest: Race and The Assault on Blackness* (SUNY Press, 2012) and *Screens Fade to Black: Contemporary African American Cinema* (Praeger, 2006). Leonard is a regular contributor to popular outlets including the *Chronicle of Higher Education*, *The Huffington Post*, and *Feminist Wire*.

Heidi R. Lewis, PhD is assistant professor of Feminist and Gender Studies at Colorado College. She earned a PhD in American Studies from Purdue University, where she also earned a Graduate Certificate in Women's Studies. Her research and teaching interests include feminist, gender and sexuality studies, critical media studies and popular culture, critical race theory, critical whiteness studies, and African American culture.

Monica R. Miller is assistant professor of Religion and Africana Studies at Lehigh University. Miller is coeditor and contributor of a 2009 special issue of *Culture & Religion Journal* (Routledge) on Hip Hop and Religion and author of *Religion and Hip Hop* (Routledge). Miller is currently cochair of a new American Academy of Religion (AAR) Group, Critical Approaches to Hip Hop and Religion, and is a senior research fellow with The Institute for Humanist Studies.

Mark Anthony Neal is professor of Black Popular Culture in the Department of African and African-American Studies at Duke University and Harvard Hip Hop Archive Fellow. Dr. Neal is a prolific author of five books including his recent project, *Looking for Leroy for New York University Press* (2013). *New Black Man: Rethinking Black Masculinity* (2005), coauthored, *That's the Joint!: The Hip-Hop Studies Reader* (2004) and more. He is the host of the weekly webcast, "Left of Black" and can be found at http://newblackman.blogspot.com/.

Tim'm West has been featured voice in many documentaries about hip-hop and masculinity because of his ground-breaking work as a gay-identified hip-hop artist, AIDS activist, and youth advocate. He is author of several books, is heavily anthologized, and has also produced and released nearly 10 hip-hop albums. Professionally, he serves as associate director of Youth Programs at Center On Halsted in Chicago, Illinois.

Discussion Questions

Chapter 1

1. What is crate digging and its importance to deejay culture in hip-hop? How would you assess Kanye West's use of the older music in his productions? How can and/or do cultural and generational sonic divides affect any listener's interpretation of rap music, specifically Kanye West and his preeminent use of the soul archives of the late 60s and 70s?

2. What is the soul archive, and how does Kanye West use its aesthetic traditions to produce a "community theater" for contemporary audiences both inside and outside black America?

3. The change in copyright laws in the late 1990s drastically changed the way music was produced and shifted greater control of rap production to the hands of corporations. Political-economic analyses of rap industry charts between 1990 and 2005 suggest that the influence and control of music corporations altered the content of rap music. Some scholars have argued that rap has been corporatized. In what other ways and areas of life in the United States has the influence and financial control by corporations visibly or noticeably affected society and the way things are done—or not done?

Chapter 2

1. According to the author, what is an "asterisk" genius, and how is this idea consistent with other contemporary areas of cultural production (music, sports, etc.)?

2. How does baseball and athletic competition in general outline a similar cultural and industrial representation of racial politics in both historic and present circumstances like that of rap and other musical genres such as jazz, soul, and funk?

3. Considering the industrial production of rap music, does the author's suggestion of evolutionary stagnation of the art form hold true? Is the author romanticizing or holding sound critiques? Additionally, search for interviews of Kanye as he discusses himself as an artist; do they support, along with Kanye's corpus of work, the author's designation of Kanye West being an asterisk genius?

Chapter 3

1. Describe the concept of "urban nihilism" in the context of the development of both hip-hop and rap musical genres. How has "urban nihilism" been articulated as an intrinsic component of the Afrofuturist aesthetic? Discuss how the digital revolution in the emergence of the postmodern era has impacted the scope and aesthetic intensity of "urban nihilism".

2. The authors describe the theme of Kanye West's video for "Stronger" as ultimately a triumph over adversity and therefore one of transcendence. How can the themes of transcendence and the concept of urban nihilism, which by definition is hollow and despairing, be reconciled?

3. The gothic symbolism employed by Kanye West in both album covers and videos depicts images that are frequently grotesque and often violent. The authors argue that these digital creations are highly effective in that they are intensely introspective and serve as an aesthetic expression of West's internal conflicts. Discuss the validity of this position and describe how West's portrayal of the issue of black male disassociation might differ from that of other rap artists.

Chapter 4

1. Do media representation and public perception of Kanye West undermine our ability to see his protests and interventions? Is it possible to understand his protests without being a fan of Kanye?

2. In what ways does this article suggest that the "conscious rapper" versus "gangsta rapper" is an inadequate paradigm for black American rhetoric and political enunciations?

3. In what ways does Kanye West embody the possibilities and limitations of hip-hop as a method and technology of social change?

Chapter 5

1. Beyond encouraging dialogue between the academy and those outside the academy, in what ways does Kanye West offer (or fail to offer) solutions to the issues he illustrates in the trilogy? Can his highlighting of the situation be seen as assisting the search for solutions, or does exposing the issue in this manner merely worsen them?

2. The academy is in effect a system created by and descended from privileged, white classes. The author suggests that black students, particularly young men, labor under the presumption that they are inherently inadequate college students, one might even say intruders in this privileged space. What effect can this preexisting internalized assumption of intellectual inferiority have when combined with the insistence on the importance of a college education and the reality that this education may not in fact guarantee material success?

3. The author argues for further engagement on the part of academics in their communities, in an effort to change the narrative and assist black youth in finding a suitable career path, whether or not the academy is involved in this. What form might this engagement take? How would it answer the accusations the author identifies in West's Higher Education Trilogy?

Chapter 6

1. West purports to embrace the militancy of the Black Power movement popularized by Malcolm X., going so far as to refer to himself as "Malcolm West." How does the substantive ideology of the Black Power–consciousness-raising movement differ from the contemporary rap interpretation of its fundamental tenets? Does the music of Kanye West further the discourse on "black liberation," or is he a poor example of a conscious artist?* Consider Chapter 10 also here.

2. How does the popular interpretation of rap music contribute to the negative profiling of young black males in contemporary society? Is the perpetuation of these stereotypes simply the result of the pervasive adoption of the fashion associated with the genre by young black males? Or, is it driven by a more deep-rooted racial bias perpetrated by the industry for the purposes of profit? Is "shock value" a shallow commercial manipulation?

3. Why does rap continue to be an almost exclusively male musical genre? How is Kanye West part and parcel of the homogenization of the art form? Discuss why the voice of black women in a supposedly liberationist and militant art form is remarkably reduced to a whisper. Identify some women rappers and cultural trailblazers who challenge the male-dominated voices.

Chapter 7

1. How does Kanye West use sound to include or set himself apart from expectations of black masculinity associated with hip-hop? *See also Chapters 6 and 8.

2. The search for cosmopolitanism is not new in Western society. The elites have been mocking the nouveau riche for centuries. In late nineteenth-century Europe, the American rube with riches but no class who came to Europe to acquire a veneer of respectability was a constant source of fun. This led to curious situations when impoverished European aristocrats would marry their sons to the daughters of American industrialists, essentially exchanging an aristocratic title for money. How does Kanye West's search for cosmopolitanism play into or play against this narrative?

3. By sampling unexpected music, is Kanye West attempting to join the world he takes it from, or to conquer it? Should he be seen as integrating or as displacing?

Chapter 8

1. The author uses the phrase "masculine anxiety" as he refers to hip-hop's preoccupation with heteronormative sexuality. Discuss various examples wherein the author argues that hip-hop and Kanye both promote and exacerbate this idea.

2. In 2014, Macklemore and Ryan Lewis won a Grammy award for "Same Love" a hip-hop song of the year affirming same-sex marriage by two white, straight "allies" of the LGBTQ community. The author suggests a particular racialized dynamic to "masculine anxiety," and that black hip-hop artists run particular risks by being gay affirming. Could Kayne have done such a song with as much success? Why or why not?

3. Define "no homo." How does the author explain the "affirmation versus negation" dialectic? How does Kanye operate within this tension? Discuss other identity relationships that we find this tension.

Chapter 9

1. Research the names Angel Perez (Illinois), Eric Glover and Terrance Rankins (Illinois), and Darrin Manning (Pennsylvania). When we think of sexual violence and racism, why does such an imagining intuitively draws us to the black female body? How does the author push us to conceptualize the violence and rape of black men similarly?

2. Using terms such as "mandingos" and "bucks," American culture has seen black men and boys as hypersexual predators that devour, with animalistic tendencies, the bodies of women. These racial stereotypes feed off themselves and often promote racial bias. Do you find hip-hop as being a hypersexual medium that supports or exacerbates these stereotypes? Explore the ways in which female rappers "flip the (cultural) script" and engage in their own form of misogyny against men.

3. Do a close reading of Kanye's "New Slaves" with particular attention to the "Hamptons" reference. The author argues that West is challenging the reader to see this white woman not as passive object, but as a perpetrator of anti-black racism and sexual violence against black men. How does the author make this claim? Where do you see its racial merits, its flaws?

Chapter 10

1. Singer, Frank Ocean's hook to "No Church in the Wild" offers a startling redefinition of power based on traditional views of the

relationship between classes. From individuality to a mob, to a king, to a God, to a nonbeliever results in the nonbeliever dethroning the God and robbing the king of his legitimacy. What effect does this nonbelief have on the mob? Does it increase or decrease its individuality?

2. The author reads the message of the "first tattoo, no apologies" as a justification of brute force, of the dark side of anarchism. It is also a hallmark of a certain type of authoritarian figure. It suggests that West is arguing for the freedom to do what one wills, not for the freedom to be spared of what others choose to do. How does this play into West's description of what he is doing as "[forming] a new religion"? If the old religion was overthrown for its oppressiveness, is West's calling its replacement a church imposing a new, different form of oppression, or something else? See chapter 11 for more on this.

3. Imagine, contrary to the message of "No Church in The Wild," a person who acts according to strict morals. Can we see this behavior as desirable? Would it be seen as a transgression with respect to the enjoyment appeals? Can you imagine an ethics that encourages both the need for enjoyment and the desirability of moral behavior?

Chapter 11

1. The author maintains that the sacred and the profane are a social construct, that is, objects of the theorist's imagining. Do you agree with such a staunch distinction within the black musical tradition in general and hip-hop in particular? Do you see any potential politicization being formed by adhering to this construct?

2. Additionally, the essay argues that talk of religion is merely "ordinary talk about the social world and simply something reflective of larger social and cultural interests." Describe how this position explains the indignation that Rap lyrics often provoke.

3. By definition, avant-garde movements are critical of, and attempt to subvert the, accepted social norms of their era, particularly institutionalized religious convictions. Is the music of Kanye West avant-garde? Discuss how his often contradictory and highly controversial approach to religious ideas and symbols may be seen as

reflective of the rhetoric of the avant-garde. *See also Chapter 10 in this regard.

Chapter 12

1. Can one justifiably study an artist in the light of a different artist's creation? Does reading Kanye West the person through the lens of Jay Gatsby attempt to reduce West to a character in a story?

2. Are similarities between two cultures—in this case the jazz age and hip-hop, respectively—enough to afford parallels between them? Can they be equated, or is it only possible to trace resemblances?

3. Considering the extent to which hip-hop is invested in black culture (and vice versa), what does the paralleling with the extremely white world of *The Great Gatsby* tell us about either culture? Are the similarities sufficient to imply something universal, or are they likely to remain separate despite these similarities?

Chapter 13

1. What is neoliberalism, and what does it have to do with Kanye West and his interruption of Taylor Swift?

2. What kind of reactions to the interruption do you yourself recall, if any at all, and how do they compare to the reactions of the larger mass media and each artist in both their own artwork and in public commentary respectively?

3. Why is an examination of the various reactions to the interruption of Taylor Swift by Kanye West important, and how can the study of hip-hop and neoliberalism help to enlighten the polarizing opinions attached to differing interpretations of the interruption?

Chapter 14

1. What are the themes or periods the author uses as shifts in Kanye's corpus of work? Do you agree with these as viable distinctions? Since the essay ends at 2013, what has 2014 and beyond meant for his "cultural impact" in any differentiated way from before? Think about branding, marketization, and family as being influential.

2. This essay posits Kanye's West status as a modernist as being based very much on his background and upbringing. The author views modernity as being a reflection or refraction of the past, or certainly, as not dissolvable from it. How do these influences from the past alter the concept of modernity? What is the effect of a modernity that relies for full comprehension of a knowledge and consideration of the past?

3. "Runaway," the fifth track from My Beautiful Dark Twisted Fantasy, is a very visual and artistically drawn out short film. Based on a close review of this video and the other tracks in the album, discuss Kanye as a lover, a dreamer, a sadist, and a narcissist. How does this album fit with 808s & Heartbreaks? How do you feel about pathos and hip-hop?

Index

Printed and bound in the United States of America